The Web As Corpus

Corpus and Discourse

Corpus linguistics provides the methodology to extract meaning from texts. Taking as its starting point the fact that language is not a mirror of reality but lets us share what we know, believe and think about reality, it focuses on language as a social phenomenon, and makes visible the attitudes and beliefs expressed by the members of a discourse community.

Consisting of both spoken and written language, discourse always has historical, social, functional and regional dimensions. Discourse can be monolingual or multilingual, interconnected by translations. Discourse is where language and social studies meet.

The *Corpus and Discourse* series consists of two strands. The first, *Research in Corpus and Discourse*, features innovative contributions to various aspects of corpus linguistics and a wide range of applications, from language technology via the teaching of a second language to a history of mentalities. The second strand, *Studies in Corpus and Discourse*, is comprised of key texts bridging the gap between social studies and linguistics. Although equally academically rigorous, this strand will be aimed at a wider audience of academics and postgraduate students working in both disciplines.

RESEARCH IN CORPUS AND DISCOURSE

Conversation in Context
A Corpus-driven Approach
With a preface by Michael McCarthy
Christoph Rühlemann

Corpus-Based Approaches to English Language Teaching
Edited by Mari Carmen Campoy, Begona Bellés-Fortuno and Mª Lluïsa Gea-Valor

Corpus Linguistics and World Englishes
An Analysis of Xhosa English
Vivian de Klerk

Evaluation and Stance in War News
A Linguistic Analysis of American, British and Italian television news reporting of the 2003 Iraqi war
Edited by Louann Haarman and Linda Lombardo

Evaluation in Media Discourse
Analysis of a Newspaper Corpus
Monika Bednarek

Historical Corpus Stylistics
Media, Technology and Change
Patrick Studer

Idioms and Collocations
Corpus-based Linguistic and Lexicographic Studies
Edited by Christiane Fellbaum

Investigating Adolescent Health Communication
A Corpus Linguistics Approach
Kevin Harvey

Meaningful Texts
The Extraction of Semantic Information from Monolingual and Multilingual Corpora
Edited by Geoff Barnbrook, Pernilla Danielsson and Michaela Mahlberg

Multimodality and Active Listenership
A Corpus Approach
Dawn Knight

New Trends in Corpora and Language Learning
Edited by Ana Frankenberg-Garcia, Lynne Flowerdew and Guy Aston

Rethinking Idiomaticity
A Usage-based Approach
Stefanie Wulff

Working with Spanish Corpora
Edited by Giovanni Parodi

STUDIES IN CORPUS AND DISCOURSE

Corpus Linguistics in Literary Analysis
Jane Austen and Her Contemporaries
Bettina Fischer-Starcke

English Collocation Studies
The OSTI Report
John Sinclair, Susan Jones and Robert Daley
Edited by Ramesh Krishnamurthy
With an introduction by Wolfgang Teubert

Text, Discourse, and Corpora. Theory and Analysis
Michael Hoey, Michaela Mahlberg, Michael Stubbs and Wolfgang Teubert
With an introduction by John Sinclair

Corpus and Discourse

The Web As Corpus

Theory and Practice

MARISTELLA GATTO

BLOOMSBURY
NEW DELHI • LONDON • OXFORD • NEW YORK • SYDNEY

First published in India 2019
First published 2014

Bloomsbury Academic India
An imprint of Bloomsbury Publishing Plc
BLOOMSBURY, Bloomsbury Academic India and the Diana logo are trademarks of Bloomsbury Publishing Plc

This edition published with permission from Bloomsbury Publishing Plc, 50 Bedford Square, London, WC1B3DP, UK

British Library Cataloguing-in-Publication Data
A catalogue record for this book is available from the British Library.

Library of Congress Cataloging-in-Publication Data Gatto, Maristella.

The Web as Corpus : theory and practice / MaristellaGatto. pages cm.-- (Corpus and Discourse) ISBN 978-1-4411-5098-1 (hardback)-- ISBN 978-1-4411-6112-3 (pbk.)-- ISBN 978-1-4411-3413-4 (epdf) 1.Language and the Internet. 2. Computational linguistics. I. Title.
P120.I6G38 2014 410.1'88--dc23
2013036238

ISBN 978 93 88002 14 1

For sale in the Indian subcontinent only

Bloomsbury Publishing India Pvt. Ltd
Second Floor, Building No. 4
DDA Complex LSC, Pocket C – 6 & 7
Vasant Kunj, New Delhi 110070
www.bloomsbury.com

Typeset by Fakenham Prepress Solutions, Fakenham, Norfolk NR21 8NN
Digitally Printed and bound in India by Replika Press Pvt. Ltd.

Two roads diverged in a wood, and I—
I took the one less traveled by,
And that has made all the difference.
(Robert Frost)

Contents

List of Figures

List of Tables

Preface

The web is changing many, many things. It is changing how we check the weather, book train tickets, go shopping for books, clothes, music, even groceries, do any kind of research, and vote. It is mostly text. Not surprising, then, that it is changing linguistics, and in particular corpus linguistics – the approach to linguistics that starts from large samples of languages.

Until this book, introductions to corpus linguistics have left the web to 'final chapters' and 'future developments'. But this is a future that is now. In 2013 half of the world's population has grown up in a world in which the web (along with, often inextricable from, the mobile phone) is a central part of how we communicate, do business and conduct our lives. More and more of the language we encounter is in and through these technologies. If we see a corpus of newspapers and books as the staple, with a corpus of blogs and chats as a marginal novelty, we are coming from a past age, an age of going to libraries and vast, heavy volumes of indexes and catalogues. Now, the language is online, the means of accessing it is online, and the ways to explore, process and analyse it are online.

Maristella Gatto places the web centre stage. She introduces and addresses corpus linguistics largely using corpora drawn from the web, accessed through the web, built with web tools of one kind and another. She acknowledges that Google has a central place in our lives and is not so different to a corpus tool. Perhaps the first question that a corpus linguist has to answer when they start explaining what they do to a non-specialist is 'why don't you just use Google?'. The reader of this book will have a full and wide range of responses to offer.

Many people come to the study of language because they are interested in what people believe (and, quite likely, want to change it). The language that people use will tell us about their attitudes and worldview, and an analysis of the language will give insights into the view underlying it. Corpus linguistics has recently engaged with Discourse Analysis to chart the linguistic networks around complex concepts such as 'culture', 'immigration', 'asylum' and 'Islam', and Gatto shows us how to study links between language, discourse and society from the perspective of web-derived corpora.

The Web as Corpus: Theory and Practice is a timely and well-presented introduction to corpus linguistics in the age of the web. It revisits traditional corpus linguistics concepts and shows how the development of methods has to keep up with changes in the language and discourse under investigation.

Adam Kilgarriff
Lexical Computing Ltd
Brighton, UK
March 2013

Acknowledgements

Writing this book was a bit of a challenge for me, and I would have probably never seen its end without constant support and insightful advice on every aspect of this work by the series editor, and true friend, Michaela Mahlberg. I feel also indebted to Adam Kilgarriff for writing the preface. His writings fuelled my imagination from the start, and shed light on my first steps in this research field. It is easy to imagine what his preface means to me.

Special thanks go to Andrew Kehoe for reading parts of the manuscript, and to two anonymous reviewers for providing useful feedback. I would also like to express my gratitude to Federico Zanettin, for giving me the opportunity to share aspects of this research with a wider research group. A word of thanks is due to all the staff at Bloomsbury, especially Andrew Wardell who guided me through the final steps of putting the book into production.

Finally, it would be unfair to forget all my colleagues at the University of Bari, in particular Franca Dellarosa, Gaetano Falco, Sara Laviosa, Annamaria Sportelli, Alessandra Squeo and – last in alphabetical order, but truly not least – Maristella Trulli, for supporting me throughout. Lisa Adams and Eileen Mulligan read the English manuscript with their usual accuracy and competence and I thank them for this. My thanks go also to all those students who accepted to write their thesis on topics which relate to the present research, and to a lively group of PhD students in Translation Studies at the University of Bari, all of whom I feel in some way or other to be part of this research. With all these people I have spent every single working day, and it is to the people with whom we share our everyday life that – more often than not – we are mostly indebted. That's why my deepest gratitude is for my husband Antonello, who constantly supported me with his patient and loving care, and for my three children, Francesco, Serena and Stefano, who (unwillingly) accepted to share their mother with a never-ending book. Without all of them nothing would be worthwhile.

***

This volume is partly based on a previous publication by the same author, *From body to web. An introduction to the web as corpus* (2009), which was distributed online between February 2009 and June 2012 by Editori Laterza (Roma – Bari) in the University Press Online Series, a project involving Editori

Laterza and the University of Bari. I wish therefore to thank the University of Bari, Editori Laterza, and the University Press Online series editor Annamaria Sportelli, for allowing me to reuse material from that book.

Introduction

The aim of this book is to provide a comprehensive introduction to the key issues that have been raised and the tools and resources that have been developed in the multifaceted research field known as 'Web as Corpus'. More specifically, the book tries to present, explain, and – whenever possible – question some of the theoretical implications of using the web as a corpus, while introducing the different methods that have become standard in this field.

The basic assumption behind the whole book is that while the web cannot be considered as a corpus in its own right, at least in the traditional sense of the word *corpus*, it is nonetheless of crucial importance to be aware of the many different ways in which its enormous potential can be exploited from a corpus linguistics perspective, and to acknowledge the fruitful interaction between established methodological standards in corpus linguistics and novel ways to tap into the inexhaustible source of authentic language which the web undoubtedly is.

While closely related to the parent disciplines of corpus linguistics and computational linguistics, this introduction to the Web as Corpus will hopefully also be of benefit to readers having little familiarity with both. This book is in fact written from the perspective of university students, teachers or researchers in the humanities, without any indulgence in technical issues which they might feel unable to 'control' for lack of specific knowledge and skills. As a consequence, it deals primarily with already-existing tools and resources, rather than with the development of new ones. When specific aspects concerning corpus compilation, statistics, or technical aspects relating to the development of tools and resources are addressed, this is always done from the perspective of the end user, not the developer.

Given its non-technical orientation, this book aims to provide an introduction to the Web as Corpus that will also be useful to language students even if their main interest is not in corpus linguistics – such as, for instance, students on programmes in English as a Foreign Language, English for Special Purposes, or Translation Studies. In all such courses students require the skills and tools to find examples of naturally occurring language and in this context the web may well emerge as an accessible resource to be used in ways that may border – or openly address – corpus linguistics methods. The examples and case studies included in this book come precisely from the author's experience in the above-mentioned teaching contexts, and so do the suggested practical activities. Each chapter also includes examples from published articles or original research carried out for this book and provides the reader with suggestions for further reading.

As to the book's content, it is perhaps a truism to say that the web is itself a sprawling, gargantuan, inexhaustible entity, so it would be foolish to think that all areas concerning its use as a corpus could be covered in one book. It is therefore with no claim at exhaustiveness that the methods and tools discussed in the applied sections of this work were selected. Their purpose is mainly that of providing a number of significant examples for different ways of using the web as a corpus. Drawing on the four meanings for the umbrella term, web as/for corpus, as suggested by Baroni and Bernardini (2006), three areas have been covered: namely 'web as corpus shop', 'web as corpus surrogate' and 'mega-corpus mini-web'. The fourth meaning, 'web as corpus proper', relates to the use of the web as a corpus representative of web language and was left outside the present work since it would require – if appropriately pursued – a book-length study in itself. It is also worth mentioning that the work takes, to some extent, a diachronic approach, moving from the earliest vision of the web as 'the corpus of the Millennium' to the methods, resources and tools that have actually been developed in corpus linguistics under the impact of the web. To some extent the book charts the steps that have turned the ideal of the web as a ready-made corpus into something closer to reality.

The focus has constantly been as much as possible on both the theoretical implications and challenges underlying each new development, and on the practical aspects. Though apparently at odds with traditional good practice in corpus linguistics, no development in web as corpus studies has ever really questioned the fundamental tenets of corpus linguistics, neither has it been the aim of researchers working on the web as corpus to dispense with traditional corpus linguistics altogether. On the contrary, as for any other field of human knowledge, research in this field has rather profited from the force field created in the tension between traditional theoretical positions and the new tools and methods developed to meet practical needs, between the gravitational pull of existing standards and the promises of the web. Indeed, the challenge of using the web as a corpus has more often than not foregrounded important theoretical issues in corpus linguistics, thus contributing to the growth of the discipline as a whole.

Outline of the book

The introductory chapter, **Chapter 1. Corpus Linguistics: Basic Principles**, provides basic notions in corpus linguistics for those who are approaching the discipline for the first time or are only superficially familiar with it. The chapter introduces corpus linguistics as a research field, also from a historical perspective, discussing the interaction between linguistic theory, the corpus linguistics approach and the methods devised to carry out research in this field. In this chapter key definitions and standards are provided and basic concepts are introduced as the background for the book as a whole. As can be imagined, this chapter is highly selective, since its main aim is by no means to provide a comprehensive overview of corpus linguistics as such – for which the reader can refer to many excellent introductions to the field – but rather to provide those basic notions which uses of the web as corpus at different levels would imply.

Some of these basic concepts and issues are revisited in **Chapter 2. The Body and the Web: An Introduction to the Web as Corpus**, from the perspective of the web as a 'spontaneous', 'self-generating' collection of texts. The chapter also explores some of the new issues that the notion of the web as corpus has inevitably raised. More specifically, the chapter shows how the notion of the web as corpus might have changed, over the past few years, the very way we conceive of a linguistic corpus, moving from the somewhat reassuring standards subsumed under the corpus-as-body metaphor to a new, more flexible and challenging corpus-as-web image.

This chapter inevitably also touches on aspects which have been studied more extensively in the field of computational linguistics and NLP or that fall in the domain of computer science; in all these cases the approach has been to leave aside details that would not be perceived as immediately useful to the wider audience of students and teachers in the humanities to whom this book is addressed. The target audience also accounts for the choice made to extensively deal with the use of web search for linguistic purposes in **Chapter 3. Challenging Anarchy: Web Search from a Corpus Perspective.** Here the focus is on the web as an immediate source of corpus-like linguistic information via commercial search engines. While this approach is not particularly favoured in traditional corpus linguistics, given its obvious shortcomings, it is one that is instead gaining prominence in language teaching, and indeed it is possibly one of the most widespread – albeit unacknowledged – uses of the web as corpus even beyond the corpus linguistics community. Also in mainstream corpus linguistics, the use of web search results as data to complement data from more controlled resources is now being often advocated with interesting results (Mair 2007, 2012; Lindquist 2009). In this section – as in all the applied sections of the book – examples mostly concern English usage so as to be comprehensible to a wide readership, but the methods described and the perspective adopted can be adapted to different languages.

Chapter 4. Beyond Search Engines: Concordancing the Web and **Chapter 5. Building and Using Comparable Web Corpora** finally introduce some of the tools devised to exploit the web's potential from a corpus linguistics perspective, showing how different ways of using the web as/for corpus can really help overcome the obvious limitations of the web as a linguistic resource and provide information that is immediately useful and appropriate in specific contexts and for specific tasks. Emphasis is laid on the defining characteristics of each tool with the aim of suggesting how each different approach and tool can be used to address diverse needs or questions. It should also be borne in mind that tools and resources themselves are constantly evolving – and improving. This is why the evaluation of the tools introduced in this book focuses on what can actually be done with them rather than on a detailed assessment of their shortcomings. Limitation will be discussed in more general terms that relate to the user's needs. The tools discussed in these two chapters include WebCorp *Live*, WebCorp*LSE*, BootCaT and WebBootCaT. Finally, particular attention is paid to several general reference mega-corpora from the web for many languages in **Chapter 6. Sketches of Culture from Large Web Corpora**. These corpora definitely open up new perspectives for those who are fascinated by the enormous potential of the web but are not going to give up the high methodological standards which years devoted to research in corpus linguistics have set. The case studies reported in the chapter show how some of the tools and data sets developed in the context of research on the web as corpus can be used to obtain not only information about language use but also fresh insights into discourse and society. In particular, the chapter illustrates some uses of the Sketch Engine by commenting on 'sketches' for the word *culture* from the 1.5 billion words corps of English ukWaC. The data are discussed through comparison with evidence from the British National Corpus in order to describe similarities and differences between data from a web-derived corpus and more traditional resources. The final chapter, **Chapter 7. From Download to Upload: The Web as Corpus in the Web 2.0 era**, briefly tries to sketch further developments enabled through the technologies of the so-called second generation web. The chapter points to research areas which are still evolving and leaves the door open for further developments.

1

Corpus Linguistics: Basic Principles

Introduction

This chapter provides basic notions in corpus linguistics for those who are approaching the discipline for the first time or are only superficially familiar with it. Section 1 presents corpus linguistics as a research field, discussing the interaction between linguistic theory, the corpus linguistics approach and the methods devised to carry out research in this field as the background for the book as a whole. Section 2 focuses on electronic corpora, also from a historical perspective, highlighting key definitions and standards. Section 3 introduces concordancers, concordance lines and the Key Word in Context (KWiC) format as the typical ways to access corpus data for analysis, and discusses such key issues as collocation, colligation and semantic associations.

1. Theory, approach, methods: Corpus linguistics as a research field

Today, it is certainly no exaggeration to maintain that the slow yet steady rise of corpus linguistics in the past fifty years has brought about a revolution in the study of language, the impact of which is now fully acknowledged. By changing the 'unit of currency' (Tognini Bonelli 2001: 1) of linguistic investigation to encompass extended units of meaning, corpus linguistics has proven over the years an invaluable way of exploring language structures and use, while opening up new perspectives in language teaching, in the study of language for special purposes, in translation studies, in historical linguistics and even in critical discourse analysis and conceptual history.

While the impact of corpus linguistics on 'a qualitative change in our understanding of language' (Halliday 1993: 24) was perhaps clear from the start, it was a matter of debate for a long time whether corpus linguistics should be regarded primarily as a 'method' to be applied in a variety of fields, or as a 'theory', 'because it is in a position to contribute specifically to other applications' (Tognini Bonelli 2001: 1). It was soon deemed necessary to account for the special status of corpus linguistics as a methodology which is nonetheless 'in a position to define its own set of rules and pieces of knowledge *before* they are applied'. To this end, Tognini Bonelli devised the notion of 'pre-application methodology' (2001: 3), thus paving the way for all subsequent interest in the theoretical implications of corpus studies. Such a focus on the theoretical consequences of corpus findings, which clearly hint at a possible theoretical status for the discipline as a whole, led to the notion of corpus linguistics as 'a theoretical approach to the study of language' (Teubert 2005: 2), which means that 'corpus linguistics is not merely seen as a methodology but as an approach [...] with its own theoretical framework' (Mahlberg 2005: 2).

A view of corpus linguistics as an approach – 'a new philosophical approach' (Leech 1992: 106) – seems to be the most fruitful to explore the complex relation between the theoretical implications of corpus linguistics and the emergence of methods that profit from the web's immense potential as a linguistic corpus. An approach, as the very word suggests, is 'the act of drawing near', and corpus linguistics – as an approach – has undoubtedly brought us closer to language models which try to overcome old paradoxes in traditional linguistics, pointing to a new dimension where repeated language behaviour seems to bridge the gap between the brute facts of individual *parole*/performance/instance and the abstraction of such notions as *langue*/competence/system (Stubbs 2007: 127ff.). By allowing us to look at language from a new point of view, corpus linguistics not only provides 'new and surprising facts about language use', but also – and more crucially – 'can help to solve paradoxes which have plagued linguistics for at least one hundred years [...] and therefore help to restate the conceptual foundations of our discipline' (Stubbs 2007: 127). Indeed, in the words of McEnery and Hardie, it has the potential to 'reorient', 'refine' and 'redefine' theories in linguistics, also enabling us to use 'theories of language which were at best difficult to explore prior to the development of corpora of suitable size and machines of sufficient power to exploit them' (McEnery and Hardie 2012: 1), ultimately facilitating the exploration and validation of theories which draw their inspiration from attested language use.

An approach, however, needs to be implemented through methods, where a method is a specific way (from the Greek *–οδοσ*), a set of steps, a procedure for doing something. Thus, in a Janus-like position between theory and method, the corpus linguistic approach seems to stand in an osmotic relation between a theory, i.e. a 'contemplation' of the nature and reality of language, and several methods (i.e. ways) to explore that reality. With this in mind, it is easy to see how the corpus linguistic approach can profit from the emergence of the web as a pervasive medium. Corpus linguistics has increased awareness of the fact that repetitions across the language behaviour of many speakers are a significant fact for the study of language, and one which can be fruitfully investigated to come to a deeper understanding of its nature. As a social phenomenon whose currency is language, the web – even when easily accessed through a common search engine – makes such repetitions immediately evident and readily available to any user, providing the linguist with countless instances of repeated 'social' and 'shared' linguistic behaviour. This vast amount of data only requires that appropriate methods be devised to exploit its significance from a corpus linguistics perspective.

It is against this background that the present book aims to deal with the emergence of the research field now commonly labelled as 'web as corpus'. By no means itself a new theory or approach, 'web as corpus' is an umbrella term for a number of methods that look at the web as their main resource to implement the corpus linguistic approach. The methods devised to exploit the web's potential from a corpus linguistics perspective must not be seen therefore as competing with one another or competing with more traditional ways for corpus work, but as a useful complement to established practices in corpus linguistics. So, while the very possibility of considering the web as a corpus has only apparently questioned, over the past few years, some fundamental issues within corpus linguistics, it has factually contributed to the growth of the research field as a whole, and has thus indirectly contributed to reshaping our view of language.

2. Key issues in corpus linguistics

Before plunging directly into the main topic of this book, it is perhaps useful to provide some introductory information on corpus linguistics as a research field. Today corpus linguistics could be very loosely defined as an exploration of language based on a set of authentic texts in machine-readable format. The set of texts, namely the *corpus*, is usually of a size which would not allow manual investigation but requires the use of specific tools to perform a quantitative and qualitative analysis of the data, through such tasks as producing frequency lists of all the words appearing in the corpus, providing data concerning recurring patterns, and computing statistics about relative frequency by comparing different data sets.

On the basis of such a loose definition, the idea of what constitutes a corpus might appear to be more inclusive than it is generally perceived to be in contemporary corpus linguistics. Indeed, as McEnery and Wilson (2001) suggest, drawing on the Latin etymology of the word, virtually any collection of more than one text could, in principle, be called a 'corpus'. The Latin word *corpus* means 'body', and hence a corpus should be by definition any body of text. In language studies, however, this term has acquired more specific connotations than this simple definition implies. Even though some branches of linguistics have always been to some extent 'corpus-based' (i.e. based on the study of a number of authentic texts), and concepts such as corpus and concordance have been for many years the daily bread of scholars studying the Bible or Shakespeare's works (Kennedy 1998: 14), corpus linguistics as a distinct research field is a relatively recent phenomenon which rests on certain basic assumptions about what a corpus is, and also – perhaps more crucially for the purpose of the present book – what a corpus is not. A corpus, according to Sinclair's definition, 'is a collection of naturally-occurring language *chosen* to characterize a state or variety of a language' (Sinclair 1991: 171, my italics). In modern linguistics this also entails such basic standards as finite size, sampling and representativeness (McEnery and Wilson 2001: 29). Thus, as Francis observes, an anthology cannot be properly considered as a corpus; neither can, despite its name, the *Corpus Iuris Civilis* instigated by the Emperor Justinian in the sixth century (Francis 1992: 17), because their purpose is other than linguistic. And while it is doubtful whether a collection of proverbs can be considered as a corpus in its own right, it may eventually be considered as such if it is the object of linguistic research carried out using corpus linguistics tools (Tognini Bonelli 2001: 53). Thus the notion of what may constitute a corpus seems to defy simple definitions based on the corpus-as-object alone and is best approached in a wider perspective including considerations on both form and purpose (Hunston 2002: 2), the latter being a very basic criterion, almost a watershed, to discriminate between a linguistic corpus and other collections of language texts.

In the light of what has been said so far, it is not surprising that great pressure was felt to establish standard criteria for corpus creation and corpus investigation. These issues were partly implicit, and necessarily in progress, in the work of most early corpus linguists, and have come to be clarified and established over the years, creating the foundation of 'good practice' in corpus work. As a consequence, each new study in corpus linguistics assumes – implicitly or explicitly – a definition of corpus which entails fundamental criteria and standards. Despite some differences, it is now safely assumed that a corpus is a collection of machine-readable authentic texts (McEnery and Xiao 2006), authenticity of the language data and electronic format being the basic *sine qua non* of a corpus in the modern linguistics sense of the word. One could find instead diverging opinions concerning the other elements which can be regarded as constitutive of a corpus, such as representativeness, balance, sampling, size and composition. These issues always enter the debate, at different levels, whenever the notion of a linguistic corpus is at stake and will be briefly surveyed in the following pages.

2.1 Authenticity

Corpus linguistics is by definition an empirical approach to the study of language based on the observation of authentic data. As such, it can well be considered as the most evident outcome of the resurgence in popularity of language studies grounded on real examples of language in use, rather than on introspection, enabled by the possibilities and affordances provided by computer storage of data (McEnery and Wilson 2001: 2ff.). In its exclusive focus on authentic language use, corpus linguistics represents the legacy of early twentieth-century, *ante-litteram*, corpus-based methodologies (such as those by American structuralists and field linguists, who carefully recorded empirical data on language use). It can therefore be safely stated that while not using the term corpus linguistics, which is in fact relatively recent, linguistics has to some extent always been interested in examples of authentic, i.e. 'real-life', language, using a methodology that could well be defined *a posteriori* as largely corpus-based (Harris 1993: 27; McEnery and Wilson 2001: 3). According to Leech (1992: 106), for most older linguists the term corpus linguistics may indeed be evocative of the times when 'a corpus of authentically occurring discourse was *the* thing the linguist was meant to study'; for them 'corpus linguistics was simply linguistics'.

However, such an ideal continuity between the heyday of what McEnery and Wilson (2001: 2) term 'early corpus linguistics' and contemporary computerized corpus linguistics was apparently broken in the middle of the twentieth century by the emergence of Chomsky's cognitive approach, which revived a long-standing dichotomy in linguistics between rationalism and empiricism (Stubbs 2001: 220ff.). The observation of authentic data, the 'brute facts' of linguistic performance, which is a valuable practice in corpus linguistics, as it was for the early field-workers of American structuralism, was seen in the Chomskyian tradition as devoid of any significant theoretical implications. A study of mere linguistic behaviour, it was objected, would only provide data for a theoretical model based on the contingencies of linguistic performance, rather than provide access to absolute linguistic competence.

Yet, where Chomsky saw irreducible qualitative difference between the limits of individual performance and a potentially unlimited, universal competence, so that performance could never yield significant insight into competence, corpus linguistics came to see how the two things are instead found on a continuum. Performance, or external language (E-language), may well be seen as representing a crucial, indispensable manifestation of competence, or internalized language (I-language), with I-language made somehow discernible as a summation of E-language events tending to infinity (Leech 2007:135). From the perspective of corpus linguistics, as Halliday has persuasively argued through his powerful 'weather' metaphor, the relationship between *visible* authentic real-life instances of language use and the *invisible* abstract system can be compared to the relationship between the *weather*, relating to the next few hours or days, and the *climate*, as the summation of each day's weather (Halliday 1991: 45). With the possibility of handling many millions of words (or weather reports, to keep to Halliday's metaphor), modern computerized corpora have provided the linguist with greater possibilities than in the past for insight into the language system (the climate), i.e. into the social, public and shared features of language.

2.2 Representativeness

Closely related to authenticity is the 'vexed question' (Tognini Bonelli 2001: 57) of representativeness, which can be considered as important as authenticity in defining a corpus. Representativeness is no doubt the standard that most clearly connects to the underlying 'body' metaphor. Reference to some of the most frequently quoted early definitions such as those by Francis (1992), Biber *et al.* (1998), or again McEnery and Wilson (2001), shows that representativeness is almost invariably mentioned as *the* key issue. According to Francis, for instance, a corpus is 'a collection of texts assumed to be *representative* of a given language, dialect, or other subset of a language, to be used for linguistic analysis' (Francis 1992: 17, my italics). Biber *et al.*, instead, state that:

> A corpus is not simply a collection of texts. Rather, *a corpus seeks to represent* a language or some part of a language. The appropriate design for a corpus therefore depends upon what it is meant to *represent*. The *representativeness* of the corpus, in turn, determines the kinds of research questions that can be addressed and the generalizability of the results of the research. (Biber *et al.* 1998: 246, my italics)

Similarly, McEnery and Wilson see sampling and representativeness as the goal to which all the other characteristics of the modern corpus are subordinate:

> A corpus in modern linguistics, in contrast to being simply any body of text, might more accurately be described as a finite-sized body of machine-readable text, sampled *in order to be maximally representative* of the language variety under consideration. (McEnery and Wilson 2001: 32, my italics)

A crucial issue in determining the value of a corpus as an object of linguistic study, the notion of representativeness concerns 'the kind of texts included, the number of texts, the selection of particular texts, the selection of text samples from within texts, and the length of text samples' (Biber 1992: 174). It also entails careful considerations concerning the users of the language which a corpus aims to represent, a task which Sinclair aptly considered 'hardly a job for linguists at all, but more appropriate for the sociology of culture' (Sinclair 1991: 13). Sinclair himself stressed again the same point by stating that 'the contents of a corpus should be selected [...] according to their communicative function in the community within which they arise' (Sinclair 2005: online). Putting it more simply, he voiced these concerns through the following questions:

> What sort of documents do they write and read, and what sort of spoken encounters do they have? How can we allow for the relative popularity of some publications over others, and the difference in attention given to different publications? How do we allow for the unavoidable influence of practicalities such as the relative ease of acquiring public printed language, e-mails and web pages as compared with the labour and expense of recording and transcribing private conversations or acquiring and keying personal handwritten correspondence? How do we identify the instances of language that are influential as models for the population, and therefore might be weighted more heavily than the rest? (Sinclair 2005: online)

Criteria for representativeness should thus be mainly text-external, i.e. situational and not purely linguistic (Biber 1992: 174). From a practical point of view this entails in the first place a clear view of the texts to be included in a corpus in terms of register and genres, rather than merely in terms of content or domain. This makes it self-evident that, as we will see later in this book, representativeness cannot apply in these same terms to the web as a corpus; it should also be made clear, however, that even in traditional corpora representativeness has come to be viewed in non-absolute terms. Representativeness is better seen as a heuristic notion, a goal which, however difficult to attain in practice, is worth being pursued in a sort of gradual approximation (Leech 2007: 143).

The reason why the issue of representativeness is so crucial in corpus linguistics is that it is – like authenticity – rich in implications from the point of view of linguistic theory as a whole. Corpus linguistics is considered as 'the natural correlate of the language model upheld by Firth, Halliday and Sinclair' (Tognini Bonelli 2001: 57), a model in which repeated events noticed in language samples at the level of individual performance are an essential element in the formulation of generalization about language. It is therefore on the representativeness of the corpus that the value of generalizations about language informed by the corpus linguistic approach ultimately rest. And this is also why early criticism of corpus linguistics by Chomsky was focused precisely on this issue. The typical charge against corpus linguistics was simply that, however large a corpus, the data would only be a small sample of a potentially infinite population, and that any corpus would be intrinsically unrepresentative and 'skewed':

> Any natural corpus will be skewed. Some sentences won't occur because they are obvious, others because they are false, still others because they are impolite. The corpus, if natural, will be so wildly skewed that the description would be no more than a mere list. (Chomsky 1962: 159; quoted in Aijmer and Altenberg 2004: 8)

While Chomsky's much-quoted criticism of early corpus linguistics – which might be equally applied to any other type of scientific investigation based on sampling – was to some extent valid at that time, it can also be considered precisely as a 'child of its times'. As McEnery and Wilson convincingly argue, Chomsky's rejection of corpus linguistics dates back to the 1950s when corpora were really small entities. While size is not in itself a guarantee of representativeness, it is a factor which obviously – albeit indirectly – contributes to it. As corpora became larger and larger, and the issue of size was no longer the problem it used to be in the beginning, it became reasonable to think that there could be 'much more representative corpora than Chomsky could dream of when he first criticized corpus-based linguistics' (McEnery and Wilson 2001: 78).

2.3 Balance and sampling

As a sample of a language or language variety aimed at being representative of something larger than itself, a corpus needs to be designed on the basis of some form of balance and sampling criteria.

A balanced corpus is supposed to cover a wide range of text categories considered to be representative of the language or variety under scrutiny. Such categories are sampled proportionally so as to offer 'a manageably small scale model of the linguistic material which the corpus builders wish to study' (Atkins et al. 1992: 6). By way of example, an overview of the design criteria behind the compilation of the British National Corpus (BNC) might be useful to indicate what is assumed to be corpus balance (McEnery and Xiao 2006: 18). The BNC contains nearly 100 million words of British English, from spoken and written texts dating from 1975 to 1991. The spoken section amounts to 10 per cent of the whole corpus and is composed of informal encounters recorded by volunteer respondents selected by age group, sex, social class and geographical region, as well as of formal encounters such as meetings, lectures and radio broadcasts. Written texts make up 90 per cent of the corpus and were selected on the basis of 'domain' (i.e. subject field), 'time', referring to the period of text production, and 'medium', depending on the type of text publication (e.g. books, periodicals or unpublished manuscripts), with the overall aim of achieving a balanced selection within each text category (Aston and Burnard 1998: 29–30). Table 1.1 below reports the design criteria for the written part of the BNC.

Table 1.1. Composition of the written BNC (Source: McEnery and Xiao 2006: 17).

Domain	%	Date	%	Medium	%
Imaginative	21.91	1960–74	2.26	Book	58.58
Arts	8.08	1975–93	89.21	Periodical	31.08
Belief and thought	3.40	Unclassifed	8.49	Misc. Published	4.38
Commerce/ Finance	7.93			Misc. Unpublished	4.00
Leisure	11.13			To-be-spoken	1.52
Natural/pure science	4.18			Unclassified	0.40
Social science	14.80				
World affairs	18.39				
Unclassified	1.93				

A further decision to be made in corpus design relates to the size of each sample – for example, full texts (i.e. whole documents) or text chunks. According to Biber (1992), frequent linguistic features are quite stable in their distributions and short text chunks (e.g. 2,000 running words) could be sufficient for the study of such features, while rare features are more varied in their distribution and thus require larger samples. Additionally, attention must also be paid to ensure that text initial, middle and end samples are balanced. Ideally, the proportion and number of samples for each text category should be proportional to its frequency and/or weight in the target population in order for the resulting corpus to be considered as representative. Nevertheless, such proportions can be difficult to determine objectively and the criteria used to classify texts into different categories or genres often rely on intuitions (cf. Hunston 2002: 28-30). As a result, the real contribution of sampling criteria to the representativeness of a corpus should be conceived of, again, heuristically rather than as a statement of fact.

2.4 Size

A corpus is by definition an object of finite size, from which precise quantitative data concerning the language items it contains can be derived. It is quite obvious that there cannot be a standard size for corpora, and size may indeed vary depending on the nature of the corpus and its purpose. A corpus aimed at being representative of general language certainly needs to be quite large if it is to provide evidence for a sufficiently large number of language items; by contrast, a specialized corpus, that is, a corpus aimed at representing only one restricted variety of language, can be relatively small. Furthermore, the very perception of what might constitute a large enough corpus has changed over time. The first computer corpus, the Brown Corpus, contains 1 million words of American English. It consists of 500 text samples taken from publications listed in the 1961 catalogue of library holdings of Brown University. This was considered a remarkable achievement in its time. Unsurprisingly, this same corpus came to be considered rather small by the standards of the so-called 'second generation' general corpora of the 1990s, such as the already mentioned British National Corpus (BNC). The corpora used for the compilation of dictionaries today are all larger than the BNC, such as the *Collins Cobuild Bank of English*, currently amounting to 650 million words[1] from written and spoken texts covering eight varieties of English. And when these corpora are compared with any of the over 1 billion-word web corpora compiled in the first decade of the new millennium out of internet documents (see Chapters 4 and 6), let alone with the web itself, it is evident how the issue of size is subject to relativism.

Notwithstanding all these considerations, size remains a decisive factor to be taken into account when considering the value of a corpus and the kind of evidence it can provide. It is a well-known fact, for instance, that any corpus will contain only one occurrence for about half of its words, only two occurrences for a quarter of words, and so on (Sinclair 2005: online), according to the so-called Zipf's Law (1935). If we consider that at least twenty occurrences are needed to provide a basis 'for even an outline description of the behaviour of a word to be compiled by trained lexicographers' (Sinclair 2005: online), it will appear quite obvious how size can affect the very usefulness of a given corpus. Furthermore, size decisively affects the possibility of using corpora to explore phraseology, since the number of occurrences that can be retrieved from a corpus for units of language larger than a single word is significantly affected by corpus size. This emphasizes that – especially in corpus design – the estimate of a suitable size for a corpus is subject to considerations concerning all other factors, first of all the purpose of the corpus itself, and can become a really complicated matter.

2.5 Types of corpora

A corpus is generally designed for a specific research purpose, and in view of such purposes different types of corpora can be identified. The first distinction to be made concerns general reference *vs* specialized corpora. Also crucial is the distinction between synchronic and diachronic corpora, and between monolingual and multilingual corpora.

A general reference corpus includes texts from a variety of domains, genres and registers with the aim of being as representative as possible of the whole range of variation within a language. It can contain both written and spoken language and is relatively large in size. It is often used to produce reference materials for language learning and translation (such as grammar books or dictionaries) or, as we will see later, as a baseline in comparison with smaller, specialized corpora, to produce lists of keywords. Typical examples of general purpose corpora for English are the BNC and the Bank of English, both comprising a range of sub-corpora from different sources to ensure a certain representativeness of general English. Unlike a general reference corpus, a specialized corpus aims instead at representing only a given variety or domain of language in use, such as medical discourse, or academic discourse. It is generally smaller than a general purpose corpus and restrictions may apply not only to domain, but also to genre, time, geographical variety and so on.

An important distinction is also drawn between synchronic and diachronic corpora – that is, between corpora that contain texts from a limited time period and provide a snapshot of a language variety at a given time (e.g. the BNC, which basically provides evidence of English from the 1990s) and corpora that seek to trace the evolution of language over time (e.g. the TIME corpus, which contains data from the US magazine *Time* from 1923 to the present). Special kinds of diachronic corpora are those labelled as monitor, or dynamic, corpora, which are continually updated. This approach was proposed by Sinclair (1991) and seeks to develop a corpus which constantly grows in size. The proportion of the different types of material it includes continually changes, but it is assumed that in this type of corpora sheer size can balance the need for precision: as the corpus grows, any skew in the data naturally self-corrects (McEnery and Hardie 2012: 7). Examples of monitor corpora are the Bank of English (University of Birmingham) and COCA (Davies 2009), a monitor corpus whose growth proceeds according to a sampling design. The web itself is now openly recognized as being very similar to a monitor corpus (McEnery and Hardie 2012: 7).

With regard to the number of languages covered, corpora can finally be defined as monolingual or multilingual. Multilingual corpora are especially used for translation purposes and include texts in different languages. The terminology adopted to categorize such corpora is not always consistent, but one can quite safely state that the most common types of multilingual corpora are parallel corpora and comparable corpora. Parallel corpora consist of original texts and their translations in one or more languages, whereas comparable corpora consist of two or more collections of texts similar as concerns genre, topic, time span, and communicative function. In parallel corpora, the two (or more) components are typically aligned on a paragraph-by-paragraph or sentence-by-sentence basis.

3. Corpus, concordance, collocation: Tools and analysis

3.1 Corpus creation

Compiling resources like the general reference corpora that have been mentioned in the previous paragraph is a very time-consuming and challenging enterprise, which is hardly a job for a single researcher. It is generally done in teams, in the context of academic (or commercial) research projects, and involves different stages. The first stage is a careful plan based on theoretically informed considerations concerning the texts to be included in the corpus, their size, their language variety, in view of the purpose of the corpus itself. Once the data have been collected on the basis of the specified criteria, they generally need to be processed before use with corpus query tools. Basic processing includes the production of machine-readable versions of the chosen documents, by digitizing/scanning printed text, or by converting existing electronic documents from a different format (PDF, HTML, etc.) into a suitable format (usually plain text), machine-readability of the texts in the corpus being a default for contemporary corpus linguistics. When using online documents, it is also necessary to clean up the text by separating the text proper from the typical paratextual material (the non-informative parts made up of navigation links, advertisements, headers and footers), i.e. the so-called 'boilerplate' (Bernardini et al. 2006). Also, depending on the nature of the corpus, its composition and its purpose, some form of mark-up may be necessary to compensate for the loss of information determined by the reduction of texts, or text samples, to mere strings of characters. Corpus mark-up can be defined as 'a system of standard codes inserted into a document stored in electronic form to provide information about the text itself' (Xiao 2010: 155). This information is definitely necessary to the interpretation of corpus data extracted from a corpus, and maybe more or less detailed or complex depending on the purpose of the corpus itself. Several schemes have been developed to accomplish this task, among which one of the most common is that known as TEI (Text Encoding Initiative). Also related to corpus mark-up is the problem of character encoding, which concerns the representation of special characters such as accented characters in European languages (see McEnery and Xiao 2006: 22–7).

A further step in the compilation of a corpus can be annotation, i.e. the practice of adding interpretative linguistic information to a corpus (Leech 2005: online). While corpus mark-up, as described above, provides 'relatively objectively verifiable information regarding the components of a corpus and the textual structure of each text' (Xiao 2010: 158) and can in some cases be inevitable (as is often the case with spoken corpora), annotation is by no means a necessity, since it concerns linguistic information that is added to the corpus. As a matter of fact, annotation can be defined in a broad sense, encompassing both the encoding of textual/contextual information (more precisely referred to as mark-up) and the encoding of interpretative linguistic analyses (annotation proper), and the two terms are sometimes used interchangeably in the literature. It is, nonetheless, important to keep the two as conceptually separate activities, given the greater degree of subjectivity of annotation when compared to mark-up proper.

Annotation can be at various levels, the most common forms being lemmatization and part-of-speech (POS) tagging, which are now generally performed automatically. In lemmatization each word is related to its base form, so that, for instance, *is*, *was* and *have been* are all labelled as forms of the lemma BE. Part-of-speech tagging requires instead that each single word is labelled according to the word class it belongs to – as noun, verb, adjective, etc. Thus the word *present* can be labelled as noun, adjective or verb, on the basis of its written form. Other levels of annotation concern levels below and above the word, such as phonetic/prosodic annotation (especially useful for spoken corpora) and syntactic annotation, or parsing, i.e. the attachment of syntactic categories and grammar relations to text segments at phrase level. Further delicacy of analysis is allowed by adding semantic annotation, pragmatic annotation, discourse annotation or stylistic annotation (Leech 2004: online). In more general terms it should be stressed that even though not all scholars agree on the importance of annotation, among these notably Sinclair (1992), annotation is now generally considered useful – and to some extent necessary – 'added value' to corpora (McEnery and Xiao 2006: 30). It goes without saying that choices concerning the level and delicacy of annotation are closely related to the uses of a corpus. In any case, some form of annotation definitely broadens the spectrum of the kind of analysis that can be performed (especially for very large corpora) and allows for a broader range of research questions to be answered, whether by manual, (semi)automated, or automated analysis.

3.2 Corpus analysis

Once compiled, a corpus can be explored and analysed using specific tools that provide access to the information stored in the corpus. In this respect, frequency wordlists and concordance lines can be seen to exemplify the two basic forms of the analysis, qualitative and quantitative, upon which corpus linguistics is firmly based.

A corpus is generally queried using a corpus analysis tool called a concordancer, which retrieves and displays data from the corpus. Today concordancers are easily available not only as commercial products, e.g. Wordsmith Tools (Scott 2004), but also as freeware made available to the research community, such as AntConc (Anthony 2005). As with any other aspect of corpus linguistics, concordancers have developed through the years, from the earliest which could do no more than provide concordance lines and were typically held on a few mainframe computers in one or two universities only, to the desktop applications that were developed with the spread of personal computers in the 1980s. This provided a new generation of linguists with the possibility of using corpora to experiment with corpus techniques supported by more and more sophisticated corpus query tools. However such factors as the steady increase in size of corpus resources, the problems arising in the distribution of the data because of copyright constraints, and the problems created by differing PC operating systems and by the relatively limited power of desktop applications, resulted in the development of the so-called fourth-generation concordancers (McEnery and Hardie 2012a: online). These systems allow corpus users to access the data through a web interface, thus making available to the research community a huge amount of corpus data. Typical examples are Mark Davies' corpus.byu.edu interface (Davies 2005), BNCweb (Hoffmann et al. 2008) and Sketch Engine (Kilgarriff et al. 2004). In the following paragraphs most of the examples used to exemplify typical corpus activities will be taken from the BNC, freely accessed through the web interface created by Davies at Brigham Young University (USA), and through the Sketch Engine, a service which will be explored in more detail in Chapter 6.

3.2.1 Wordlists and keywords

The first gateway to the invaluable information stored in a corpus is provided by frequency lists, that is, simple lists featuring all the word types that occur in a corpus, along with an indication of the frequency of occurrence of each item, i.e. how often that item appears in the corpus itself. This is usually referred to as raw frequency. By way of example, one can consider the first 24 word forms from the 1 million-word Brown Corpus and from the 100 million-word British National Corpus (see Figure 1.1), ordered according to their raw frequency:

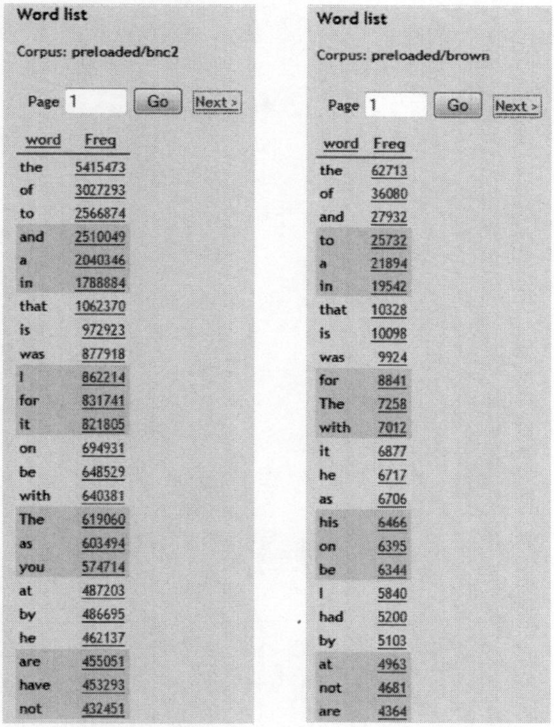

Word list

Corpus: preloaded/bnc2

Page 1 Go Next >

word	Freq
the	5415473
of	3027293
to	2566874
and	2510049
a	2040346
in	1788884
that	1062370
is	972923
was	877918
I	862214
for	831741
it	821805
on	694931
be	648529
with	640381
The	619060
as	603494
you	574714
at	487203
by	486695
he	462137
are	455051
have	453293
not	432451

Word list

Corpus: preloaded/brown

Page 1 Go Next >

word	Freq
the	62713
of	36080
and	27932
to	25732
a	21894
in	19542
that	10328
is	10098
was	9924
for	8841
The	7258
with	7012
it	6877
he	6717
as	6706
his	6466
on	6395
be	6344
I	5840
had	5200
by	5103
at	4963
not	4681
are	4364

Figure 1.1. *The first 24 word forms from the* Brown Corpus *and from the* British National Corpus

As Figure 1.1 makes clear, the most frequent words in a corpus – irrespective of difference in size – are mostly function words. Interesting phenomena occur also at the end of the frequency list, where there is a long tail of *hapax legomena*, i.e. words occurring only once in the corpus. This list includes rare words, proper names, foreign words, but also misspelt items or strings erroneously computed as words by the system. Table 1.2 illustrates a small sample of *hapax legomena* from the BNC and from the Brown Corpus:

Table 1.2. A sample of *hapax legomena* from the BNC and the Brown Corpus

BNC	Brown Corpus
Agesidamos 1	middle-Gaelic 1
Epizephyrian 1	flashback 1
filth-century 1	Meinckian 1
xii.30 1	Jungian 1
Greek-barbarian 1	Pockmanster 1
Kokalos 1	spouting 1
Segestans 1	Province 1
Kamarina 1	Bathar-on-Walli 1
Lokrian 1	nnuolapertar-it-vuh-karti-birifw- 1
Decemvirate 1	tongue-twister 1
non-Dorian 1	sweathruna 1
xi.76xii. 1	pratakku 1
river-nymph 1	salivate 1
Elymiots 1	bouanahsha 1

As seen in the examples above, if we compare at a glance the frequency of occurrence of the first function words in the BNC and in the Brown Corpus we find that they are roughly proportional to the overall size of each corpus. The BNC is about 100 times larger than the Brown Corpus and, according to data reported in the table above, it contains 6,054,238 occurrences for the definite article *the*, which means a normalized frequency of 53,968.5 per million; similarly, the Brown Corpus has 69,971 occurrences for *the*, which amount to 59,515.6 per million. If we compare not the quantitative data *per se* ('raw frequency') but their normalized frequency, *the* appears to be roughly as frequent in the Brown Corpus as in the BNC. A more significant example could be comparing the number of occurrences of the word *American* in the Brown Corpus and in the BNC. In this case we would find that there are only 570 hits for *American* in the Brown Corpus, set against the 18,845 hits in the BNC, but this obviously does not mean that the word *American* is more frequent in the BNC than in the Brown Corpus! It is only a comparison between the normalized frequency of *American* in the Brown Corpus (484.8 per million) and the normalized frequency of *American* in the BNC (168.0 per million), which suggests that the word *American* is – as expected – nearly four times more frequent in the Brown Corpus than in the BNC.

As will be clarified later, the usefulness of word lists goes well beyond these simple, or even simplistic, statistics. If properly investigated, word lists can also give an indication of genre and register (Scott and Tribble 2006), and can reveal ideological concerns (Baker 2006). At a more basic level, an overview of frequency lists can, at a glance, provide evidence of the content of a corpus. For specialized corpora, for instance, frequency lists may provide immediate insights into domain and terminology. Table 1.3 below shows how the first 20 content word forms from a 500,000-word specialized corpus on ORAL CANCER are crucially related to this specific subject field. Numbers to the left of each word refer to the position in the word list (function words have been removed) whereas numbers to the right refer to raw frequency and normalized frequency.

Word lists can be useful in themselves, as seen above, but even more useful is comparison of different word lists from different corpora to reveal the items which are characteristic of each list. This corresponds to the retrieval of 'keywords', defined as 'words which occur unusually frequently in comparison with some kind of reference corpus' (Scott 2010: 35), i.e. words that occur with higher (or lower) frequency in a text or corpus, given the frequency of occurrence of the same words and expression in a corpus which is larger or of equal size. Keywords can thus be defined as words or expressions that are statistically more, or less, frequent than expected in a text or corpus when compared to another corpus taken as a point of reference. For instance, the keywords retrieved by comparing the word list obtained from a single text, or corpus of texts, and the word list from a general reference corpus like the BNC would result in clear evidence of the words characterizing the text or corpus under investigation. An example is the list of keywords resulting from a comparison between Shakespeare's *Othello* and the word list from a general reference corpus, as reported in the Wordsmith Tools Manual (Scott 2010a: 165). See Figure 1.2.

Table 1.3. The first 20 content word forms from a specialized corpus on Oral Cancer (Source: Gatto 2009: 119)

N	Word	Freq.	%
10	CANCER	4.096	0,93
23	ORAL	1.590	0,36
25	PATIENTS	1.546	0,35
30	TREATMENT	1.352	0,31
31	CELL	1.153	0,26
35	NECK	1.082	0,24
37	SURGERY	1.069	0,24
39	PAIN	1.041	0,24
42	LUNG	1.001	0,23
44	CELLS	960	0,22
45	DISEASE	935	0,21
47	LYMPH	913	0,21
48	USE	840	0,19
51	BLOOD	813	0,18
52	BIOPSY	797	0,18
59	BODY	746	0,17
60	THERAPY	745	0,17
61	RISK	744	0,17
69	NODES	653	O,15
71	BREAST	634	0,14
72	RADIATION	626	0,14

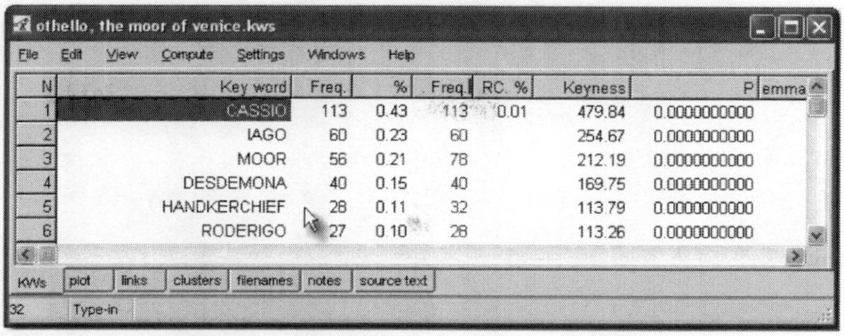

Figure 1.2. *The keywords of Shakespeare's* Othello *as reported in the Wordsmith Tools Manual*

3.2.2 Concordances

If quantitative frequency data are the first, and in some respects most important, aspect of the kind of analysis that can be performed in corpus linguistics, concordances are the most typical. Indeed corpus linguistics itself is strongly associated, today, with the image of a scholar searching through screen after screen of concordance lines (McCarthy and O'Keffee 2010: 3), and concordances have been at the heart of corpus exploration from the very beginning. Again, however, it is perhaps useful to remind us that what is relatively new are the electronic tools used to explore concordance lines, whereas the methodology itself is not. Detailed, painstaking, and certainly passionate, search for words and phrases in multiple contexts and across large amounts of text can actually be traced back to the Middle Ages, when biblical scholars manually indexed all the words in the Bible, page after page.

Despite having been around for centuries, concordances have no doubt radically changed their face in the computer age, with the shift related to the new medium entailing a more radical change than might appear at first glance. Through electronic concordances the qualitative difference between reading a corpus and simply reading a text has become finally evident. In the words of Tognini Bonelli (2001: 3):

> the text is to be read *horizontally*, from left to right, paying attention to the boundaries between larger units such as clauses, sentences and paragraphs. A corpus [...] is read vertically, scanning for the repeated patterns present in the co-text of the node.

By allowing simultaneous access to the individual instance of language use at the level of syntagmatic patterning as well as to patterns of repetition across many texts and to the alternatives available on the paradigmatic axis, concordancers have provided a radically new point of view for the observation of linguistic facts. This new point of view allows the linguist to take the analysis a step further from simple computation, and perform a qualitative/quantitative analysis in which each word is investigated in its immediate co-text, i.e. with the possibility of seeing which words occur before and after it in the limited span of fixed number of words (e.g. five words to the right and to the left).

In more practical terms, concordancers are tools that search for given words or phrases in a corpus and display them in their immediate textual environment. All occurrences of the search word, or 'node' word, are displayed in the centre of the computer screen, aligned and highlighted, in the so-called Key-Word-in-Context (KWiC) format. Figure 1.3 shows a sample from the 754 occurrences of the word *scenery* from the BNC with a certain amount of co-text to its left and to its right.

```
east to west one may see more varieties of scenery than are to be found in many bigger countrie
ly placed to appreciate the relationship of scenery and structure, for few other parts of the ea
es on the way to the district hospital. The scenery throughout the rugged mountain areas is dram
ather bought houses there, feeling that the scenery would be a good influence on their children;
rowded world. Both regions include splendid scenery and wildlife, for which a possible wise use
bly sunny, photograph. Historical dates and scenery all conveyed the objective, factual nature o
 region for recreation and the enjoyment of scenery and wild life which, being open to the publi
pressed on north-westwards, passing through scenery of a wild grandeur and beauty he had never k
e, such strenuous activities amid inspiring scenery appealed particularly to Anglo-Saxon intelle
t rather for the fresh air and breathtaking scenery . They do not want commercialisation, if any
 followed by yet another enquiry. True, the scenery has changed. For instance, government may ha
w of sea and river. Thereafter, the coastal scenery reminded me increasingly of lowland Scotland
ractions almost, along with the surrounding scenery . In this case the native Lake District popu
ooking and gives your guest some variety of scenery . THE DINNER OR LUNCHEON PARTY Whatever time
covers six hundred square miles of dramatic scenery , with picturesque villages, purple moorland
meandering rivers flow through breathtaking scenery and beside magnificent abbeys and castles. A
 Big Country Wide open spaces, breathtaking scenery , great company, superb horses -- that's Nor
oliday -- amidst some of the most beautiful scenery in the world. Glenborrodale, on the northern
ncluded) travel through attractive woodland scenery to the fortified city of Naarden with its st
 course mile after mile of wonderful alpine scenery to walk or run through. And for those who pr
ide villages, breathtaking river and forest scenery and Llanybydder Mountain to the east of the
its stands of tall, dark pines. Some of the scenery is very Scottish-looking with clumps of birc
tarring Boris Karloff. It was given without scenery , and the music was played on the Wurlitzer
to their use. The beauty and novelty of the scenery , the luxuriance of the shrubs and above all
t 59 per cent of the visitors mentioned the scenery as the main attraction of the area. Cumbria
ar hundred miles through some of the finest scenery in the British Isles with the freedom of the
ope of a hill commanding a great variety of scenery and had given each bedroom its own special v
ad in the Kurpark. For a complete change of scenery , a 1520 minute bus ride (buses run every ha
oliday in some of the most beautiful alpine scenery there is, including some excellent bars and
deal centre for walking in beautiful alpine scenery , with every route you choose offering fanta
e whole journey is filled with breathtaking scenery . What to see and do Excursions: Take the lo
med Edelweiss is surrounded by the dramatic scenery of the Bernese Alps. This stone built hotel
```

Figure 1.3. *A sample out of the 754 occurrences of* scenery *from the BNC.*

As the sample shows, the function of the KWiC format is to enable 'vertical' reading, i.e. 'scanning for the repeated patterns present in the co-text of the node' (Tognini Bonelli 2001: 3). In order to make repeated patterns more easily discerned, the user can sort the words left or right of the node word under analysis, so as to explore different areas of the co-text. For example, they can be sorted alphabetically according to the first (or second or third, etc.) word to the left or to the right. In the case of *scenery*, it only takes a quick glance to see how some words (adjectives, nouns, verbs...) repeatedly occur left and right of the node word, providing evidence for subtler levels of analysis. In Figure 1.4. below, which reports the same sample as in Figure 1.3 now sorted to the first word on the left (L1 co-text), one can see how the left co-text clearly features such adjectives as *beautiful*, *breathtaking*, *dramatic*, etc.:

```
ibly sunny, photograph. Historical dates and scenery all conveyed the objective, factual nature
:d staff who will design and build props and scenery to specification. Production Services Phone
inch -- has other attractions too. Beautiful scenery , fresh air and good food, a chance to live
ioliday -- amidst some of the most beautiful scenery in the world. Glenborrodale, on the norther
is an excellent way of seeing such beautiful scenery . We went back to college for lunch and cha
 harbour. (e) St Abb's Head Some of the best scenery of the Scottish E coast. (g) Visitor centre
 that it was back into the " chocolate box " scenery of western Norway, the fabulous fiords and
it rather for the fresh air and breathtaking scenery . They do not want commercialisation, if an
 meandering rivers flow through breathtaking scenery and beside magnificent abbeys and castles.
i Big Country Wide open spaces, breathtaking scenery , great company, superb horses -- that's No
ie whole journey is filled with breathtaking scenery . What to see and do Excursions: Take the 1
iw of sea and river. Thereafter, the coastal scenery reminded me increasingly of lowland Scotlan
 away) takes you through spectacular coastal scenery . Another, from the harbour to St Juliot's
iy night. For the ocean may provide dramatic scenery but it does not, in itself, belong centre-s
iast of Majorca, gives the island a dramatic scenery in contrast to the soft beaches below. Our
 covers six hundred square miles of dramatic scenery , with picturesque villages, purple moorlan
imed Edelweiss is surrounded by the dramatic scenery of the Bernese Alps. This stone built hotel
 An easy mistake. She was used to fashioning scenery for the background. In Dreams, you always p
iur hundred miles through some of the finest scenery in the British Isles with the freedom of th
 day, guy ropes were needed to hold the flat scenery upright. Gabriel quickly discovered why a r
iide villages, breathtaking river and forest scenery and Llanybydder Mountain to the east of the
 then along the Gadmen valley to the gentler scenery of the valley of the Aare at Innertkirchen
is on a large scale. Or there is the grander scenery , and the more spectacular engineering, of
:s. Treat it with respect through -- hitting scenery and objects costs time, and eventually impa
. But we were drawn by the Romantic taste in scenery , what Bertrand Russell called " wild torre
:e, such strenuous activities amid inspiring scenery appealed particularly to Anglo-Saxon intell
:what slipshod -- with cameras crashing into scenery , sound effects drowning out voices, etc --
Ind villain with very good memory, who loves scenery . Still looking for his Woodbines even thou
irnoon is at leisure to enjoy the marvellous scenery . Day 4 BanffJasper Travel north on the Gla
.ne " of Norway through spectacular mountain scenery to Trondheim. Much of the country was woode
 of carved marble mosques, dramatic mountain scenery and spectacular coastline. Reverence for th
intain in the world. In magnificent mountain scenery , the country's capital of Kathmandu stradd
```

Figure 1.4. *A sample out of the 754 occurrences of* scenery *from the BNC sorted to the first word on the left (L1 co-text).*

As the screenshot above suggests, concordancers can present language data in a corpus in a way that helps bridge the gap between quantitative and qualitative analysis, showing evidence of co-occurrence that indicates typical and frequent patterns in language. However, the computer can only act as a facilitator, since the interpretation of the data depends only – and critically – on what Leech called 'the observational and generalizing skills of the investigator' (Leech 1992: 114). The challenge then is to provide a qualitative analysis of quantitative data, and the best way to start is to consider each word's lexico-grammatical context, starting from other words appearing in its immediate textual environment, i.e. to its 'collocates'.

3.3 Collocation and basic statistics

As already argued above, the visual output and functionality of concordancers have enabled researchers to discover aspects of language uses that could have remained invisible. It also gave them access to empirical data to support views that had been held for years, but for which no evidence could be found. It is indeed one of the advantages of using a computer corpus that it can provide reliable, objective, quantitative data concerning phenomena that are only intuitively grasped. Particularly fruitful in this respect has proved the interaction between the theoretical notion of collocation, 'the company a word keeps', put forward by Firth (1957: 11), and its computational counterpart. Collocation is the tendency of words to co-occur. More specifically, the collocates of a word are words that frequently occur in its immediate co-text (e.g. within five words to the left or to the right of that word). Going back to the example of *scenery* (see Figures 1.3 and 1.4), it is quite easy to see how a computer could in a matter of seconds give an exact measure of collocation. In Figure 1.5, the twelve adjectives most commonly collocating with *scenery* in the BNC are reported in order of frequency:

		CONTEXT	TOT		ALL	%	MI
1		BEAUTIFUL	54		8394	0.64	6.68
2		SPECTACULAR	39		1929	2.02	8.33
3		DRAMATIC	27		3817	0.71	6.82
4		MAGNIFICENT	20		1972	1.01	7.34
5		BREATHTAKING	17		333	5.11	9.67
6		STUNNING	15		935	1.60	8.00
7		WILD	14		5401	0.26	5.37
8		COASTAL	13		1425	0.91	7.19
9		WONDERFUL	13		4670	0.28	5.47
10		ALPINE	10		481	2.08	8.37
11		SUPERB	9		2063	0.44	6.12
12		IMPRESSIVE	9		2915	0.31	5.62

Figure 1.5. *The first twelve adjectives collocating with* scenery *in the BNC*

As Figure 1.5 shows, collocations in corpus linguistics are not based on raw frequency data only, but are generally computed through a statistical approach based on the comparison between actual patterns of co-occurrence for words in a given corpus and the patterns that could have been expected if those words were to occur randomly. The significance of each co-occurrence is computed using statistical formulae such as Mutual Information (MI) or other formulae like *t*-score, and log-likelihood. In Figure 1.5 above, the numbers appearing on the right-end column report MI-score, which shows – for instance – that *breathtaking* is the most significant collocate of *scenery*, though not the most frequent. This suggests that quantitative analysis 'goes well beyond simple counting' (McEnery and Wilson 2001: 81) and that, however intimidating it can be for people in the humanities, some basic statistics is essential in corpus linguistics.

The most commonly used formula to identify significant collocations is, as mentioned before, the MI-score. This is a formula borrowed from information theory and basically measures collocational strength, i.e. the probability of two words occurring close to each other in a given span (e.g. 4 or 5 words). The higher the MI-score, the stronger the bond between the two words. Following Hunston (2002: 72) it is generally accepted that an MI-score of 3 or higher can be taken as evidence of a collocation. It has been argued, however, that MI-score alone is not entirely reliable in identifying significant collocations since it is too sensitive to the size of the corpus. It is also necessary to take into account the amount of evidence, i.e. how certain a collocation is. This can be done through another statistical measure, the *t*-score, which considers the actual frequency of occurrence of the collocation. In the words of McEnery and Xiao, again, 'while the MI test measures the strength of collocations, the *t*-test measures the confidence with which we can claim that there is some association' (Church and Hanks 1990; McEnery and Xiao 2006). In other words, the *t*-test, or *t*-score, measures the certainty of a collocation, whereas the MI-score compares the actual co-occurrence of two words with the expected co-occurrence if the words were to occur randomly, i.e. it computes the non-randomness of a collocation. However, as observed in Kilgarriff and Kosem (2012: 40), one possible flaw of MI-score is that it tends to emphasize rare words. In order to solve this problem, a number of different statistics have been proposed, including such formulae as log-likelihood ratio and the Dice coefficient (Manning and Schütze, 1999). Among the most recent collocation statistics is logDice (Rychly 2008), which is currently implemented in the Sketch Engine (see Chapter 6 of this book).

In order to appreciate some practical implications of what has been said so far, we can now compare the list of collocates for the word *culture* from the BNC, ordered according to their mere frequency of occurrence, and then in terms of MI-score and *t*-score, to see the difference. See Table 1.4.

As the table makes clear, the *t*-score measures the 'certainty' of the collocation, favouring high-frequency items and almost replicating raw frequency data, whereas the MI-score foregrounds the 'non-randomness' of the collocation, bringing up words which are not frequent in the corpus and almost exclusively occur together with the node word. The word *Plesu*, for example, occurs only 3 times in the BNC, always in the immediate co-text of *culture*, since it is the name of the Romanian Minister of Culture in the years 1990–1. It would, however, be an over-simplification to draw the conclusion that Plesu is a significant collocate for culture in British English! This is why other statistical tests are required to provide evidence of more sophisticated – and reliable – forms of attraction between words. This is the case of the already mentioned

Table 1.4. List of collocates for *culture* in the BNC, ordered according to Frequency, *t*-score, MI-score

Frequency	*t*-score	MI-score
of	of	Plesu
the	the	MG3
,	and	Gubenko
.	,	reaggregate
and	.	Yevgeniy
in	in	middle-brow
a	a	Sidorov
to	to	serum-free
is	is	hybridoma
that	the	spectatorship
The	that	CULTURES
'	'	confluency
`	which	12h
as	`	Lérins
which	as	Spheroplasts

logDice (Rychly 2008), which adjusts the results so as to foreground the most significant pairs. By way of example, Table 1.5 reports the list of collocates for *culture* from the BNC according to logDice.

As seen in Table 1.5, logDice has highlighted such typical collocations as *popular culture* or *western culture*, *language and culture*, as well as *tissue culture* and *culture cells*, which refer to the two most common meanings of culture, thus contributing to a more consistent profile for the node word. The role that these statistics can play in lexicography will appear quite obvious now, and the usefulness of information of this kind for any language student is self-evident.

Collocation, as this section has shown, is thus a crucial concept in corpus linguistics. It is certainly a concept that is heavily dependent on statistics, and as such it can provide the linguist with significant quantitative data concerning

Table 1.5. List of collocates for *culture* form the BNC according to logDice

logDice
culture
popular
language
Western
youth
dominant
Education
Ministry
tissue
society
history
religion
political
cells
Enterprise

patterns of usage, but it always requires a well-informed qualitative analysis to go beyond superficial suggestions.

3.4 Colligation and semantic associations

Besides focusing on collocations, corpus linguistics also studies colligation, defined as the '[t]he occurrence of a grammatical class or structural pattern with another one, or with a word or phrase' (Sinclair 2003:173). Colligational relations are more difficult to observe especially with large amounts of data and could not be identified at a glance from the observation of a list collocates but would require a thorough investigation of concordance lines. A clear example of colligation can be found in Figure 1.6 where one could consider an evident tendency of the lemma ENMESH to occur in the passive form. See Figure 1.6:

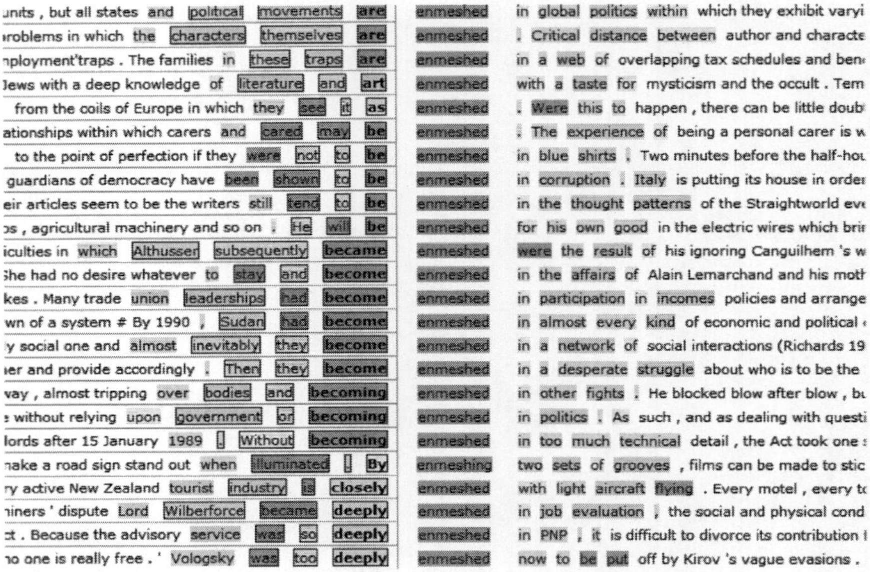
units , but all states and political movements are enmeshed in global politics within which they exhibit varyi
problems in which the characters themselves are enmeshed . Critical distance between author and characte
nployment'traps . The families in these traps are enmeshed in a web of overlapping tax schedules and ben
Jews with a deep knowledge of literature and art enmeshed with a taste for mysticism and the occult . Tem
from the coils of Europe in which they see it as enmeshed . Were this to happen , there can be little doub
ationships within which carers and cared may be enmeshed . The experience of being a personal carer is w
to the point of perfection if they were not to be enmeshed in blue shirts . Two minutes before the half-hou
guardians of democracy have been shown to be enmeshed in corruption . Italy is putting its house in order
eir articles seem to be the writers still tend to be enmeshed in the thought patterns of the Straightworld eve
ps , agricultural machinery and so on . He will be enmeshed for his own good in the electric wires which brir
iculties in which Althusser subsequently became enmeshed were the result of his ignoring Canguilhem 's w
She had no desire whatever to stay and become enmeshed in the affairs of Alain Lemarchand and his moth
kes . Many trade union leaderships had become enmeshed in participation in incomes policies and arrange
wn of a system # By 1990 , Sudan had become enmeshed in almost every kind of economic and political
y social one and almost inevitably they become enmeshed in a network of social interactions (Richards 19
ier and provide accordingly . Then they become enmeshed in a desperate struggle about who is to be the
vay , almost tripping over bodies and becoming enmeshed in other fights . He blocked blow after blow , bu
without relying upon government or becoming enmeshed in politics . As such , and as dealing with questi
lords after 15 January 1989 , without becoming enmeshed in too much technical detail , the Act took one
nake a road sign stand out when illuminated . By enmeshing two sets of grooves , films can be made to stic
ry active New Zealand tourist industry is closely enmeshed with light aircraft flying . Every motel , every to
niners ' dispute Lord Wilberforce became deeply enmeshed in job evaluation , the social and physical cond
ct . Because the advisory service was so deeply enmeshed in PNP , it is difficult to divorce its contribution
no one is really free . ' Vologsky was too deeply enmeshed now to be put off by Kirov 's vague evasions .

Figure 1.6. *Concordance lines for the lemma ENMESH from the BNC*

However difficult to observe in some cases, colligational relations are of crucial importance in determining the behaviour of a word, and this is an area that greatly benefits from information automatically extracted from lemmatized and POS tagged corpora.

Besides providing insight into patterns of habitual co-occurence of a word with other word forms and with words sharing the same word class, namely collocation and colligation, concordance lines can also provide evidence of the semantic associations concerning a word, because of recurrence with other words belonging to specific semantic areas. A word's tendency to co-occur with words evoking a specific semantic field is generally referred to as 'semantic preference'. Anderson and Corbett (2010: 59) report the examples of *stricken*, a word that typically collocates with words like *grief*, *panic*, *terror*. Another typical example found in the literature is the phrase *with/to the naked eye*, generally occurring with collocates suggesting visibility, such as 'visible to the naked eye', 'you can see with the naked eye', and 'look at with the naked eye' (Sinclair 2004: 32).

Also fundamental is the notion of 'semantic prosody' (Louw 1993), or 'discourse prosody' (Stubbs 2002), which refers to the tendency of words to take on special connotations deriving from collocational patterns. It is generally revealing of the speaker's communicative intentions and pertains therefore to the discourse functions. The word *cause* is an excellent example discussed in Stubbs (2002) and Anderson and Corbett (2011: 59–62). Despite its apparently neutral significance, *cause* can be said to have a negative semantic prosody because of its usual co-occurrence with words having negative connotations, as shown in Figure 1.7.

an increase in earnings , when these	cause	benefits to be lost and tax to be
on all pesticides with the potential to	cause	cancer or to damage a developi
by Indian Airlines pilots is starting to	cause	chaos on the sub-continent with
jain . ' The Mahdi 's skull had been a	cause	clbre . At the conclusion of the S
ch as sodium , from the plastic , and	cause	corrosion inside the chip . Indus
al radioactive isotopes in the air and	cause	dangerous levels of alpha radia
jood for Pricewell 's public image (a	cause	dear to his heart) , but he was u
eceived wisdom that it is people who	cause	desertification . Deserts are th
t explains that these toxins probably	cause	diarrhoea by stimulating the ph
le the child himself in his daily life or	cause	distress to his family or commu
hile having a quiet read as this may	cause	drowsiness . A nap after lunch ,
just being realistic . Even that would	cause	enormous difficulties . I could n'
gh the crystal . The absorbed X-rays	cause	excitation of the electrons in th
f times ... " The Vikings certainly did	cause	extensive damage to property i
k is better , but that should not be a	cause	for complacency . Examine whet
t have , and it becomes yet another	cause	for concern and an occasion for
. This was a genuine and reasonable	cause	for concern at a time when the p

Figure 1.7. *Concordance lines for* cause *from the BNC*

Unlike collocation and colligation, and to some extent also semantic preference, which are more prone to being assessed computationally, semantic prosody requires a greater interpretative effort on the part of the linguist (Stewart 2010), and can rely much less on the usefulness of quantitative data alone, than other aspects of qualitative analysis.

Taken together, collocation, colligation, semantic preference and semantic (or discourse) prosody are generally recognized as the typical steps involved in the analysis of concordance lines and represent the basics of data interpretation within the corpus linguistics approach.

Conclusion

In this chapter some basic notions concerning corpus linguistics as a research field have been introduced, also from the perspective of the interaction between linguistic theory and the corpus linguistic approach. Definitions and standards have been discussed in order to make the reader familiar with key issues in corpus linguistics at both a theoretical and practical level before introducing the typical ways of accessing corpus data for qualitative/ quantitative analysis. With no pretence at exhaustiveness, the notions given in this chapter were especially selected in view of the remainder of the book. The reader may wish to refer to more comprehensive introductions to corpus linguistics by choosing from those listed in the suggestions for further reading section.

Study questions and activities

- What do you think are the advantages of quantitative analysis for linguistic research?
- How does the KWiC format of concordance lines contribute to a qualitative analysis of language data?
- Imagine you are planning the compilation of a corpus for a research project and define its aims. What type(s) of texts, registers or genres would you include? Why? Discuss issues of representativeness with reference to your planned corpus.
- This activity will help you get familiar with basic corpus issues using the British National Corpus (BNC) through the search interface made available by Mark Davies at BYU-BNC. Please note that very limited use is here made of the many options made available by the system. If interested in exploring the service in detail take the 'five minute guided tour' provided in the website to learn more about the corpora and the tool and refer to the list of publication included in the website.

1. Go to http://corpus.byu.edu/bnc/ and register as a user.
2. Set the Display function on KWIC and input the word *dramatic* in the search string. Now press the 'Search' button and read the first 50 concordance lines. What do the results displayed suggest as to possible collocates for the node word?
3. Reset the Display function on KWIC and input the word *risk* in the search string to obtain concordance lines. Then sort concordances to the left and to the right using the 'Display/Sort' utility. What do different areas of co-text suggest as to the colligational profile of *risk*? Are there any patterns that are particularly evident?

4 Now input the verb *incur* in the search string. Sort the concordance lines to the left and to the right using the 'Display/Sort' utility. What do different areas of the co-text suggest as to the semantic associations of *incur*?

Finally set the Display function on 'List', click on 'Collocates' and choose a part of speech (POS) tag to look for specific grammar categories among collocates for *incur* (e.g. nouns). What do the results suggest?

Suggestions for further reading

Anderson, W. and Corbett, J. (2009), *Investigating English with Online Corpora*. Basingstoke: Palgrave Macmillan.

Lindquist, H. (2009), *Corpus Linguistics and the Description of English*, Edinburgh: Edinburgh University Press.

McEnery, A. and Hardie, A. (2012), *Corpus Linguistics: Theory, Method, and Practice*. Cambridge: Cambridge University Press.

—(2012), 'Support website for *Corpus Linguistics: Method, theory and practice*'. Available online at http://corpora.lancs.ac.uk/clmtp [accessed 5 June 2013].

McEnery, A. and Xiao, M. (2006), *Corpus-based language studies: an advanced resource book*. London: Routledge.

Note

1 Source http://www.mycobuild.com/about-collins-corpus.aspx [accessed 1 June 2013].

2

The Body and the Web: An Introduction to the Web as Corpus

Introduction

In this chapter the web's controversial nature as a corpus is explored in the light of its properties as a spontaneous, self-generating collection of texts. More specifically, the chapter shows how the notion of the web as corpus might have changed, over the past few years, the very way we conceive of a linguistic corpus moving from the somewhat reassuring standards subsumed under the corpus-as-body metaphor to a new, more flexible and challenging corpus-as-web image. On the one hand, the traditional notion of a linguistic corpus as a *body* of texts rests on some correlate issues, such as finite size, balance, part-whole relationship and permanence; on the other hand, the very idea of a *web* of texts brings about notions of non-finiteness, flexibility, de-centring/re-centring, and provisionality. The thorny relationship between corpus linguistics and the web as a *body* of texts is discussed from a theoretical standpoint in Section 1 and Section 2. Section 3 revisits in more detail such standards as 'authenticity', 'representativeness', 'size' and 'composition', and briefly discusses 'copyright', in order to envisage the changing face of corpus linguistics under the impact of the web. Section 4 finally explores some new issues specifically relevant to the web as corpus, such as 'dynamism', 'reproducibility' and 'relevance/reliability'.

1. Corpus linguistics and the web

At the beginning of the new millennium, in a brief, seminal paper on 'The Web as Corpus', attention was called for the first time to the value of the web as a linguistic resource:

> The corpus resource for the 1990s was the BNC. Conceived in the 80s, completed in the mid 90s, it was hugely innovative and opened up myriad new research avenues for comparing different text types, sociolinguistics, empirical NLP, language teaching and lexicography.
>
> But now the web is with us, giving access to colossal quantities of text, of any number of varieties, at the click of a button, for free. While the BNC and other fixed corpora remain of huge value, it is the web that presents the most provocative questions about the nature of language. (Kilgarriff 2001: 344)

In his stimulating paper, Kilgarriff envisaged a more significant connection between corpus linguistics and the web than was at the time safely recognized, on the basis of the actual impact of the web on corpus linguistics. He was indeed voicing a hope that one day the largest collection of authentic machine-readable texts could be used by linguists, freely and ubiquitously, as a corpus in its own right. And it was perhaps more hope than certainty that made him conclude his paper with the challenging and controversial statement: 'The corpus of the new millennium is the web' (Kilgarriff 2001: 345).

Despite such enthusiastic claims, the way to treating the web as a linguistic corpus was by no means straightforward. It was often landmarked by false starts, disappointment and disillusion, and for a long time faced harsh criticism in the context of more traditional corpus linguistics. Only a few years ago, on the opening page of one of the earliest volumes fully devoted to *Corpus Linguistics and the Web*, the editors – provocatively of course – still wondered 'why should anyone want to use other than carefully compiled corpora?' (Hundt et al. 2007: 1). This was indeed a legitimate question and one that is also relevant to the object of the present book. Why should one even consider taking the risk of using a database as anarchic and chaotic as the World Wide Web? Why should linguists, translators, language professionals of any kind, turn their attention to a collection of texts whose content is largely unknown and whose size is difficult to measure? As the editors of the above-mentioned volume argue, there are a number of obvious answers to these questions. For some areas of investigation within corpus linguistics, such as lexical innovation or morphological productivity, or for investigations concerning ephemeral points in grammar, one might need a corpus larger than the traditional reference corpora of the BNC type. Then, there are language varieties for which carefully compiled corpora are not always viable, but which are extensively represented on the web. Last, but not least, there is the problem of updating, which requires that profit and loss are carefully balanced in the compilation of a conventional corpus, which obviously runs the risk of being out of date before it is finished (Hundt et al. 2007: 1–2).

Judging from these considerations, the notion of the web as corpus would seem to have developed for opportunistic reasons, which have resulted in different ways to exploit the web's potential from a corpus linguistics perspective. In rather general terms, most uses of the web in corpus linguistics can be summed up under the label 'web as/for corpus' (De Schryver 2002; Fletcher 2007), depending on whether the web is accessed directly as a source of online language data or as a source for the compilation of offline corpora. More precisely, in their introduction to the collection of papers from the First International Workshop on the Web as Corpus (Forlì, 14 January 2005), Baroni and Bernardini (2006: 10–14) focused on four basic ways of conceiving of the web as/for corpus:

1 The Web as a corpus surrogate: researchers using the web as a corpus *surrogate* use it for linguistic purposes either via a standard commercial search engine, mainly for opportunistic reasons (e.g. as a reference tool for translation tasks), or through linguist-oriented metasearch engines (e.g. WebCorp).

2 The Web as a corpus shop: researchers using the web as a corpus *shop* select and download texts retrieved by search engines to create 'disposable corpora' either manually or in a semi-automatic (e.g. using a toolkit which allows crawling and extensively downloading from the web, such as BootCat).

3 The Web as corpus proper: researchers using the web as a corpus *proper* purport to investigate the nature of the web, and more specifically they look at the web as a corpus that represents Web English.

4 The mega-Corpus mini-Web: the most radical way of understanding the web as corpus refers to attempts to create a new object (mini-Web/mega-Corpus) adapted to language research and combining web-derived (large, up-to-date, web-based interface) and corpus-like features (annotation, sophisticated queries, stability).

This overview shows how rich the relationship between corpus linguistics and the web can be and undoubtedly testifies to a variety of approaches and methods. And yet this is probably not the whole story. While the reasons for turning to the web as a corpus were no doubt mainly practical (size, open access, low cost) at the outset, there appear also to have been less obvious reasons for taking the patently risky decision to use the web as a resource for linguistic research. It can be argued, indeed, that if the web has been considered as the corpus of the new millennium, this must also be due to qualitative considerations concerning the nature of the web itself, so that there may have been further reasons for turning it into an object of linguistic investigation. In the words of linguist David Crystal, language is 'at the heart of the Internet'; and as a 'social fact', rather than simply a 'technological fact', where 'the chief stock-in-trade is language' (Crystal 2006: 271), the web has paradoxically been brought to the attention of linguists almost against their will. 'Wherever we find language,' Crystal argues, advocating the emergence of what he calls Internet Linguistics, 'we find linguists. [...] So when we encounter the largest database of language the world has ever seen, we would expect to find linguists exploring it, to see what is going on' (Crystal 2011: 1). It is clear that one could explain, in not dissimilar terms, the convergence between a social phenomenon existing independently from linguistic investigation (the web) and the corpus linguistics approach, where the web itself is seen as a huge amount of machine-readable authentic texts which both 'tantalize and challenge linguists and other language professionals' (Fletcher 2007: 27).

With the advent of the web in the new millennium, the relationship between (corpus) linguistics and information technology seems thus to have entered into an exciting stage that has been envisaged in terms of a role reversal between 'giving' and 'taking'. While web technologies in the past drew extensively on language research through computational linguistics and natural language processing, it seems that today the relationship has been reversed in a sort of '"homecoming" of web technologies, with the web now feeding one of the hands that fostered it' (Kilgarriff and Grefenstette 2003: 336–7). In this context, it is no surprise that such characteristics as multilinguality and multimediality, dynamic content and distributed architecture, all clearly linked to the emergence of the web as a key phenomenon of our times, should also be seen as the standard for all linguistic resources in the twenty-first century (Wynne 2002: 1204), and should accordingly affect the way we conceive of a linguistic corpus.

It is against this background that the web's nature as a 'body' of texts, which provides the material basis for its controversial and intriguing status as a corpus, deserves some further investigation from the perspective of corpus linguistics as a whole.

2. The web as corpus: A 'body' of texts?

The very idea of treating the web as a linguistic corpus presupposes a view of what a corpus *is*, and entails a redefinition of what a corpus *can be*. As seen in the previous chapter, virtually any collection of more than one text can be called a corpus, but the term has acquired a specific meaning in contemporary linguistics, including considerations on both form and purpose (Hunston 2002: 2), the latter being a fundamental criterion in discriminating between a linguistic corpus and other collections of language texts (Francis 1992: 17). Accordingly, the idea of considering the World Wide Web as a ready-made corpus by virtue of its very nature as a collection of authentic texts in machine-readable format is called into question by the evident lack of any linguistic purpose, let alone theoretically informed design. It is not surprising, therefore, that in a publication aimed at clarifying and divulging the 'good practice' of corpus work, Sinclair should explicitly declare that '[a] corpus is a remarkable thing, not so much because it is a collection of language text, but because of the properties that it acquires if it is well-designed and carefully constructed', consistently denying corpus dignity to the web:

> The World Wide Web is not a corpus, because its dimensions are unknown and constantly changing, and because it has not been designed from a linguistic perspective. (Sinclair 2005: online)

Notwithstanding doubts concerning the hypothesis of considering the web as a corpus, made explicit by one of the founding fathers of contemporary corpus linguistics, linguists from all over the world have been increasingly turning their attention to the web not only as a source of language text for the creation of conventional (well-designed and carefully constructed) corpora, but also as a corpus in its own right. The relationship between corpus linguistics and the web seems to have become all but marginal, to the extent that this could well be envisaged as a new stage in the penetration of the new technologies in corpus linguistics. According to Tognini Bonelli, the computer was, at first, only a tool for speeding up processes and systematizing data; then it offered a methodological frame by providing evidence of patterns of regularity which would never otherwise been noticed or elicited by mere introspection; finally, information technology immensely contributed to the creation of new corpora, simplifying the work of corpus builders and potentially turning corpus linguistics from an area of investigation for specialists only to a research field virtually open to all (Tognini Bonelli 2001: 43ff.). Now, over the past decade, the web has claimed the right of being considered a corpus by virtue of its very nature as a collection of machine-readable and searchable authentic texts, thus opening up new perspectives and offering new challenges.

Acknowledging the undisputable role that the web has played so far in corpus linguistics and its potential as a ready-made corpus can, however, by no means obliterate the difference between the textual *mare magnum* which constitutes the web and a corpus where texts are gathered 'according to explicit design criteria, with a specific purpose in mind, and with a claim to represent larger chunks of language selected according to a specific typology' (Tognini Bonelli 2001: 2). While taking for granted the irreducible qualitative difference between a corpus designed and compiled as an object of language study and the web, it is possible to break this *impasse* by pointing out the fundamental difference between attempts at answering the 'ontological' question relating to what a corpus is – which implicitly points to a 'deontological' notion of what a corpus should be – and more empirical, yet legitimate, attempts to test the web's potential as a corpus by answering the practical question 'Is corpus *x* good for task *y*?'. This is what Kilgarriff and Grefenstette did in their influential editorial for the 2003 special issue of *Computational Linguistics* on 'The Web as Corpus':

> We wish to avoid the smuggling of values into the criterion of corpus-hood. McEnery and Wilson (following others before them) mix the question 'What is a corpus?' with 'What is a *good* corpus (for certain kinds of linguistic study)?', muddying the simple question 'Is corpus *x* good for task *y*?' with the semantic question 'Is *x* a corpus at all?'. The semantic question then becomes a distraction, all too likely to absorb energies that would otherwise be addressed to the practical one. So that the semantic question may be set aside, the definition of corpus should be broad. We define a corpus simply as a 'collection of texts'. If that seems too broad, the one qualification we allow relates to the domain and contexts in which the word is used, rather than its denotation: A corpus is a collection of texts when considered as an object of language or literary study. (2003: 334)

Going for a 'broad definition of corpus' as 'a collection of texts when considered as an object of language or literary study', the notion of 'corpus-hood' was implicitly shifted to the intention of the researcher rather than being seen as intrinsic to the text collection itself. Committed to the practical task of seeing whether the web could be profitably used as a corpus, research carried out under the label 'web as corpus' was apparently limited, for a long time, only to the practical question of seeing whether, as Kilgarriff put it, a web corpus is 'good' for a certain task, while in fact each new study in this controversial field was imperceptibly contributing to reshaping the way we conceive of a corpus in the new millennium. As a result, it is no longer simply a matter of highlighting the advantages and disadvantages of using the web as a corpus, but it may also be necessary to reinterpret some key issues in corpus linguistics in light of the specific features of the web as a 'spontaneous', 'self-generating' collection of texts, and to explore the new issues the emerging notion of the web as corpus has raised. Indeed, all uses of language material from the web seem to present a challenge to 'established empiricist notions such as reliability, representativeness and authoritativeness' (Bergh and Zanchetta 2009: 311); even more, the by now well-established notion of the 'web as corpus' requires a careful revision of some basic definitions and standards, if one is not simply going to equate a corpus to 'a helluva lot of texts' (Leech 1992: 106).

When surveying the most common definitions of a corpus in the literature produced over the last twenty years, as seen in the previous chapter, some issues emerge as criteria of paramount importance in determining the nature of a corpus as an object of language study. These issues have to be carefully reconsidered when exploring the position of the web as a corpus and can be readdressed from a new perspective. With this in mind, it can be argued that the challenge of using the World Wide Web in corpus linguistics has by no means pushed key questions to the background, but has rather served as 'a magnifying glass for the methodological issues that corpus linguists have discussed all along' (Hundt et al. 2007: 4). Indeed, no development in web-as-corpus studies has ever aimed at questioning the fundamental tenents of corpus linguistics, neither is the aim of research focused on the web as corpus to replace 'traditional' corpus linguistics. As in any other field of human knowledge, research in corpus linguistics can only profit from the force field created by the tension between traditional theoretical positions and the new tools and methods developed to meet practical needs. It is therefore more than desirable that corpus linguistics and studies on the web as corpus coexist and interact for a long time to come, providing the linguistics community with a wider spectrum of resources to choose from.

3. The corpus and the web: Key issues

While the emerging notion of the web as corpus apparently questions some basic standards in corpus linguistics, it provides, in fact, an opportunity to further explore some of the theoretical and methodological issues on which the good practice of corpus work rests. Such issues can be profitably revisited from the perspective of the web in order to envisage, if possible, the 'changing face' of corpus linguistics under the impact of the World Wide Web. The most relevant, for the purposes of the present book, are authenticity, representativeness, size and composition, and will be discussed in the following pages, along with a brief survey of copyright issues.

3.1 Authenticity

It is a basic assumption of corpus linguistics that all the language included in a corpus is authentic, and certainly the most prominent feature of the web to have attracted the linguist's attention is its undisputable nature as a reservoir of authentic, purposeful language behaviour. The web is, in essence, a collection of authentic texts produced in authentic human interactions by people whose aim 'is not to display their language competence, but rather to achieve some objective through language' (Baroni and Bernardini 2006: 9). Regardless of its size and easy availability as a collection of texts in machine-readable format, there would be no reason to turn to the web as an object of linguistic study were it not for its being comprised of authentic texts that are the result of genuine communicative events, produced by people going about their normal business. Attention to the web as a source of linguistic information must therefore be seen as deeply rooted in the context of that 'growing respect for real examples' (Sinclair 1991: 5) that has been gaining new prominence thanks to the possibilities offered by computer data storage. If then, to paraphrase Sinclair, it has now become fashionable to look outwards to society rather than inwards to the mind (Sinclair 1991: 1) in the search for linguistic evidence, the web seems to be there, ready at hand, to provide such evidence of language use as an integral part of the 'society' it mirrors. Furthermore, as is often the case with research domains related to some form of technology, there may be traces of a mutual influence between the exponential growth of easily accessible authentic data in electronic format caused by the digital revolution and a preference for empiricism; it is therefore not far from the truth to state that the web itself, as a repository of huge amounts of authentic language in electronic format, freely available with little effort, has contributed to making the corpus linguistics approach so popular and accessible.

It can well be argued, then, that the authenticity of the web makes it 'a fabulous linguist's playground' (Kilgarriff and Grefenstette 2003: 345), a hitherto unavailable open space to explore the interplay between what is formally possible in language and what is actually performed. Its very unplanned inclusiveness makes it a site where data gained through introspection can be tested against the background of what has been actually performed. A simple Google search for phrases easily demonstrates, for instance, how the web can make repetitions across the language behaviour of many speakers immediately visible, thus highlighting not only the repetitive and routine nature of language, but also providing evidence for what Teubert has defined as the 'autopoietic' and inherently 'diachronic' nature of the discourse (Teubert 2007: 67).

In this context, however, it is important to remember that while authenticity is the most obvious strength in the similarity between a corpus and the web, it is also one of the latter's major flaws and the main reason for being extremely cautious. Owing to its nature as an unplanned, unsupervised, unedited collection of texts, authenticity in the web is in fact often related to problems of 'authoritativeness'. Everyday experience suggests that 'authentic' in the web often means inaccurate (misspelt words, grammar mistakes, improper usage by non-native speakers), i.e. texts are almost certainly authentic in terms of their communicative intent but may be unreliable and lacking authority at the level of code. Thus, it is of crucial importance that linguists purporting to look at the web from a corpus linguistics perspective become aware of some of its basic features (and pitfalls) so that they can profit from its potential without running the risk of being 'tangled' in the web itself.

3.2 Representativeness

Closely related to authenticity is – as seen in the previous chapter – the 'vexed question' (Tognini Bonelli 2001: 57) of representativeness. Certainly the standard of representativeness is the one that puzzles those who claim corpus dignity for the web the most, and, in the words of Leech, it might seem that 'the web as corpus makes the notion of a representative corpus redundant' (2007: 144). Early research in the field, mainly within computational linguistics, seemed indeed to dispense altogether with the notion of representativeness on the grounds that it is quite impossible to achieve, and that the researcher's efforts could be more profitably devoted to the solution of practical problems (Kilgarriff and Grefenstette 2003: 343).

Exploring the web's potential for representativeness has thus remained the most crucial concern for scholars interested in investigating the value of the web as a corpus-like collection of texts. The real problem is that the notion of representativeness is the issue most closely bound up with the organic metaphor of the corpus-as-body, based on the assumption that each part of a 'body' can be representative of the whole. As a consequence, while the enormous size of the web and its inclusiveness apparently make it a gateway to a potentially representative heterogeneous amount of language events, its imbalances and potential un-representativeness impair its value as a language resource. It has been stressed, for instance, that while the web certainly gives access to a wide range of genres, some of which are undeniably well-established in the written medium, such as academic writing, and others which are newly evolving and closer to speech, such as blogs, it gives little access to private discourse, such as everyday exchanges, telephone conversations and the like (Leech 2007: 144–5). By contrast, the emergence of social media networks has started to provide insight into new forms of Computer Mediated Communication, in which such distinctions as written and spoken, private and public are blurred. Furthermore, it has been noted that certain major areas of language use are under-represented while other varieties are definitely over-represented; for instance, as noted in Lew (2009: 294), an inordinately high proportion of web-based texts are about the web itself or about high-technology in general. Apart from this intrinsic imbalance of web content, a new threat to the already precarious claim to representativeness of web texts is the practice of some web content creators to include repeated keywords in their pages in a manner that is unobtrusive to the human reader but that further affects the balance of content in the web (Lew 2009: 294). Thus, even though the web's textual universe (at least as far as the English language is concerned) largely overlaps with the non-electronic textual universe of the English language itself, its status as a 'representative sample' remains non-existent: ' It is a textual universe of unfathomed extent and variety, but it can in no way be considered a representative sample of language use in general' (Leech 2007: 145).

As Leech's thoughts on the subject suggest, the notion of representativeness, as it is generally conceived of in corpus linguistics, can only pertain to corpora which have been designed and created out of selection from carefully chosen material. This is patently not the case with the web which already exists, independently of the linguist's intentions, as the result of a wide range of (but not all) everyday activities which imply knowledge exchange, communication, interaction, and for which the web is proving to be, more and more, a privileged mode. Paradoxically, however, this is precisely where its real potential for representativeness may lie. The web is not constructed by a human mind, but is the direct result of a number of human interactions taking place – significantly from a linguist's perspective – mainly through written texts which in the very act of their production are made available worldwide as authentic machine-readable texts. Accordingly, the web's textual content inevitably reflects – if not actually represents – the international community at large. In some way it could be argued, as some researchers have, that the web can be considered as 'an increasingly representative and unprecedented in scale machine-readable sample of interests and activity in the world' (Henzinger and Lawrence 2004: 5186). Even though such a view of representativeness is not necessarily significant from the point of view of language, it cannot be dismissed as altogether irrelevant. The increasing prominence of the web in contemporary culture, the very fact that it is 'directly jacked into the culture's nervous system' (Battelle 2005:

2), along with its evident ability to mirror changes in real time, thanks to its intrinsic dynamism, seems on the contrary to mitigate the problems arising from lack of representativeness in the corpus linguistics sense of the word. Certainly, the web cannot be considered a representative sample of language use in general, but its scope, variety and, above all, its immense size seem to legitimize the opinion that these characteristics can counterbalance the limits of representativeness. As already noted for monitor corpora – to which the web has been compared – the proportion of the different types of material it includes may continually vary, but it can be assumed that as the corpus grows in size any skew will tend to self-correct (McEnery and Hardie 2012: 7). In this respect the web's impossibility of being representative of nothing else but itself (Kilgarriff and Grefenstette 2003) does not altogether destroy its value as a source of linguistic information from a corpus linguistics perspective.

3.3 Size

Intrinsically related to representativeness, the issue of size is fundamental in determining the value of a corpus as an object of language study and affects the kind of generalizations that can be made from corpus data.

While enormous size and virtually endless growth are the most notable characteristics of the web when compared to traditional corpora, this is precisely where its limitations as an object of scientific enquiry lie, if it is to be considered as a source of data for quantitative studies. As McEnery and Wilson suggest, the notion of corpus should by default imply 'a body of text of a finite size' (2001: 30), whereas the web is, by its very nature, bound to perpetual expansion. This soon gained the web a reputation as 'the ultimate monitor corpus' (Bergh 2005: 26), i.e. a corpus which – according to Sinclair's definition – 'has no final extent because, like language itself, it keeps on developing' (Sinclair 1991: 25). And a monitor corpus is by nature a more opportunistic and less balanced corpus where 'quantity of data replaces planning of sampling as the main compilation criterion' (Kennedy 1998: 61).

The problem of the web's non-finiteness brings with it uncertainties and doubts concerning its value in a research field, like corpus linguistics, which is based on the investigation of quantitative data. How can an object of uncertain size provide the basis for objective quantitative investigation? Unsurprisingly, one of the earliest attempts to establish the exact size of the web – an effort which entailed, as the author acknowledged, 'difficult qualitative questions concerning the Web, and attempts to provide some partial quantitative answers to them' (Bray 1996) – opened with a famous quotation from mathematician and physicist Lord Kelvin (1824–1907) on the poverty of knowledge which is not based on exact measures:

> When you can measure what you are speaking about, and express it in numbers, you know something about it; but when you cannot express it in numbers, your knowledge is of a meagre and unsatisfactory kind; it may be the beginning of knowledge, but you have scarcely in your thoughts advanced to the state of science. (Lord Kelvin, quoted in Bray 1996: 993)

The problem with the web's size is indeed extremely complex, both from the perspective of information technology and from a linguistic perspective. What is the current size of the web? How many websites are there? How many bytes of data? And, more specifically, how many running words does the web contain when considered as a text corpus? It is certainly a truism to say that the size of the textual content of the web is somewhat difficult to grasp, and it is also quite obvious that any possible answer to the above questions would be, by necessity, approximate and ephemeral, owing to the intrinsically dynamic nature of the web. Nonetheless, attempts have been made at 'measuring' the web by adopting different metrics, and tentative answers relating to its nature as a textual corpus have been provided. Some of these answers will be briefly surveyed below.

On the eve of the new millennium, a much-quoted pioneer study published in *Nature* (Lawrence and Giles 1999) estimated that in the World Wide Web there were, at that time at least, 800 million publicly accessible pages, amounting to 6 terabytes of text (mark-up and white space excluded), which, according to calculation by Meyer et al. (2003), meant over 800 billion words. In 2000, a study conducted by Inktomi & Nec Research Institute verified that the web had grown to include at least 1 billion unique documents (Inktomi, 2000), while in 2002 Google claimed to index 3 billion pages. Building on these attempts to measure the size of the web, computational linguists started to assess its significance as a corpus. In 2003 Kilgarriff and Grefenstette estimated 20 terabytes of non-markup text amounting to 2000 billion words of running text (2003: 337). After only two years, in October 2005, Google's CEO Eric Schmidt estimated the size of the internet at roughly 5 million terabytes of data and suggested that it was expanding by 100 terabytes per month. These data, of course, do not include the so-called 'invisible' or 'hidden' web, the much larger section of the web which is not directly accessible, and which is, according to Levene (2010: 10), approximately 550 times larger than the 'tip of the iceberg' that can be accessed through search engines.

In terms of running words, interesting estimates of the web's size come again from the people at Google, with Peter Norvig, current Director of Research at Google Inc., indicating in the now-famous video lecture *Theorizing from data* (2008) that the size of the internet amounts to 100 trillion words (i.e.10^{14}). Peter Norvig's lecture is indeed rich in hints and suggestions concerning the web as a corpus. As he says, it took nearly 30 years to go from a linguistic text collection of 1,000,000 million words like the Brown Corpus to the approximately 100,000,000,000,000 words of the web and, as an example of the immense potential of the web as a corpus, he comments on data released from Google in 2005. In 2005 Google harvested one billion words (the term billion was used in this case adopting the long scale, i.e. 10^{12}) from the net, counted them up and published them. The data was obtained by processing 1,024,908,267,229 words of running text and apparently included 13,588,391 unique words, after discarding all the words appearing less than 200 times. Figures from the complete data set are reported in Table 2.1 below.

Table 2.1. Data from Google LDC N-gram Corpus (Source: Norvig 2008)

Number of tokens: 1,024,908,267,229
Number of sentences: 95,119,665,584
Number of unigrams: 13,588,391
Number of bigrams: 314,843,401
Number of trigrams: 977,069,902
Number of fourgrams: 1,313,818,354
Number of fivegrams: 1,176,470,663

Even more significant is the sample of 3-grams reported below in Table 2.2.

Regardless of their ephemeral nature, these figures are no doubt indicative of the steady, dramatic growth of the web as a repository not only of information but – more crucially for the linguist – of language text. In the words of Crystal, 'there has never been a language corpus as large as this one', a corpus which contains 'more written language than all the libraries in the world combined' (Crystal 2011: 10). Whatever its exact size, it is clear that the web presents linguists with a collection of texts definitely larger than any other existing corpus and probably larger than any linguist might need, a fact that definitely alters the meaning of size as a basic corpus requirement.

In the early days of corpus linguistics, anyone could testify to what extent size mattered. It was a painstaking task to reach the minimum size required for a corpus to yield significant evidence. Even today, when corpora are enriched by extensively downloading from the web, the 'Shandian paradox' of creating something which seems to be getting old at a faster pace than it grows is still an everyday experience for corpus

Table 2.2. Data from Google LDC N-gram Corpus (Source: Norvig 2008)

serve as the indication 72
serve as the indicator 120
serve as the indicators 45
serve as the indispensable 111
serve as the indispensible 40
serve as the individual 234
serve as the industrial 52
serve as the industry 607
serve as the info 42
serve as the informal 102
serve as the information 838
serve as the informational 41
serve as the infrastructure 500
serve as the initial 5331
serve as the initiating 125
serve as the initiation 63
serve as the initiator 81

linguists, leaving corpus compilers with the strange feeling of working at something which could be deemed old or inadequate by the time it is released. When it comes to the web as corpus, however, the role played by size seems to be reversed. If early corpus linguists had to strive for size, with the dimension of the corpus being of prime concern to researchers constantly asking themselves 'is the corpus we are building large enough?', the web as corpus revolution seems to push the problem to the other extreme by providing a collection of texts which can be literally overwhelming in terms of running words, and hence potentially useless. Thus, while Sinclair could safely suggest, in the early 90s, that 'a corpus should be as large as possible, and should keep on growing' (Sinclair 1991: 18), looking at the web as a corpus in its own right makes linguists revise such slogans as 'the larger the better'. That bigger is better is a truth that cannot hold when big actually means gargantuan and uncontrollable, as is the case with the World Wide Web. This is not only the case from a corpus linguistics perspective but also from the point of view of information retrieval, where it has been explicitly argued that with the exponential growth of the internet, it has become disputable whether bigger is better, even though it is undeniable that a large quantity of data accessible through the web can be of great help when seeking unusual or hard-to-find information (Sullivan 2005). The same applies to linguistics, where 'sheer quantity of linguistic information can be overwhelming for the observer' (Hunston 2002: 25). Nonetheless, there is also ample evidence, especially from Natural Language Processing research, that probabilistic models of language based on very large quantities of data, even if very 'noisy', are better than ones based on estimates from smaller and cleaner datasets (Banko and Brill 2001; Keller and Lapata 2003; Nakov and Hearst 2005).

3.4 Composition

The exponential growth of the web in size since its inception in the early '90s has also had an impact on its composition – another key issue to be explored when determining the web's value as a corpus.

As far as the web as corpus is concerned, the issue of content becomes even more 'indigestible' given the intrinsic difficulties of characterizing the web in any of its aspects. As pointed out by Chakrabarti in the late '90s, 'the Web has evolved into a global mess of previously unimagined proportions. Web pages can be written in any language, dialect or style, by individuals with any background, education, culture, interest and motivation' (Chakrabarti 1999: 54). Today, as noted in Baeza-Yates and Ribeiro-Neto (2011), the data is surely growing in size, but also in complexity. This is why the focus can no longer be only on the question of size but on the interplay among the web's three different dimensions of growth: Volume, Variety, Velocity (Gartner Research 2011).

Indeed, web content and the categorization of such content changes from day to day, so that while some estimates may suggest that there are some 155 million websites in the web, a number fluctuating wildly from month to month, what exactly constitutes a website is cast into doubt. As recently argued, it is perhaps worth asking whether a person's individual Facebook page should be counted as a website. And what about blogs? And what if the blog is hosted by a blog service? (McGuigan 2011). Things are no better when one addresses the web's more recent bent towards visual content. How, for example, can one simply imagine the 2 billion videos being watched on *YouTube* each and every day? How is it possible that 35 hours of video can be uploaded to the site every minute? What do 36 billion photos look like? (Catone 2011) The patent impossibility of reaching any conclusive result in terms of description of the web's content is, again, a serious limitation when seen from a corpus linguistics perspective. It is recognition of this intrinsic, irreducible 'anarchism' that not only makes the 100 million words of the British National Corpus resemble, in comparison, 'an English country garden', as imaginatively argued by Kilgarriff, but, more importantly, seems to put an end, from the very start, to any hope of relying on the web as an object of scientific enquiry. Nothing possibly voices better the puzzlement and bewilderment of the (corpus) linguist when confronted with the web than the words of one of the earliest and most influential supporters of the web as corpus:

> First, not all documents contain text, and many of those that do are not only text. Second, it changes all the time. Third, like Borges's Library of Babel, it contains duplicates, near duplicates, documents pointing to duplicates that may not be there, and documents that claim to be duplicates but are not. Next, the language has to be identified (and documents may contain mixes of language). Then comes the question of text type: to gain any perspective on the language we have at our disposal in the web, we must classify some of the millions of web pages, and we shall never do so manually, so corpus linguists, and also web search engines, need ways of telling what sort of text a document contains: chat or hate-mail; learned article or bus timetable. (Kilgarriff 2001)

While this might sound like an argument against the web as corpus, for Kilgarriff this is precisely where the challenge really lies: 'For the web to be useful for language study, we must address its anarchy' (Kilgarriff 2001). Anarchy is thus the original sin of a virtual space which, as its very name reveals, is more 'global' than anything else on earth. In the World Wide Web anyone, regardless of country or language, is free to make information and services available, and this is achieved – significantly from a linguist's perspective – mainly through written texts produced and made available, often in real time, as authentic machine-readable format texts.

Despite, therefore, all the limitations of any attempt to confront the anarchy and idiosyncrasy of the web, and with no pretence at exhaustiveness, in the following pages the issue of content has been conveniently split into four basic components: medium, languages, topic, register/genre. Referring to these issues, various attempts at characterizing the web have been reported, with the aim of giving an idea of the scope of the web as a corpus from the point of view of its textual content.

3.4.1 Medium

While a traditional corpus may contain only written texts or only spoken texts, or a variable proportion of both, it must be acknowledged that it is becoming increasingly difficult to conceive of web texts in terms of only one medium, and the composition of the web in this respect is not easily investigated. The web has indeed largely contributed to a blurring of clear-cut distinctions between spoken and written language, and the very way we talk about the internet suggests 'an uncertainty over the relationship between these two mediums'. In the words of Crystal (2011: 20):

> On the one hand we talk about having an email 'conversation', entering a 'chat' room and 'tweeting'. On the other hand we talk about 'writing' emails, 'reading' web 'pages', and sending 'texts'. Is Internet language closer to speech or to writing, or is it something entirely different?

Some of the forms of interaction which are native to the new digital environment (e.g. instant messaging), though written, display core properties of speech, in the sense that 'they are time governed, expecting or demanding an immediate response'; they are 'transient' because messages may be deleted or lost to attention as they scroll off the computer screen; they display 'the urgency and energetic force which is characteristic of face-to-face conversation' (Crystal 2011: 21). But this cannot be said of 'all' the language that is available on the internet, which – as noted again in Crystal – varies greatly with respect to linguistic idiosyncrasy and complexity. 'At one extreme', he argues,

> we find the web, which displays the same range of written constructions and graphic options as would be found in the corresponding texts of traditional print. Online government reports, newspaper editions, or literary archives (such as Project Gutenberg) have a great deal in common with their offline equivalents (though there is never identity, as screen and page offer different functionalities and constraints). At the other extreme, the character limits of texting and tweeting reduce the grammatical and graphic options, ant the more elaborate sentence patterns do not appear. In between we found outputs, such as blogging, that vary greatly in their constructional and graphic complexity. Some blogs are highly crafted; others are wildly erratic, when compared to the norms of the standard written language. (Crystal 2011: 20)

Considerations concerning the specific properties of internet language should thus be taken as no more than a new *caveat* to the great linguistic complexity of the web, rather than as precise descriptive categories. Certainly, the language used in blogs, Facebook, Twitter, closely resembles oral interaction, and being aware of this is of paramount importance whenever dealing with web data. But it is also important to remember that this kind of language would mostly emerge from the web as part of corpora created *ad hoc* to study these specific forms of interaction, since it is mainly stored in those parts of the web that are not indexed by search engines, and cannot be considered as representative of the web as a whole.

These issues are all relevant to the nature of the web as a corpus of (predominantly) written texts, which is the perspective adopted in the present work. This choice is justified not only by the large amount of written texts found on the internet which still display the same range of grammar and graphic options of traditional printed texts but also by the fact that, even when featuring aspects of spoken language, internet language 'is better seen as writing which has been pulled some way in the direction of speech, rather than as speech which has been written down' (Crystal 2011: 22). Indeed, Crystal goes on,

> Internet language is identical to neither speech nor writing, but selectively and adaptively displays properties of both. It is more than an aggregate of spoken and written features. It does things that neither of the other medium does. (Crystal 2011: 22)

This ability to re-mediate and incorporate the existing media, Bolter and Grusin (2000) would suggest, is precisely what makes the web a 'new' medium.

3.4.2 Language

Since English soon established itself as the *lingua franca* of the internet, one might be misled into thinking of the web as a predominantly English language corpus. On the contrary, one of the most interesting characteristics of the web is its multilinguality, which, from a corpus linguistics perspective, means that the web contains virtually endless corpora in almost any language on earth. In Crystal's words, again,

> The Web is an eclectic medium, and this is seen also in its multilinguistic inclusiveness. Not only does it offer a home to all linguistic styles within a language; it offers a home to all languages – once their communities have a functioning computer technology. (Crystal 2006: 229)

Since the inception of the web as a multilingual environment, several techniques have been implemented for estimating the number of words available through web browsers for given languages by applying to the web the most common techniques used to estimate the size of a language-specific corpus based on the frequency of commonly occurring words in the corpus itself. In their much-quoted article published in 2000, Grefenstette and Nioche estimated English and non-English language use on the World Wide Web; though clearly faced with a predominantly English language 'corpus', with over two-thirds of the pages written in English, the authors were able to report that non-English languages were growing at a faster pace than English (Grefenstette and Nioche 2000: 2). Today, the exponential growth of non-English languages is easily explained by the growth of websites providing news in different languages (such as newspaper websites), of official government websites, and of collaborative enterprises such as Wikipedia, together with the growing number of personal or corporative homepages or blogs. Nonetheless, the relative growth of languages other than English does not necessarily imply that access to the benefits of the internet are more evenly distributed around the world, and the persistence of differences in the 'weight' of individual languages on the web points to more general problems concerning the so-called 'digital divide' between rich and poor countries. The internet seems to have rather disappointed hopes for a 'global village' where even 'the poor countries would be able to benefit, with unprecedented ease, from a myriad of databases, from training, from online courses, all of which would provide access to the knowledge society and allow these countries to catch up progressively with the pack of prosperous nations' (Mouhobi 2005). The digital divide between the first and third world is an issue made even worse by the technical problems relating to the encoding of non-Latin alphabets using a system (ASCII codes) devised for Latin alphabets only (Crystal 2006). But while the problem of non-Latin alphabets on the internet still calls for a solution capable of redressing imbalances in access to the internet, the web has paradoxically proved to be a language resource precisely for some 'minor' or 'endangered' languages (Ghani R. et al. 2001; De Schryver 2002; Scannel 2007).

Certainly, as has been argued, there are imbalances in access to the web, with some areas – Africa especially – being under-represented, but participation is extended every day, and, what is more, the web has given people who had previously never had the opportunity to see their writing in print a chance to share their language and writing. The web has even been profitably used as a 'phonological corpus' (Zuraw 2006) for a language like Tagalog, whereas in recent years a number of web corpora have been compiled for languages as diverse as Swahili, Welsh or Latvian, precisely by exploiting the web's multilingualism. In this context, the current debate on the possibility of establishing access to the internet as a basic human right can do much in redressing the remaining imbalances (Sengupta 2012).

As far as the present distribution of languages used on the web is concerned, relatively recent estimates[1] of the top ten languages report that in 2010 English and Chinese were the most widely used languages, with 536.6 and 444.9 million internet users respectively, followed by Spanish, Japanese, French, Portuguese, German, Arabic, French, Russian and Korean. See Figure 2.1:

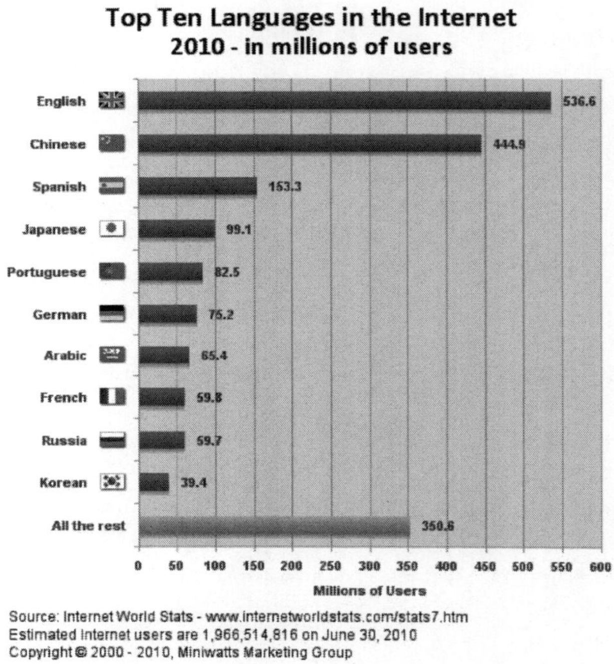

Figure 2.1. *Top 10 internet languages (Source: Internet World Stats)*

While interesting, these data are obviously not significant in themselves, since they only provide a snapshot of a constantly changing reality. As Figure 2.2 shows, it is mainly in terms of percentages that numbers can help us assess how the World Wide Web is changing in an increasingly global and multilingual environment, with changes in the relative growth of languages possibly mirroring changes taking place at different levels in society.

Taking the presence of Arabic on the internet as an example, the most recent estimates available suggest that as of May 2011 there were 65,365,400 Arabic-speaking people using the internet, representing 3.3 per cent of all internet users. This means that out of an estimated 347,002,991 world population that speaks Arabic, 18.8 per cent use the internet. Overall,

Top Ten Languages Used in the Web
(Number of Internet Users by Language)

TOP TEN LANGUAGES IN THE INTERNET	Internet Users by Language	Internet Penetration by Language	Growth in Internet (2000 - 2011)	Internet Users % of Total	World Population for this Language (2011 Estimate)
English	565,004,126	43.4 %	301.4 %	26.8 %	1,302,275,670
Chinese	509,965,013	37.2 %	1,478.7 %	24.2 %	1,372,226,042
Spanish	164,968,742	39.0 %	807.4 %	7.8 %	423,085,806
Japanese	99,182,000	78.4 %	110.7 %	4.7 %	126,475,664
Portuguese	82,586,600	32.5 %	990.1 %	3.9 %	253,947,594
German	75,422,674	79.5 %	174.1 %	3.6 %	94,842,656
Arabic	65,365,400	18.8 %	2,501.2 %	3.3 %	347,002,991
French	59,779,525	17.2 %	398.2 %	3.0 %	347,932,305
Russian	59,700,000	42.8 %	1,825.8 %	3.0 %	139,390,205
Korean	39,440,000	55.2 %	107.1 %	2.0 %	71,393,343
TOP 10 LANGUAGES	1,615,957,333	36.4 %	421.2 %	82.2 %	4,442,056,069
Rest of the Languages	350,557,483	14.6 %	588.5 %	17.8 %	2,403,553,891
WORLD TOTAL	2,099,926,965	30.3 %	481.7 %	100.0 %	6,930,055,154

NOTES: (1) Top Ten Languages Internet Stats were updated for May 31 2011. (2) Internet Penetration is the ratio between the sum of Internet users speaking a language and the total population estimate that speaks that specific language. (3) The most recent Internet usage information comes from data published by Nielsen Online, International Telecommunications Union, GfK, and other reliable sources. (4) World population information comes from the U.S. Census Bureau . (5) For definitions and navigation help in several languages, see the Site Surfing Guide. (6) Stats may be cited, stating the source and establishing an active link back to Internet World Stats.

Figure 2.2. *Internet users by language (Source: Internet World Stats)*

the number of Arabic-speaking internet users has grown by 2,501.2 per cent in the eleven years between 2000 and 2011; an interesting comparison can be drawn from estimates dating back to 2000, as reported in Table 2.1:

Table 2.3. Web pages by language (Source: Pastore 2000)

Web Pages By Language		
Language	**Web Pages**	**Percent of Total**
English	214,250,996	68.39
Japanese	18,335,739	5.85
German	18,069,744	5.77
Chinese	12,113,803	3.87
French	9,262,663	2.96
Spanish	7,573,064	2.42
Russian	5,900,956	1.88
Italian	4,883,497	1.56
Portuguese	4,291,237	1.37
Korean	4,046,530	1.29
Dutch	3,161,844	1.01

Sweden	2,929,241	0.93
Danish	1,374,886	0.44
Norwegian	1,259,189	0.40
Finnish	1,198,956	0.38
Czech	991,075	0.32
Polish	848,672	0.27
Hungarian	498,625	0.16
Catalan	443,301	0.14
Turkish	430,996	0.14
Greek	287,980	0.09
Hebrew	198,030	0.06
Estonian	173,265	0.06
Romanian	141,587	0.05
Icelandic	136,788	0.04
Slovenian	134,454	0.04
Arabic	127,565	0.04
Lithuanian	82,829	0.03
Latvian	60,959	0.02
Bulgarian	51,336	0.02
Basque	36,321	0.01

These estimates published at the millennium give us an idea of how the presence of each single language is subject to change. One cannot help noticing, for instance, the macroscopic growth of Arabic as a language for internet communication, moving up from 27th position in these 2000 estimates to 2nd position in the more recent 2011 estimates, perhaps mirroring the recent socio-political evolution of the Arab world. Other languages that have significantly changed position are Portuguese and Korean (9th and 10th position in 2000), which have now overtaken Italian, and Spanish (6th position in 2000 and now immediately following Chinese as the third language for internet communication). Finally, one should notice the growth of Chinese, leaving its 4th position in 2000 to become the 2nd language in 2011.

The astonishing variety of languages on the web and the impressive growth of non-English and also non-Western languages show the importance of the web as a multilingual environment which is ready to reflect changes taking place in society at large. While variety should not make us forget the problems relating to the 'digital divide', it is unquestionable that, from a linguistic point of view, the web can be considered as a vast, dynamic, easy to access, multilingual language resource, whose significance is further enhanced by the astonishing diversity of the topics covered.

3.4.3 Topics

The web has become such a pervasive communication medium that there seems to be no field of human activity that is not, in some way or other, covered by it. This has probably made us forget that the web has its origins in the world of US defence and that only subsequently did it develop as a way to share knowledge and research within the academic world. Today it continues to play a major role in governmental and scientific communication, but the fact that it has become increasingly easy to use has meant that more and more people outside research and political institutions have begun to develop other uses for the web, making it a more inclusive, but also a more chaotic, environment.

This situation is made even worse by the evolution of the so-called Web 2.0 technology. As stated in the much-quoted article 'We are the web', published in *Wired* in 2005,

> the scope of the Web today is hard to fathom. [...] Today, at any Net terminal, you can get: an amazing variety of music and video, an evolving encyclopedia, weather forecasts, help wanted ads, satellite images of any place on Earth, up-to-the-minute news from around the globe, tax forms, TV guides, road maps with driving directions, real-time stock quotes, telephone numbers, real estate listings with virtual walk-throughs, pictures of just about anything, sports scores, places to buy almost anything, records of political contributions, library catalogs, appliance manuals, live traffic reports, archives to major newspapers – all wrapped up in an interactive index that really works.
>
> Furthermore, the web's scope is not only spatially but also temporally ubiquitous. You can switch your gaze of a spot in the world from map to satellite to 3-D just by clicking. Recall the past? It's there. Or listen to the daily complaints and travails of almost anyone who blogs (and doesn't everyone?).

In order to profit from diversity of content on the web, several attempts have been made to implement some principles of classification based on topic[2]. In the beginning this was generally performed through directories, which group web pages on the basis of content into a number of categories. An apparently trivial task, the classification of web pages into directories relating to their content is something which ordinary search engines have trouble coping with, given the nature of the web as a democratic, or rather 'anarchic', space, apparently free of any form of organization and planning.

The earliest attempt at organizing the content of the web from the point of view of topics was made in the mid-90s by two Ph.D. students at Stanford University, Jerry Yang and David Filo, who created the Yahoo! directory to help their friends locate useful websites. In a matter of months, their initially informal project was incorporated as a fully fledged company. As Chakrabarti argues, the partial success of this enterprise was due to the attempt at 'reviving the ancient art of organizing knowledge into ontologies' – an art which 'descends from epistemology and philosophy and relates to the possibility of creating a tree like hierarchy as an organizing principle for topics' (Chakrabarti 2003: 7). The paradigm of browsing topics arranged in a tree is a pervasive one and the average computer user is generally familiar with hierarchies of this kind through directories and files. This familiarity, Chakrabarti suggests, carries over rather naturally to topic taxonomies.

At Yahoo!, the decision whether to include a site in the directory is made by human editors, who monitor pages before inclusion, and the inclusion process may also be subject to a fee. Despite providing an important support to categorization of web content, directories suffer from poor coverage and, when manually maintained, cannot keep up with the dynamics of the web; in the long run their contents may not be as fresh as they should be (Levene 2010: 152). In this respect, a more interesting approach is taken by the Open Directory Project. The Open Directory (dmoz.org) was created to provide the internet with a means to organize itself, profiting from the cooperative spirit of the Open Source movement. 'As the Internet grows,' it is stated in the project's home page, 'so do the number of net-citizens. These citizens can each organize a small portion of the web and present it back to the rest of the population, culling out the bad and useless and keeping only the best content' (Open Directory Project).

Whatever the approach taken, a survey of the 'directories' listed by a search engine is useful to appreciate the wide range of topics covered by the web. In Figure 2.3 are reported the topics listed by Yahoo! Directories.

As is well known, each topic label in the directory takes the form of a hyperlink and is to be considered as a gateway to subdirectories, expanding in a sort of Chinese box structure. Thus, choosing 'Chemistry' from the directory

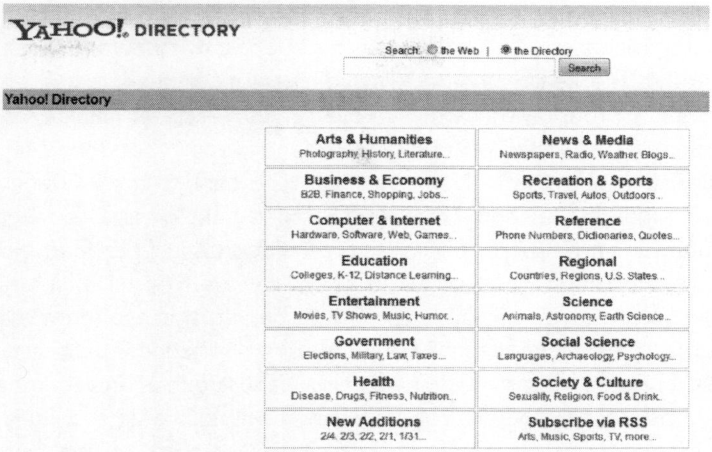

Figure 2.3. *List of directories in Yahoo! (Source: www.yahoo.com/directories)*

'Science' in Yahoo!, the user is projected into a new set of topics, which are in turn open doors to other topics (see Figure 2.4):

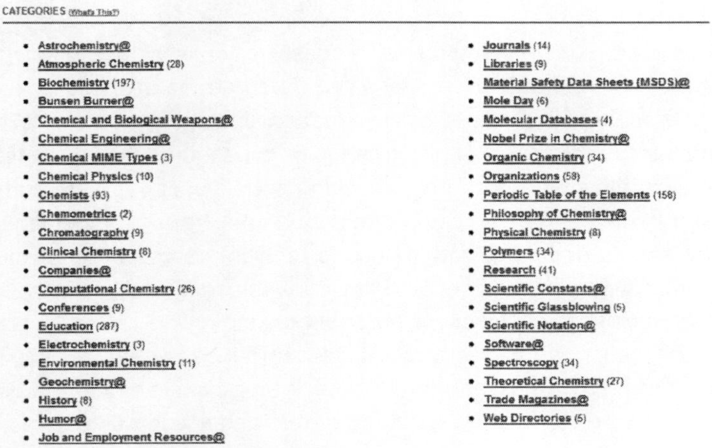

Figure 2.4. *Directory 'Science' from Yahoo! (Source: www.yahoo.com)*

From the categories listed above, it is clear that directories could play a significant role in identifying subsets of web pages clustered around a single topic. Each directory could – theoretically at least – be considered as a 'virtual' corpus including texts all dealing with the same topic, so that to find evidence of usage of a certain phrase in a specific domain (e.g. Health), one could restrict the search to the relevant directory instead of searching the whole web. On the other hand, however, it should be stressed that 'topic' or 'domain' are themselves notoriously controversial categories in corpus linguistics (EAGLES 1996). As a matter of fact, despite their attractiveness, web directories can answer the linguist's need only in part. As research by Biber and Kurjian (2007) has shown, the categorization provided by search engine directories, while considered as indicative in terms of reference to general topical domains, still remains well behind the minimum standards required for linguistic research. It is of crucial importance in fact for (corpus) linguists to identify texts on situational/linguistic grounds, i.e. to know what kind of texts are included in a corpus (even in a 'virtual' one, such as a search engine directory) in terms of register, genre, text type. A label generically referring only to topic or domain is not enough for a linguist to discriminate (web) content, and as the web grows in size and anarchy, classification of web pages by topic only seems to be insufficient to maintain acceptable standards of effectiveness even from the point of view of general purpose information retrieval. For this reason more and more interest is being paid to web categorization by genre as a complement to topic classification, and it is precisely on this issue that current research in the field of information retrieval and the interests of the corpus linguistics community seem to have finally converged.

With the growth of the web as 'a massive loosely organized library of information' (Boase 2005: 1), it has in fact become increasingly evident that new forms of 'representation' of information, including genre, are needed (Crowston and Kwasnik 2004). Information on the web now so vastly exceeds users' needs that even a common search runs the risk of being frustrating just on the ground of genre/text type. What are we looking for, for instance, when we ask a search engine to return results for San Francisco? Information on the city? Accommodation? Flights? People searching for information (whether general or specifically linguistic) do not simply look for a topic but also have implicit generic (i.e. genre-related) requirements (Kessler et al. 1997: 32). The problem of matching a user's query with the relevant answers in terms of text types and genres is anyway bound to remain an issue unless more information is integrated by web designers in their web pages, or unless users formulate more explicit and complex queries, or unless – and this is a crucial point – web information retrieval applications (i.e. search engines) themselves are modified so that they can focus not only on topic and content but also on features of form and style as a gateway to genre and text types (Boase 2005: 3–4). As a category 'orthogonal to topic' (Boase, 2005: 6) genre would thus make it possible to find documents that match the user's search terms from the point of view of topic, including (or excluding) documents of a given genre or genre cluster.

3.4.4 Registers, (web) genres, and text types

While it is clear that languages and topics alone can only partially represent the web's content in a way that is meaningful from the linguist's point of view and greater attention is being paid to the issue of register and genre, it is also essential to acknowledge that technological development has resulted in the emergence of new textualities, such as chat rooms, blogs and home pages, along with the re-mediation of traditional genres, which call for new attention, since they seem to blur old distinctions between written/spoken, formal/informal registers and require new categories of approach.

In traditional corpora, texts are generally classified in terms of topic/domain and genre, an approach which is difficult to reproduce with the web, even though there seems to be no more universally accepted typology for classifying texts in traditional corpora than there is for the internet (Sharoff 2007: 84). From a corpus linguistics perspective, discriminating texts in terms of genre, register and text type has always been a fundamental concern (Lee 2001), and identifying web genres/registers would certainly pave the way towards a more methodologically sound use of the web as a corpus. Indeed, the very impossibility of getting to know anything about the web in this respect is one of the reasons why its representativeness from a corpus perspective has been radically questioned. While the linear organization of most paper documents and the apparent fixity of most traditional genres can still be reflected in traditional electronic corpora, such as the BNC, a similar approach would be hardly applicable to a corpus of web documents, which are more complex and unpredictable than paper documents, and where the very notion of genre seems to be undergoing a process of democratization (Yates and Sumner 1997: 3; Santini 2005: 1). However, it might be argued, genre and register, along with related concepts of text type, domain and style, on which corpus studies implicitly or explicitly rely, are themselves 'somewhat confusing terms' (Lee 2001: 37). This makes it even more difficult to thoroughly map genres and registers for the web.

Apart from the intrinsic difficulty of sorting out the plethora of highly individualized documents which make up the web, when dealing with the web in terms of genres and registers some basic prejudices also need to be addressed. It has perhaps become something of a commonplace to think of the web as a writing space that is characterized mainly by ephemeral writing, while in fact diversity is the only keyword. Certainly many texts are created in real time and do not undergo any kind of editing, but others are faithful reproductions of historical or literary texts. Some of the writing on the web can give the impression that this is a place where traditional genres and text types have been superseded by the new genres of electronically mediated communication, but there are still also many traditional genres which have been adapted to the new electronic environment without losing their basic properties as genres (e.g. newspapers, academic articles etc.). Variation of register is thought to be set permanently at the informal end on the web, but web texts actually range from the most formal legal documents to quite informal blogs and chat rooms. Even though, as has been argued, all attention is drawn to the new – or not-yet-standard – text types and styles that have clearly emerged in recent years in computer mediated communication, these are in fact only a part of all the text available on the web (Crystal 2006: 84). From the point of view of registers and genres, the problem with the web is therefore not so much what it actually contains, but rather how to discriminate and take advantage of its 'sprawling' content. In a world where 'the dream of creating an information-rich society has become a nightmare of information overload' (Kwasnik and Crowston 2000) because information has exceeded the limits of our ability to process it, and the advantages of a huge store of information like that of the World Wide Web seem to be outweighed by the difficulties of accessing it, the problem of categorizing web content in terms of genre, register and text type as a complement to topical principles of classification has become a common priority for information retrieval, computational linguistics, and also corpus linguistics. However, methods for achieving this have not yet been fully established. Researchers involved in web genre analysis have long recognized the need for new categories of approach, based on the awareness that the web, as a dynamic environment, is more prone to centripetal forces which result in constant genre evolution (Santini 2007; Mehler et al. 2010). On the one hand, it is clear that the web hosts a number of traditional genres which have simply changed medium (from paper to electronic) without any further modification of their intrinsic features (reproduced genres); on the other hand there are text types and genres that are undergoing processes of 'remediation' which make them definitely hybrid genres (adapted novel genres), as well as completely new genres (emerging genres). On the basis of this evolutionary pattern, and drawing on earlier classifications, Santini (2007) proposes a list of five recognizable genres typologies:

1 reproduced/replicated genres,

2 adapted/variant genres,

3 emergent/novel genres,

4 spontaneous genres,

5 unclassified web pages.

In this new and varied context, the notion of genre is clearly undergoing a process of hybridization in which traditional criteria for text categorization and genre identification cannot hold. Previously clear-cut distinctions between spoken/written, formal/informal seem inappropriate ways to address the registers used in most instances of computer-mediated communication, whose complexity requires multidimensional approaches. In order to ride the 'rough waves' of web genres, as the authors of a recent contribution to the debate suggest, a more flexible genre classification scheme is required, capable of making sense of the composite structure of web documents, the complexity of interaction they allow, the different naming conventions and the tendency towards rapid change and evolution (Mehler et al. 2010: 13). What is needed is a system in which genres and text types on the web are not identified in terms of their adherence to *a priori* determined genres, but are rather determined *a posteriori*, as a post-coordination of co-occurring features. These methods are proving more flexible and hospitable to the many hybrid genres which characterize the web as a new medium, and make researchers hope for a real possibility to implement genre categorization within web search systems, from which both information retrieval and corpus linguistics would greatly benefit.

3.5 Copyright

As is the case with language resources of a different kind, and specifically with language corpora, accessing web data for linguistic purposes poses obvious copyright problems. This was clear from the start, and the problem was soon addressed in a specific paper by Hemming and Lassi (2002), and in Kilgarriff and Grefenstette's much-quoted introduction to the special issue of *Computational Linguistics* on 'The Web as Corpus'. Even though copyright constraints were mentioned as mainly pertaining to traditional corpora, and – in some respects – the web was initially seen, by contrast, as apparently less constrained in terms of copyright, it was clearly acknowledged that 'legal issues for Web corpora are no different from those around non-Web Corpora' (Kilgarriff and Grefenstette 2003: 335).

Certainly, when using the web as a corpus in its own right, or as a source for offline corpora, it is more difficult not only to obtain permissions of any kind from authors, but also to identify specific pages protected by copyright.

Also, the use made of web data in corpus linguistics may vary. As suggested in Fletcher (2004a), including entire webpages in a corpus distributed on CD-ROM would obviously be illegal, but using web data to provide online concordances may fall within currently accepted practice. It is also self-evident that the limited use of web data that can be made through any web-as-corpus approach is nothing when compared to what search engines actually do every day, on the basis of an implied consent from webpage owners in accordance with the Digital Millennium Copyright Act (2001). As stated in the specific section devoted to copyright infringement liability by online service providers, entitled 'Online Copyright Infringement Liability Limitation Act', the latter are protected against copyright infringement provided that they meet specific requirements. One of these is that access to online material should be blocked immediately if notified of an infringement claim from a copyright holder or from the copyright holder's agent. This means that, as a rule, copyright material that is included/used in web-as-corpus resources can be removed upon request from the copyright holders. Furthermore, while the wider copyright issues concerning the information industry at large might still need to be clarified, it can perhaps be safely assumed, with Fletcher (2004a: 281), that 'a Web-accessible corpus for research and education derived from online documents retrieved by a search agent in ad-hoc searches will fall within legal boundaries'.

Be that as it may, copyright issues remain a grey area and a thorny issue for web-as/for-corpus resources, since free access to the web by no means implies a right 'to download, retain, reprocess and redistribute web content'. It could indeed be argued that the legal and ethical issues arising from corpus construction, distribution and use 'have become more pressing over time as vast amounts of textual data have become available to collect easily over the World Wide Web' (McEnery and Hardie 2012: 57ff.). This problem has been addressed in several ways. The first is the traditional way of contacting copyright holders and requests permission to use and redistribute the texts. It is quite obvious that this approach can work only if interested in data from limited sources, because, otherwise, asking millions of potential copyright holders for usage permission would be impossible (Baroni et al. 2009: 18). A second approach is using data only from sites whose content is explicitly declared as public domain. The third approach is to collect data regardless of copyright infringement but avoid distributing them. This is the case of a number of large web-corpora created by crawling under the mega-corpus miniweb approach devised by the Wacky group (see Chapter 6). The solution to copyright problems adopted for these corpora included providing clear information to potential copyrights holders on how to request the removal of their documents from the corpora, and bypassing the problem of redistribution of the data by giving access to the data only through online interfaces, which means that the user can never 'possess' a 'copy' of the texts. In this case what is actually 'distributed' is only a few words of context around the node word so that it is virtually impossible to reconstruct the original texts. Furthermore, it should be noted that the data extracted from webpages is, in any case, made available in a linguistically processed format unlikely to be of use for non-linguists. Also, it is a well-known fact that it is seldom the case that copyright owners have requested the removal of specific pages from web-based language resources.

McEnery and Hardie (2012) also mention a fourth approach, which entails redistribution of web addresses only, rather than texts, with no infringement of copyright – an approach which has as many disadvantages (e.g. broken links) as advantages. The third approach appears therefore to be the one that is dominant at the moment, with many large corpora created out of web documents made accessible through web interfaces. This is the case of the corpora made available through the aforementioned website created by Davies, corpus.byu.edu (Davies 2005) or through the Sketch Engine (Kilgarriff et al. 2004).

4. From 'body' to 'web': New issues

The attempts to analyse the web as a linguistic corpus have obviously highlighted certain characteristics, such as constant change, non-finite size and anarchy, which in turn indicate the need to address some radically new issues if web-as-corpus research is to be pursued on sound methodological bases. It is worth stressing, however, that some of these new issues are, to some extent, to be considered as not specifically related to the web as corpus but rather as a natural consequence of the impact of new technologies on linguistic resources as a whole, and can be related to those changes predicted by Wynne (2002: 1204) as typical of language resources in the twenty-first century: multilinguality and multimodality, dynamic content, distributed architecture, connection with web searching. While it is clear that a corpus is by no means the same as a text archive, for which Wynne envisaged the above-mentioned changes, these new characteristics of language resources embody all the consequences of the shift from real to virtual and are closely linked to the emergence of the web as a key phenomenon in contemporary society. In this respect, they inevitably relate to the web as corpus too. More specifically, Wynne's idea of an inescapable shift towards virtual corpora is illuminating. The old scenario of the researcher 'who downloads the corpus to his machine, installs a program to analyse it, then tweaks the program and/or the corpus mark-up to get the program and the corpus to work together, and finally performs the analysis' (Wynne 2002: 1205) is now replaced by a new model where replicating digital data in a local copy and installing the software to analyse the data becomes redundant, as all the processing can be done over the network. This also changes notions of permanence/stability for corpora. As Wynne, again, argues,

> In the traditional model a corpus is carefully prepared, by taking a sample of the population of texts of which it aims to be representative, and possibly encoded and annotated in ways which make it amenable for linguistic research. The value and the reusability of the resource are therefore dependent on a bundle of factors, such as the validity of the design criteria, the quality and availability of the documentation, the quality of the metadata and the validity and generalisability of the research goals of the corpus creator. (Wynne 2002: 1205)

In the new scenario, the relative importance of design criteria may well change, as it might become the norm to create a collection of texts (the corpus) on an *ad hoc* basis – such as 'all seventeenth-century English fiction' or 'all Bulgarian newspaper texts' – by simply choosing from within larger existing text archives (Wynne 2002: 1205).

Over ten years on, these issues seem to have really affected the notion of what constitutes a corpus, prompting a shift away from the somewhat 'reassuring' conventional features subsumed by the corpus-as-body metaphor itself, to a new corpus-as-web metaphor. While the notion of linguistic corpus as a body of texts still rests on some correlate issues such as finite size, balance, part-whole relationship, stability, the very idea of a web of texts brings about notions of non-finiteness, flexibility, de-centring and re-centring, provisionality. This calls into question, on methodological grounds, issues and standards which instead could be taken for granted when working on conventional corpora, such as the stability of the data, the reproducibility of the research and the reliability of the results. Some of these new issues will be briefly explored in the following pages.

4.1 Dynamism

An important characteristic of the web that has implications for its supposed nature as a corpus is its inherently dynamic nature. Firstly, the web is characterized by exponential growth, with new pages and sites appearing at a significantly high rate. Secondly, the content of existing documents is continually updated, so that sites and pages do not only frequently appear but also as frequently disappear. Thirdly, the very structure of the web is in constant flux, with new links between documents being continually established and removed (Risvik and Michelsen 2002). These factors have largely contributed to making the web the largest and most accessible information resource in contemporary society, but have also gained it a reputation for volatility. No doubt everybody has experienced such volatility through the so-called 'broken-link' problem – the most evident sign of the ever-changing nature of the web – symbolized by the well-known *HTTP Error 404 Page not found* message.

With a large fraction of existing pages changing over time, and a significant fraction of 'changes' due to new pages that are created over time, the web as a whole is constantly changing and precise estimates are not only difficult to make but are, perhaps, useless. As Fletcher argues, 'studies of the nature of the web echo the story of the blind man and the elephant: each one extrapolates from its own samples of this ever evolving entity taken at different times and by divergent means' (Fletcher 2007: 25). It goes without saying, then, that existing studies of the web's fluidity can only give us a faint idea of what we really mean when we say that the web is 'dynamic'. A study carried out in 2004 on a selection of commercial, academic, governmental and media US sites estimated, for instance, how many new pages were created every week, calculating a 'weekly birth rate' for web pages of 8 per cent. Then the authors addressed the issue of 'new content', finding that on average each week around 5 per cent of the page content was really new, coming to the conclusion that nearly 62 per cent of the content of new URLs introduced each week was actually new. Finally they estimated the life of individual web pages on the web, by combining their findings with results from a study by the Online Computer Library Center (OCLC 2002) to get a picture of the rate of change for the entire web. On the basis of the two sets of data, the authors could speculate that only 20 per cent of web pages are still accessible after one year (Ntoulas et al. 2004).

While this low rate of 'survival' of web pages has made historical archiving and long-term access to web content a crucial concern, prompting the work of institutions such as the Internet Archive or initiatives such as the Wayback machine, it is also worth considering how such dynamism affects the web's potential as a reservoir of attested usage from the linguist's point of view. Web texts certainly change over time, but there is no reason to assume that this perpetual change in content altogether alters the nature and composition of the whole. If the web is a huge collection of authentic texts which are the result of genuine human interactions, the source of each single utterance or lexical item may vary, but if these are to be considered as evidence of usage, it may not be of crucial importance whether the source is one or another document. On the contrary, evidence of attested usage of the same phrase found in different web pages at different times could testify to the social dimension of usage, providing evidence of the aforementioned diachronic nature of discourse (Teubert 2007: 67) and contributing to a richer notion of intertextuality (Kristeva 1986), by rendering visible how

> [each] new text repeats to a considerable extent things that have already been said. Text segments, collocations, complex and simple lexical items which were already in use, are being recombined, permuted, embedded in new contexts and paraphrased in new ways. (Teubert 2007: 78)

Thus, while the fluid nature of the web is often invoked as one of the main arguments against using the web as a corpus, because a result computed today may not be exactly reproducible tomorrow, one is tempted to revive a powerful analogy with water (Kilgarriff 2001), arguing that nobody would demand that the chemical composition of water in a river is exactly the same at each experiment, and nonetheless river water is undoubtedly a legitimate object of scientific enquiry. And so is the web. As Volk suggests, we only have to learn how 'to fish in the waters of the web' (Volk 2002: 9).

4.2 Reproducibility

One of the most obvious practical consequences for linguistic research of the web's dynamic nature is the impossibility of reproducing any experiment – a really serious problem, since it is one of the basic requirements of scientific research that an experiment can be replicated/reproduced so that it can also be validated or – perhaps more crucially for the scientific method – invalidated. This also applies to corpus linguistics research, which aims to be scientific. Accordingly, it is an implicit requirement of a corpus that it should be stable, so that 'the results of a study can be validated by direct replication of the experiment' (Lüdeling et al. 2007: 10). Reproducibility is in fact a serious concern in corpus linguistics, because both quantitative and qualitative approaches to corpus data require that an experiment can be repeated. Any claim made about language facts needs be either validated by experiments confirming those facts or invalidated when a replication of the same experiment brings up contradictory evidence (Lüdeling et al. 2007: 11).

While for traditional corpora this is, at least in principle, taken for granted, the problem of reproducibility and validation of experiments becomes a crucial issue when using the web as a corpus, especially if accessed through ordinary commercial search engines. As Lüdeling again argues,

> [...] the web is constantly in flux, and so are the databases of all commercial search engines. Therefore, it is impossible to replicate an

> experiment in an exact way at a later time. Some pages will have been added, some updated, and some deleted since the original experiment. In addition, the indexing and search strategies of a commercial engine may be modified at any time without notice. (Lüdeling et al. 2007: 11)

Furthermore, the wild inconsistencies and fluctuations discovered in the result counts, even for common English words, via common search engines, and the patent incapability of Google to 'count' anything in any reliable way (Veronìs 2005; Baker 2012) reveal that any linguistic study based on the web as corpus definitely calls for some form of validation. This has made the issue of reproducibility one of the new key concerns, prompting research on the web as corpus in terms of a reconsideration of tools and methods. Thus, while the problem of reproducibility has been empirically addressed by researchers using the web as corpus via ordinary search engines, who simply validate their results by repeating the same search at distant intervals in time (Lüdeling et al. 2007: 11), others have opted for different methods of using the web as a corpus, i.e. by downloading the results of the queries submitted to a search engine so as to create a more stable, and hence verifiable, object.

4.3 Relevance and reliability

The dynamic and fluid nature of the web makes it an extremely noisy environment for corpus-based research also from the point of view of relevance and reliability (Fletcher 2004), which are key concerns for corpus research based on the web, especially when web data are to be used as a basis for both quantitative and qualitative evidence (Rosenbach 2007: 168). Relevance and reliability are generally seen as aspects of 'precision' and 'recall', two issues pertaining to information retrieval which are often mentioned as worthy of consideration in studies concerning the web as corpus (Baroni and Bernardini 2004; Fletcher 2007; Lüdeling et al. 2007).[3]

The importance of precision and recall, even in the most basic use of the web as corpus, is easily explained. While any linguistic search carried out by means of specific software tools on any traditional stable corpus of finite size (such as the BNC) will certainly report *only* (precision) results exactly matching the query, and *all* (recall) the results matching the query, this is obviously not the case with the web, where recall is impaired by its 'unstable' nature as a dynamic non-linguistically oriented collection of text, whereas precision is impaired by the intrinsic limitations, from the linguist's perspective, of search tools such as ordinary search engines. If locating an item in a corpus makes sense only assuming a minimum qualitative and quantitative accuracy in the search, a web search for linguistics purposes would make sense only assuming that the search should not return too many 'wrong' hits, called *false positives* (precision), and should not miss too many correct items, called *false negatives* (recall). This is precisely what makes using search engine hits as a source of linguistic information (i.e. using frequency data from a search engine – the so-called 'Google frequencies' – as indicative of frequency of a given item in the web as corpus) more problematic than it might seem at first glance. To assume a fairly high number of hits for a query as evidence of usage is not – as will be seen later – something which can be taken for granted. For one thing, reliability and recall are made problematic by the huge number of duplicates and near-duplicates found by search engines, a fact that ultimately depends on the dynamic nature of the web itself. The presence of duplicates on the web, an issue generally alien to carefully compiled corpora, dramatically inflates frequency counts and makes numeric data obtained from hit counts on the web virtually useless from the point of view of statistics. Thus, while using page hit counts as indicative of the frequency of a given lexical item seems intuitively to be a cheap, quick and convenient way for researchers to obtain frequency data, the reliability of such data is seriously impaired by the inherent instability of the web.

As to relevance and precision, these are impaired by the very strategies that enhance the power of search engines as tools for retrieving information (not specifically linguistic) from the web. In order to retrieve as many documents as possible matching a user's query, search engines usually perform some sort of normalization: searches are usually insensitive to capitalization, automatically recognize variants ('white-space' finds *white space*, *white-space* and *whitespace*), implement stemming for certain languages (as in *lawyer fees* vs. *laywer's fees* vs. *lawyers' fees*), ignore punctuation characters and prevent querying directly for terms containing hyphens or possessive markers (Lüdeling et al. 2007; Rosenbach 2007). While such features are undoubtedly helpful when searching for information on the web, they affect the search possibilities in terms of precision and relevance, and accordingly distort frequency data. Indeed, it is out of the necessity to counteract the limits in terms of relevance and reliability of any use of the web as corpus, based on access via ordinary search engines, that the most important tools for the creation of web corpora were born.

Conclusion

In this chapter some theoretical aspects relating to the notion of the web as corpus have been explored by revisiting key issues in corpus linguistics in the light of the characteristics of the web as a spontaneous, self-generating collection of texts, and by hinting at some of the new issues which the possibility of using the web as a corpus has raised. While the notion of a linguistic corpus as a 'body' of texts rests on some correlate issues such as finite size, balance, part-whole relationship and stability, the notion of the web as corpus introduces key concepts of non-finiteness, flexibility, de-centring, re-centring and provisionality, which, while apparently calling into question the 'good practice' of corpus work, may also affect the very notion of a linguistic corpus in more radical ways. All these issues will be further explored in terms of their application in the following chapters.

Study questions and activities

- Go to Internet World Stats and focus on language statistics. Compare the most recent data you can find with data for 2000 reported in Table in section and comment on those changes which strike you as most significant.
- Go to corpora.byu.edu and open the Corpus of Contemporary American English (COCA). Search for the phrase 'serve as an indicator'. How many occurrences can you find? Now search the web for the same phrase. Make a proportion to compare the number of occurrences of this phrase in the 450.000.000 word COCA and the number of hits found of the web. How do your findings relate the estimated size of the web amounting to 100 trillion (10^{14}) words reported in Norvig's lecture?
- Go to the Home Page of the Open Directoy Project at www.dmoz.org. Choose a directory (e.g. Chemistry). How many subcategories can you find? Choose one subdirectory (e.g. Environmental Chemistry) and visit a sample of the documents it contains. Which genres are represented? Is there any genre or register that strikes you as being overrepresented (or missing)?

Suggestions for further reading

Crystal, D. (2011), *Internet Linguistics*. London: Routledge.

Kilgarriff, A. (2001), 'Web as corpus'. *Proceedings of the Corpus Linguistics Conference* (CL 2001), University Centre for Computer Research on Language Technical Paper, Vol. 13, Special Issue, Lancaster University, 342–4.

Kilgarriff, A. and Grefenstette, G. (2003), 'Introduction to the Special Issue on the Web as Corpus'. *Computational Linguistics*, 29, 3, 333-47.
Fletcher, William H. (2012), 'Corpus analysis of the World Wide Web', in C. A. Chapelle (ed.), *Encyclopedia of Applied Linguistics*. Oxford: Wiley-Blackwell.
Lew, R. (2009), 'The Web as corpus versus traditional corpora: Their relative utility for linguists and language learners', in *Contemporary Corpus Linguistics*, ed. by Baker, London: Continuum, 245-300.
Norvig, P. (2008), 'Theorizing from Data: Avoiding the Capital Mistake' (Videolecture). Available at http://www.youtube.com/watch?v=nU8DcBF-qo4 [accessed 1 June 2013].

Notes

1 Updated statistics reporting the Top Internet Languages are available at www.internetworldstats.com/stats7.htm. The website is regularly updated but, as of 7 June 2013, the most recent statistics available date back to 30 June 2011.

2 The word topic is here used as a synonym for domain in the sense of subject field. Preference for the word topic was suggested to avoid confusion with the notion of 'domain' in internet technology, where the term refers to part of the URL used to identify a website.

3 Precision and recall are defined as 'measures of effectiveness of search systems'. More specifically, 'precision is the ratio of the number of relevant documents retrieved to the total number of documents retrieved, and recall is the ratio of the number of relevant documents retrieved to the total number of relevant documents' (Van Rijsbergen 1979).

3

Challenging Anarchy: Web Search from a Corpus Perspective

Introduction

In this chapter the potential and the limitations of accessing the web as a ready-made corpus via ordinary search engines are introduced and discussed. In Section 1 some general issues concerning web search are surveyed, before providing an overview of how search engines work in Section 2. Section 3 reports on case studies based on the use of commercial search engines for linguistic purposes (such as providing evidence of attested usage, investigating phraseology, and testing translation candidates), before discussing the meaning of search engine advanced options from the linguist's point of view in Section 4.

1. The corpus and the search

The previous chapter has attempted to outline the controversial status of the web as a linguistic corpus, by revisiting key issues in corpus linguistics from the perspective of the web as a spontaneous, self-generating collection of texts. Although the web is far from being a carefully compiled corpus, and despite obvious reservations and concerns about the advisability of using such a haphazard repository of digital text for linguistic purposes, it has often been used as a corpus in a variety of research, professional and teaching contexts. Especially in the field of computational linguistics, the web was immediately seen as the obvious and only source to go to in many cases. As a text collection of unprecedented size and scope, freely and ubiquitously accessible, the web provided data that could be crucial for the solution of typical Natural Language Processing tasks (Banko and Brill 2001; Keller and Lapata 2003: 459). Particularly for Machine Translation and Word Sense Disambiguation, the idea of using large text collections as an alternative (or complement) to sophisticated algorithms has become popular since the advent of the web, with an increasing body of studies showing that simple algorithms using web-based evidence can out-perform sophisticated methods based on smaller but more controlled data sources (Lüdeling et al. 2007: 7). In the specific field of corpus linguistics, the web is increasingly used as a source of evidence of attested language use (Hundt et al. 2007; Mair 2012), and more recently this use of the web has also received attention in the context of Computer Aided Language Learning (Shei 2008; Wu et al. 2009; Sha 2010; Geluso 2011), sometimes even labelled as Google Assisted Language Learning (Chinnery 2008). While the shortcomings of the web as a corpus are invariably acknowledged, its usefulness as a ready-made source of authentic language available at the click of a mouse button is clear, and makes it an extremely convenient resource to test research hypotheses and/or personal intuitions about language use. In this context, the potential of search engines is openly recognized and their use is strongly advocated and supported, especially in foreign language teaching. Furthermore, recent studies proving the usefulness of less opportunistic and more systematic approaches to using the web as a corpus (e.g. Hundt et al. 2007; Mair 2012) have gained web-as-corpus methodologies a reputation also for serious academic research in corpus linguistics.

When using the web as an immediate source of corpus-like linguistic information through an ordinary search engine, awareness of problems and limitations is, in any case, of paramount importance. The first and most obvious problem in accessing the web as a corpus in its own right is the total lack of control that the linguist has over such a huge, anarchic and unstable database. First, the web is, as we have seen, very far from a traditional 'closed' archive or database in which information content is stored in an orderly manner that can accordingly be retrieved with extreme precision and high recall; secondly, the web has become a very special mixed medium, serving many purposes and increasingly including all kinds of user-generated content. Even when considering only the textual content, one is bewildered. As seen in the previous chapter, the extraordinary inclusiveness of the web, as a heterogeneous and non-sampled body of text, creates a varied scenario that includes all kinds of texts, from literary masterpieces to pornography, from carefully drafted official documents and peer-reviewed scholarly articles to unrevised commercial ephemera and quite informal personal communication. Furthermore, online texts may consist of mere fragments, stock phrases, hot lists, and may come in a myriad of duplicates and near-duplicates which are of no use from a linguist's perspective (Fletcher 2004a: 275). In this respect one could also consider the increasing amount of content consisting of videoclips, mp3 files, and especially song lyrics, which, while authentic, are repeated and mirrored several times, undoubtedly contributing to further imbalance of the web's content. Then there is the vexed question of authorship, which today often entails 'multiple authorship' (Crystal 2011: 30), with texts being manipulated, revised and re-edited by a number of writing entities, as is, openly, the case with wikis and, covertly, with countless forms of plagiarism whereby the apparent anonymity of much of web content seems to legitimate its manipulation by other users. In addition, there is the already discussed problem of size. While working with such a huge amount of data greatly enhances the chances of finding information about any item, this advantage is counterbalanced by the fact that, in many cases, dealing with too much data may result in the impossibility of assessing the real significance of the quantitative data retrieved. Finally, there is the impossibility of relying on any form of linguistically oriented utilities or linguistic metadata, and the notorious 'volatility' of the 'webscape' (Fletcher 2007: 26). These are, no doubt, limitations which make the web an inhospitable environment for 'serious' linguistic research.

Concerns and reservations are even more crucial when attention is focused not only on the web corpus *per se* but also on the practice of accessing it as a linguistic resource only via commercial search engines. While the quantity, diversity and topicality of web documents are undoubtedly tempting, the problem of locating linguistically meaningful data through query systems that are not completely free from commercial interests represents a real challenge.

Apparently, the only problem with search engines is that they are not designed for linguistic purposes. They aim, in fact, to answer a variety of other needs, and come with a number of limitations, from the linguist's perspective, which are not easily bypassed. In the literature on the web as corpus, the problems typically mentioned are that search engines impose a limit to the number of results that can be displayed, that the results themselves are displayed in a format which is not suitable for linguistic analysis, and that results are ranked according to algorithms which escape the user's control. In addition, it is important to consider how the very strategies that enhance the effectiveness of search engines for general purposes, such as normalization of spelling, lemmatization and the inclusion of synonyms in the results, fight against precision in linguistics-oriented web search. Finally, search engines do not allow result re-sorting according to the user's specific needs – if we exclude recently implemented options that allows to sort results by relevance or date. All this makes the observation of recurring language patterns very difficult and time-consuming.

However, these limitations are only part of the picture. New generation search engines have greatly improved research for the average user but have made it even more difficult for linguists to locate useful information in other respects. In their commitment to answer the supposedly commercial need behind the average user's query, search engines are now engaged in an unprecedented effort to shift the original query-based retrieval algorithm, in which the search engine's task was to find items exactly matching the query, into a context-driven information supply algorithm, whose aim is to provide information that is supposed to be of interest to the user on the basis of elements not necessarily contained in the query itself (Broder 2006).

The scenario so far described suggests, therefore, that it would be an oversimplification to think that the problem posed by search engines is that they are not designed for linguists and that they are 'only' geared towards the retrieval of general information from the web. The real problem is that the very needs which search engines address are constantly evolving and it can no longer be assumed that search engines are constructed to respond to straightforward informational needs. On the contrary, it is quite clear today that the need behind the query is often not so much 'informational' in nature, but rather 'navigational' or 'transactional' (Broder 2002; 2006)[1] and – it could be argued – even 'social', 'affective' and 'emotive', as the growth of social networks apparently suggests. This clearly derives, as stated in Baeza-Yates (2011: 11), from the very nature of the web as not simply a repository of documents and data, but also a medium to do business. The concept of search has thus been extended beyond the mere seeking of text information to encompass such needs as the price of a book, the phone number of a hotel, the link for downloading a software. Accordingly, web search tools have evolved in the same direction, blending data from different sources, clustering results in a manner that is supposed to be of greater utility in responding to those needs, trying to learn from the searcher's behaviour, in an attempt to guess what a user is really looking for and what he or she wants to do, in order to offer personalized results (Sullivan 2009). New generation search engines do not simply 'passively' retrieve the information required but rather 'actively' supply (unsolicited and often commercial) information, not only in the form of 'banner ads' and 'sponsored links', but also through algorithms aimed at behavioural and contextual targeting (Levene 2010: 152ff.). These new algorithms clearly tend towards a strong customization of the results, creating a 'filter bubble' (Parser 2011) around each individual user, without the user even being aware of what is happening.

This is what may make the web apparently more useful, but arguably more insidious, for the average user, and definitely less reliable for linguistic research. Linguistic research could in fact be labelled as exclusively and quintessentially 'informational' and does not profit from strategies aimed at enhancing the ability of web search tools to meet other needs.

2. Search engine basics: Crawling, indexing, searching, ranking

In spite of all these drawbacks and limitations, the web has entered the scene of corpus linguistics, often providing solutions to specific problems and unique opportunities for research questions that cannot find an answer in more traditional resources. This is the reason why recent introductions to corpus linguistics include sections on the web as corpus and also, albeit briefly, comment on the use of search engines (Lindquist 2009; Baker 2009; McEnery and Hardie 2012). It is precisely against the background of the *de facto* intersection between web search as a common, non-linguistically oriented practice and linguistic research informed by the corpus linguistic approach that it is perhaps useful at this stage to survey some basic concepts concerning web search, starting from the workings of web search engines.

In essence, a search engine is 'a program designed to help people locate information on the Web by formulating simple keyword queries' (Oja and Pearson 2012). The engine thus only connects the keywords a user enters (query) to another list of keywords (index), which represents a database of web pages, to produce a list of website addresses with a short amount of context. In response to the user's query, the search engine displays the results or hits for that query with a certain amount of co-text, accompanied by links to the source page or website.

Three major steps are involved in performing this task (crawling, indexing, searching) and these steps correspond to the 'parts' of the search engine: the crawler; the indexing program; the search engine or query processor. The main task that a web search engine performs is to store information about a large number of web pages, which are retrieved from the World Wide Web itself by a web crawler, or 'spider', in keeping with the general metaphor representing the internet as a 'web' of documents. This is the program used by search engine sevices to scan the internet, locating new sites or sites that have recently changed. Once a new page is located by the search engine crawler, its content is analysed (i.e. words are extracted from titles, headings, or special fields called meta-tags) and indexed under virtually any word in the page – even though most search engines tend to exclude from the index particularly frequent words, such as articles or prepositions, the so-called stopwords. All data about web pages are then stored in an index database for use in later queries, so that when a user enters one or more search terms into the search engine, the engine examines its index and provides a list of web pages matching the query, including a short summary containing the document's title and extracts from the text. More precisely, search engines have been defined as Information Retrieval (IR) systems 'which prepare a keyword index for a given *corpus*, and respond to keyword queries with a ranked list of documents' (Chakrabarti 2003: 45, my italics). In the last phase a fundamental and challenging process is involved, i.e. determining the order in which the retrieved records should be displayed. This process is related to a relevance-ranking algorithm which takes a number of factors into account – as explained in Brin and Page's (1998) seminal contribution on this aspect. Typical factors taken into account today are the popularity of the page (measured by the number of other pages linked to it), the number of times the search term occurs in the page, the relative proximity of search terms in the page, the location of search terms (for example, pages where the search terms occur in the title page get higher ranking), and even the geographical provenance of the query (which may prompt a bias to ranking higher those websites which are closer to the user). It is, at this stage, evident that the usefulness of a search engine ultimately depends on the relevance of the result set it gives back, and it is equally evident that 'relevant' means something different to the linguist than to the average user. When searching for *harsh landscapes* a linguist might be simply trying to find evidence to validate or invalidate this collocation, whereas a geographer might be looking for specific information on geomorphology. Similarly, when searching *oral squamous cell carcinoma* or *squamous cell oral carcinoma* a translator might be trying to check the exact word order in the noun phrase referring to the disease, whereas the average user will probably be looking for information on the disease itself. The search engine's ranking algorithm uses its track of previous searches, the user's geographical positions and all other sorts of contextual data it has access to, in order to guess the potential needs behind the user's query and return customized results.

In this scenario, where both the working of search engines and the web's content definitely fall beyond the linguist's control, the only part of the search that can be controlled – for those seriously interested in using the web as a corpus – is the query. When using the web as a corpus, everything starts with the user's query, and this is another fundamental difference between web search and ordinary corpus research. There is no way, via search engines, to start from the corpus itself to produce frequency lists, or to compare corpora in order to obtain keywords. Neither can the results be ordered according to criteria other than the ranking system used by the search engine. What is more, no further processing of the results can be done of the type generally allowed by linguistic tools (e.g. sorting, statistics, annotation etc.), unless the web pages are downloaded into an *ad hoc* corpus to be analysed with more traditional corpus linguistics tools. The typical thing that a search engine can do is to produce a list of concordance-like strings for a given item, which display a number of occurrences of a certain word or group of words in context, with vague indications of frequency. This suggests quite different roles for the linguist in inductive empirical research on conventional corpora and when using the web as a corpus. As Sinclair (2005: online) suggests, it is the very 'cheerful anarchy of the Web' that places 'a burden of care' on the user. This is true with reference to the use of the web as a source of texts for conventional corpora (as Sinclair meant it), but it is even more so in cases where the web is accessed as a corpus 'surrogate'. The problem for the linguist is then to learn how to 'challenge' the anarchy of the web and the limited service provided by search engines, by finding ways to elicit from the web useful response to well-posed research questions. It should be borne in mind that the usefulness of results for the linguist does not only depend on the nature of the database or on the ranking algorithm used by the search engine, but can also crucially depend on the appropriateness of the query. The way most users – and linguists here are no exception – generally approach the act of searching the web through ordinary search engines can be very naïve and this may account not only for much of the frustration experienced by web searchers, but also for the risk of misusing the web as a linguistic resource. In the following pages useful techniques for exploiting search engines for linguistic reference will be discussed.

3. Google and the others: An overview of commercial search engines

As seen at the beginning of this chapter, a web search engine is today very different from the text-based information retrieval system it was at the beginning of the internet era. A quick overview of the search options provided by one of the most popular search engines, www.google.com, can provide at a glance insights into the wide variety of search needs a search engine responds to today, and gives clues of the position of linguistically oriented search in the wider context of web search. Needless to say, the present overview of the workings of web search engines cannot claim to be exhaustive, and is in any case bound to become out of date in a matter of weeks, given the speed of change in search engines' functions and options. Rather, it aims to suggest how complex and rich a search engine is today, and to show how much is going on behind the scenes without the user – the linguist in our specific case – ever being aware. Also, it should be noted that the options that are available directly from the search engine's home page may vary depending on the regional version (e.g. the home page of google.com is slightly different from the home page of google.co.uk or google.ie and so on), and are constantly updated or changed by the web search company itself.

In this section we will use the results page for the simple query *landscapes* in google.com to survey some characteristics of web search.[2] As Figure 3.1 clearly shows, starting from the basic act of typing in a word in the query box, a user is presented with the 'proactive' role of the search engine itself, which offers instant suggestions for the query, based on popularity, previous search by the same user and location (Sullivan 2011).

Figure 3.1. *Google query interface with instant suggestions for search* landscapes

Exploring the results in detail, as reported in Figure 3.2, prompts further considerations. On the left-hand side, a tool bar points to a number of subsections of the web, some sort of sub-corpora indeed, that could be searched directly for more focused results, reflecting the variety of needs which the search engine aims to satisfy: news, maps, blogs, videos, but also shopping, patents, apps, and even recipes. Search options also include proximity search, with the possibility of setting a specific location as reference point (e.g. a city or a ZIP code), and limit the search to a certain geographical area, two options which – albeit devised primarily for commercial purposes – might also be useful from a linguist's point of view. In the lower part of the left-hand frame, one finds other search possibilities which suggest that language issues feature quite prominently in web search engines like Google, which is proud to offer all sorts of language utilities like Dictionary search, search by Reading level, and even Verbatim, an option that allows users to temporarily neutralize spelling corrections and the default inclusion of synonyms in the results.

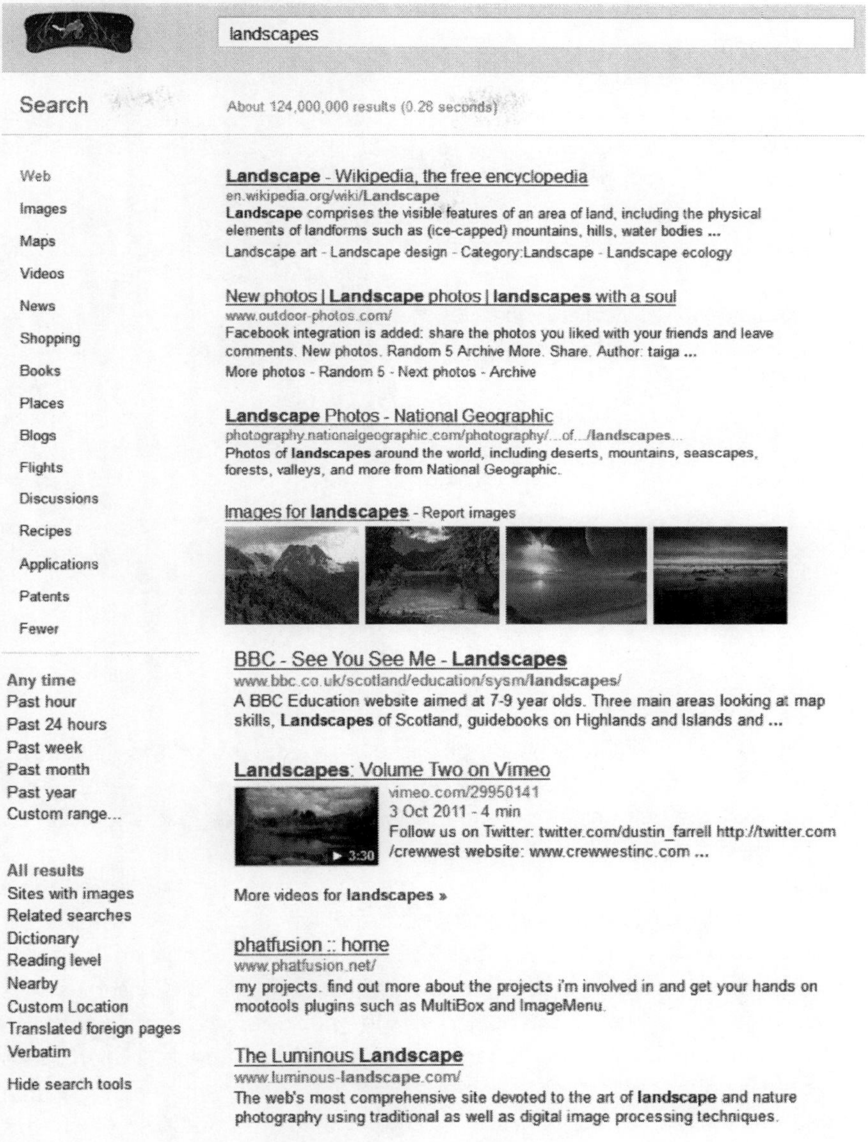

Figure 3.2. *Search results for* landscapes *from google.com*

When moving on to consider the results, these clearly reflect the variety and inclusiveness of web content featuring not only language texts, but also images, videos, and music. See, for instance, the results for the word *landscapes* from google.co.uk, as reported in Figure 3.3 overleaf.

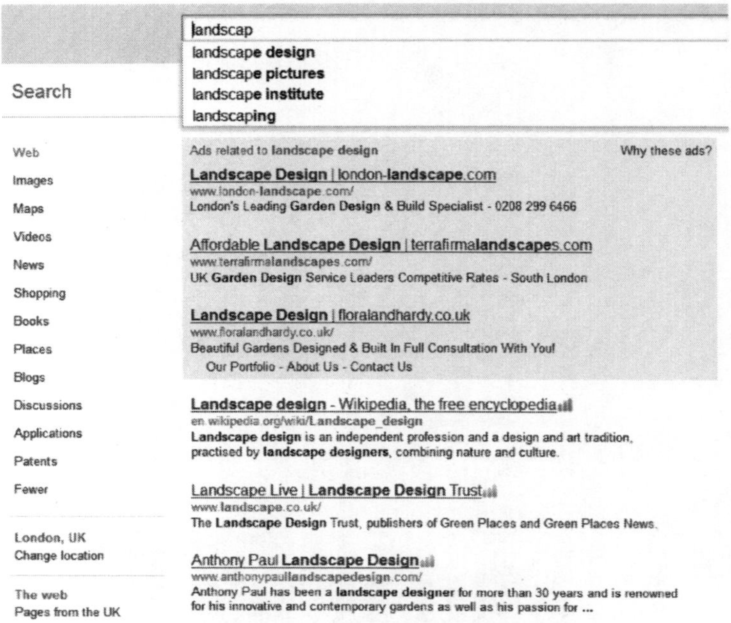

Figure 3.3. *Search results for* landscapes *from google.co.uk*

In focus position (i.e. on the right-hand side and top of the list with a different colour background) one will generally find sponsored adverts. These are definitely the parts more patently sensitive to changes in the settings for location, and are – obviously – highly dependent on the regional version of Google being used. The latter is by no means a trivial matter, since Google tends to set by default the regional version which is closest to the area in which a machine IP address is located, so the results visible to the user, and their ranking, is determined by this default position. This means that a search initiated by a user from Spain through google.es will be different from the same search initiated from Germany through google.de. The user needs to be aware of these default settings to make sure that the results are not biased regionally in a way which is not the one desired. An example of this can be seen by comparing the results page obtained for the word *shock* in google.it, google.fr, google.de, and google.co.uk (the Italian, French, German and British version of Google). While the number of hits remains the same (604,000,000 as of March 2013) the first results (i.e. the ones that are ranked higher according to the search engine algorithm) are different (with the one exception of the corresponding Wikipedia entry which always tops the results), just because of the 'geographical' bias of the search engine's default settings.

On the basis of what has been said so far, it will therefore appear obvious that, although apparently trivial, the task of searching the web as if it were a corpus poses specific problems for the researcher, and requires that cautionary procedures are adopted both in submitting the query to the search engine and in interpreting the results. The user needs to take into account basic issues which are related to the peculiar nature of the web as a huge, dynamic, multilingual 'corpus', as well as other problems specific to the gateway to information on the web, the search engines themselves. As to the latter, the first step towards a competent use of search engines from a corpus linguistics perspective is a deeper understanding of how to use a search engine's advanced options.

4. Challenging anarchy: Mastering advanced web search

Accessing the web via ordinary search engines is no doubt the most straightforward and immediate mode for using the web as a language resource. This is certainly an approach that is widely utilized also outside the corpus linguistics community itself and shows how using the web as a corpus can be viewed as a specific case of information retrieval.

In recent years researchers have developed several theoretical models to describe the way people retrieve information from the web. The classic model, as reported in Baeza-Yates and Ribeiro-Neto (2011: 23ff.) is formulated as a cycle consisting of four main activities:

- problem identification,
- articulation of information need(s),
- query formulation, and
- results evaluation.

This standard model entails, as we will see in the remaining sections of this chapter, the basic steps required for a competent use of web search engines for linguistic purposes. It should also be noted, however, that more recent models emphasize the dynamic nature of the search process, suggesting that users learn from their search, and that their information needs can be adjusted as they see retrieval results (Baeza-Yates and Ribeiro-Neto 2011: 23). Using the web as a corpus through ordinary search engines therefore engages the user in a process of progressive query refinement towards greater complexity which can only be supported by a deep knowledge of the advanced search options provided by most search engines.

4.1 An overview of web search options

A use of the web as a corpus is, indeed, implicit in the query language of most search engines, which basically allows the user to look for web pages that contain (or do not contain) specified words and phrases, together with a rough indication of how many web pages satisfy these conditions.

The simplest kind of query essentially involves a relationship between terms and documents such as:

- documents containing the word X
- documents containing the words X and Y
- documents containing the word X but not the word Y
- documents containing the word X or the word Y

These conditions represent what is generally known as a Boolean search, which, in the context of web search, refers to the process of identifying those web pages that contain a particular combination of words. More specifically, Boolean search is used to indicate that a particular group of words must all be present (the Boolean AND operator) in the web pages retrieved by the search engine; or that any word of a group is accepted (the Boolean OR operator); or that if a particular word is present in a web page, that page is to be rejected (the Boolean NOT operator). While the explicit use of the Boolean operators AND, OR and NOT has been progressively downplayed in most search engines, and searchers may not even be familiar with them, Boolean search has been partially replaced in some engines by the use of menus in the advanced search mode (see Figure 3.4 below).

Figure 3.4. *Google's advanced search user interface*

Thus, by typing your query in the box labelled 'all these words', you are implicitly using a Boolean AND; by using 'this exact word or phrase' you are asking for a sequence of words precisely matching the sequence used as an input for the query; by entering words in the 'any of the words' box you are using a Boolean OR; by selecting 'without the words' you are expressing the Boolean NOT. In most search engines, the Boolean AND is now a default in the simple search interface, so that whenever more terms are entered in the query box, they are implicitly linked by an AND operator. In Google, one can also input the following symbols directly in the simple search query box:

+ (for the Boolean AND)
" " (for 'exact phrase match')
OR (for the Boolean OR)
- (for the Boolean NOT)

Besides this explicit use of Boolean syntax, Google also provides further options to refine the query, such as 'language', 'region', 'last update', 'site or domain', and even indication of where in the page the searched term should appear, as shown in the relevant sections of the advanced search user interface reported in Figure 3.5 below.

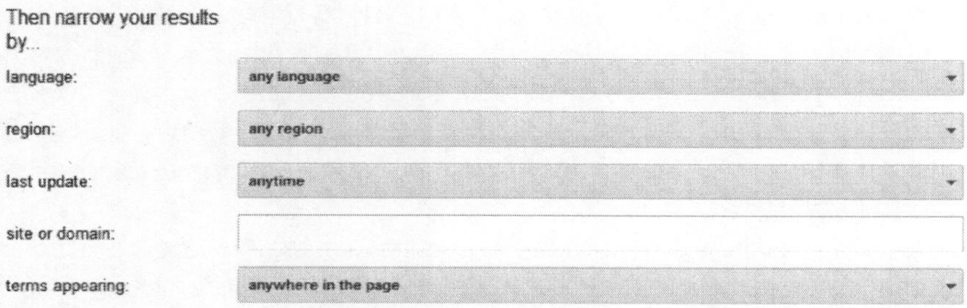

Figure 3.5. *Google's advanced search user interface*

Among these utilities for refining the user's query, the one most obviously related to a more specific use of the web for linguistic purposes is restriction by language, which means that, for most search engines, results can be limited to one among over 40 languages, ranging from Arabic to Vietnamese, including Esperanto and Belarusian. Its usefulness hardly needs to be demonstrated: by asking the search engine to retrieve only results in Italian, it is possible to prevent a search for *sole* (in Italian this means *sun*) to include English pages featuring the word *sole* (the fish). This may not, however, be enough to boost the quality of the results. The effectiveness of language options can be further enhanced by using the provenance utility implemented in some engines.

This option allows the user to obtain results only from websites registered in a given area (e.g. United Kingdom, Germany or Portugal); in this way one can also obviate the problem created by result customization based on the provenance of the query. A further option is restriction by domain, such as one of the national top-level domains (for example, .it for Italy, .fr for France, .es for Spain, .ie for Ireland and so on). While not 100 per cent reliable, this kind of regionally differentiated search has already started to provide the basis for research on change and variation in present-day English, as can be seen in studies by Mair (2007: 233–47; 2012: 245–55). Evidence of the reliability of national top-level domain in terms of specific varieties (especially as far as different varieties of English are concerned) has also recently been provided in a study by Cook and Hirst (2012), whose aim was precisely to see whether an English corpus constructed from a specific national top-level domain (e.g. .uk, .ca) could represent the English variety of the corresponding country. The results of this study indicate that top-level domains are a good proxy to national varieties, proving that a web corpus from a given top-level domain is 'more similar to a corpus known to contain texts from authors of the corresponding country than to a corpus known to contain documents by authors from another country' (Cook and Hirst 2012: 281). As a consequence, limiting a search to a specific national top-level domain may indeed boost the reliability of the results. This could be easily verified using markers of a specific variety, as in Murphy and Stemle (2011), where examples are taken from Hiberno-English, e.g. 'amn't' for the standard 'am not'. A search for the Hiberno-English form 'amn't' finds only 50,200 hits (as of January 2013) in pages in English from .uk sites registered in the United Kingdom, against the 116,000 hits found for the same search in English pages from .ie sites registered in Ireland.

The usefulness of domain restriction is not limited however to national/regional domains only. It is also very useful to search academic domains in English-speaking countries (such as .ac.uk and .edu), or limit the search to the so called generic top-level domains (.org, .com, .gov). Web search can finally be limited also to specific well-known portals for the distribution of scientific journals, or to well-known sites, like a journal, or specific sections of a newspaper (e.g. the Travel section in the *Guardian*), as an indirect way to control register and genre. Thus a query within the domain .edu could be loosely interpreted as a way of searching the web as a corpus representative of American academic discourse, whereas a search restricted to the site travel.guardian.co.uk would temporarily turn the web into a virtual corpus made up of articles from the Travel supplement of the well-know British newspaper.

The reliability of the results is also increased by the possibility of searching more controlled parts of the web, as is the case of Google Scholar (Brezina 2012), or the possibility of searching only published texts offered by Google

Books. In these cases some of the limits relating to the lack of representativeness and unreliability of the web are partly removed and the potential of the web as a ready-made corpus is greatly enhanced. As to the indication of where in the page the searched item appears, this can be useful to avoid undesired links to page-titles only or to URLs. Finally, the possibility of limiting the search to a certain date range can be exploited to turn the web into a diachronic corpus.

From the linguist's point of view, all these 'conditions' can be seen as a form of selection from among the wealth of texts that constitute the web and can, to some extent, be compared to the creation of a temporary, virtual sub-corpus from the web relating to a specific language environment.

4.2 Limits and potentials of 'webidence'

When discussing the potential of web search from a corpus linguistic perspective, reference is often made to the web as a source of evidence of 'attested usage'. More specifically, the web has been used to ascertain qualitative evidence, i.e. to show that a certain form or construction is attested, and as a source of quantitative evidence, i.e. to address, however approximately, the question of 'how many' of these forms/constructions are found (Rosenbach 2007: 168; Mair 2007, 2012). The specific evidence of attested usage that the web can provide has also been labelled by Fletcher as 'webidence' (2007: 36).

In its most basic form, this use of the web as a source of evidence of 'attested usage' could entail a simple search for a single word. A patently 'low-tech' use of the web for linguistic purposes, searching for a single word is not devoid of interesting implications, and provides a good starting point for exploring the potential and the limitations of the web as a source of quantitative and qualitative data. A case in point is spell-checking; by alternatively searching the web for two competing spelling forms, one can come to the conclusion that the word hitting more matches is likely to be the one spelled correctly, thus blending qualitative and quantitative evidence (Kilgarriff 2003: 332). This is, however, one of the most appropriate examples to show how misleading web search can be for a linguist and to what extent the bias of search engines towards a less 'mechanistic' view of users' needs determines the search engine output.

A search for one of the most commonly mis-spelt words, *accomodation*, would for instance return 473,000,000 hits, automatically including results for the normalized spelling *accommodation*, as seen in the screenshot below (see Figure 3.6).

In order to retrieve results precisely matching the mis-spelt form, one should reformulate the query, using inverted commas. The new query would still find

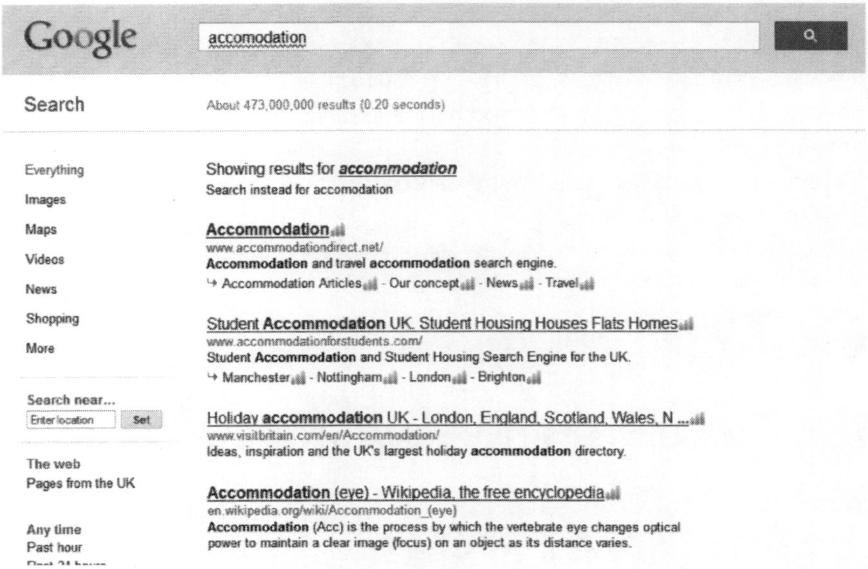

Figure 3.6. *Google's results for* accommodation

over 61,800,000 hits, which could well be mistakenly taken as evidence of attested usage, while they are in fact proof of the abovementioned issues concerning the potential unreliability and non-representativeness of web data.

Furthermore, doubts have been raised over the very capability of ordinary search engines to 'count' anything at all, i.e. to provide any reliable quantitative data. A paper by Rayson et al. (2012) has in fact shown that search engines generally do not agree on result counts, and that result counts fluctuate over time. This confirms that all kinds of quantitative information from the web must definitely be taken with a pinch of salt. The web is very noisy and it is only by a process of progressive query refinement that it can be effectively used as a reservoir of attested usage, especially for collocations, phraseological patterns, and to test translation candidates.

4.3 Phrase search and collocation

While searching the web for one single word seems not to promise much to the linguist, searching for 'phrases' is definitely a more interesting possibility offered by ordinary search engines. Here the enormous size of the web allows for a plethora of examples to be retrieved, even for phrases, collocations and grammatical constructions that are relatively sparse in other corpora (Baroni and Ueyama 2006; Wu et al. 2009; Sha 2010).

A basic way to use phrase search for linguistic reference is to check whether a certain sequence of words actually occurs in a given language. As already seen in the second chapter, the possibility of finding evidence in the web for longer chunks of language in use is orders of magnitude larger than in conventional corpora. As noted by Zanettin (2009), for instance, starting from the phrase *naked eye*, which has 150 occurrences in the BNC and over 976,000 hits on the web, one can still find a good number of results for the longer stretch *so small as to be barely visible to the naked eye*, a text chunk which is authentic and widely used in different contexts but obviously too long to be attested in the BNC or other traditional corpora.

Particularly interesting in this respect, especially for non-native speakers, is the possibility of using the web to test collocations. For instance, a web search for *rough waves* as opposed to *rugged waves* quantitatively favours the former, suggesting that *rough waves* is a more common collocation. The problem with the web, however, is that even collocations that are not attested elsewhere, or are perceived by native speakers as unnatural or untypical, still find many hits. Taking *heavy rain* vs *thick rain* as another example, among the typical collocations reported by a recently published English Grammar (Carter et al. 2011: 125) it is easy to see that the untypical collocation *thick rain* would seem nonetheless to be fairly frequent on the web, with 54,900 hits. Even allowing for a number of these results to be irrelevant (e.g. *thick rain* could be part of the phrase *thick rain forest*), the number of hits retrieved is by no means a negligible result. The problem is then how to interpret these results. Should the matches for *thick rain* be considered nonetheless as clear evidence of attested usage, or do they instead provide support to claims about the total unreliability of web frequency data as a source of linguistic information (especially if the 54,900 hits for *thick rain* are compared to the 39,200,000 hits for *heavy rain*)? It is hard to provide an answer to questions like these, since language itself constantly changes, and what is untypical today might become the standard of tomorrow. In more general terms, it is important to be constantly aware of 'noise' in the web and aim not so much at validating the initial hypothesis, but rather at invalidating it.

A case in point is the collocation *suggestive landscapes* discussed in Gatto (2009: 59–66). A new web search for this phrase from google.co.uk, as of March 2012, apparently provides evidence of attested usage with over 10,000 matches (see Figure 3.7 below), a number that might not appear at first glance a negligible part of the English web, which it is in fact.

The problem, thus, concerns again the correct interpretation of frequency data from a qualitative point of view. It requires a closer inspection into the results to probe their reliability, which is called into question, in this case, by their almost invariable provenance from sites referring to Italy (see references to the Sorrentine peninsula or to Lake Como). As a matter of fact,

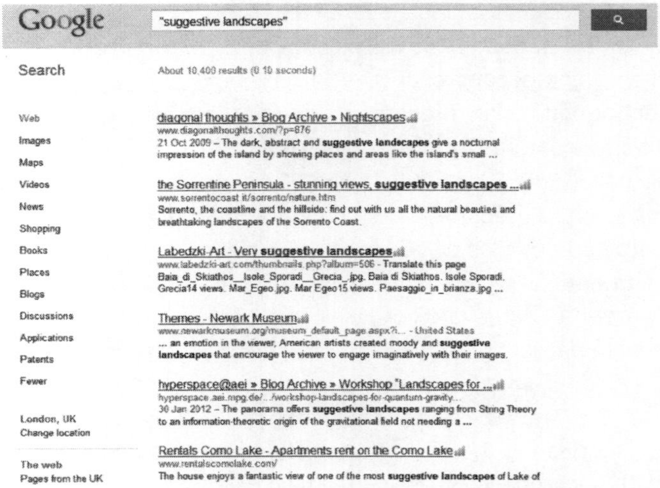

Figure 3.7. *Google's results for the query* "suggestive landscapes"

the incidence of hits for this query drops dramatically when resorting to the provenance utility, aimed at retrieving only English pages coming from the United Kingdom (see Figure 3.8 below).

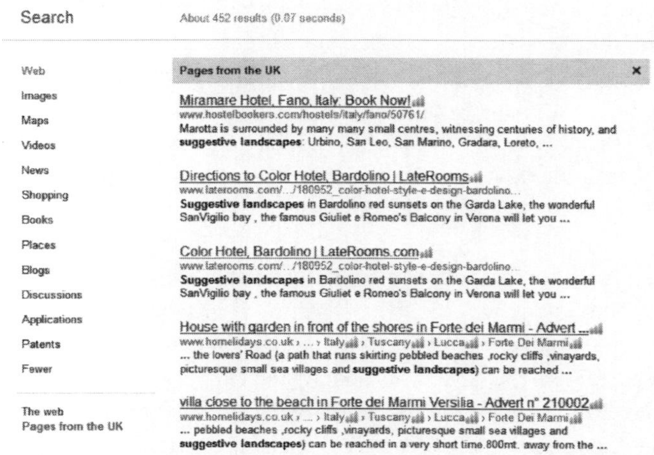

Figure 3.8. *Google's results for the query* "suggestive landscapes" *from UK pages*

As the screenshot reveals, the new query finds only 452 matches, which is very few hits indeed – at least for English, as we will see later in this chapter

– and all, again, relating to Italy. The phrase *suggestive landscapes* possibly originates in a literal translation from the Italian *paesaggi suggestivi*, meaning spectacular, or dramatic, scenery. By excluding the word *Italy* from the results (using the minus sign in the query box, or through the advanced search interface) the matches dramatically fall to 5, all again invariably relating to Italy.

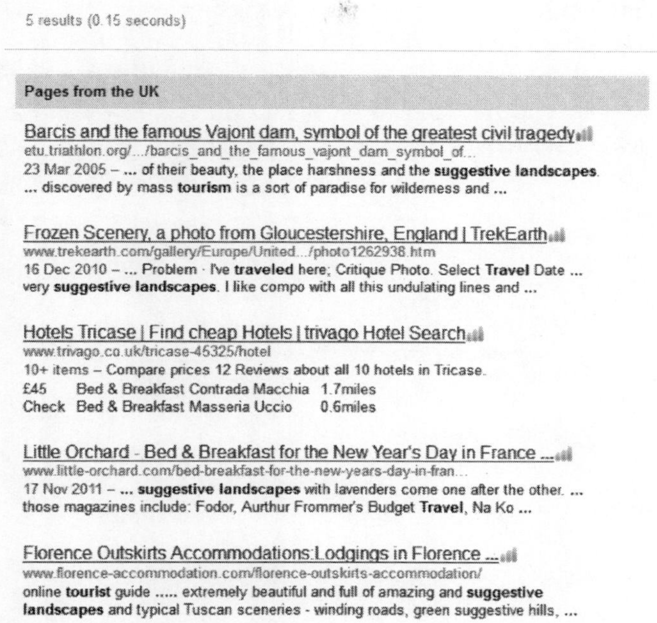
5 results (0.15 seconds)

Pages from the UK

Barcis and the famous Vajont dam, symbol of the greatest civil tragedy
etu.triathlon.org/.../barcis_and_the_famous_vajont_dam_symbol_of...
23 Mar 2005 – ... of their beauty, the place harshness and the **suggestive landscapes**. ... discovered by mass **tourism** is a sort of paradise for wilderness and ...

Frozen Scenery, a photo from Gloucestershire, England | TrekEarth
www.trekearth.com/gallery/Europe/United.../photo1262938.htm
16 Dec 2010 – ... Problem · I've **traveled** here; Critique Photo. Select **Travel** Date ... very **suggestive landscapes**. I like compo with all this undulating lines and ...

Hotels Tricase | Find cheap Hotels | trivago Hotel Search
www.trivago.co.uk/tricase-45325/hotel
10+ items – Compare prices 12 Reviews about all 10 hotels in Tricase.
£45 Bed & Breakfast Contrada Macchia 1.7miles
Check Bed & Breakfast Masseria Uccio 0.6miles

Little Orchard - Bed & Breakfast for the New Year's Day in France ...
www.little-orchard.com/bed-breakfast-for-the-new-years-day-in-fran...
17 Nov 2011 – ... **suggestive landscapes** with lavenders come one after the other. ... those magazines include: Fodor, Aurthur Frommer's Budget **Travel**, Na Ko ...

Florence Outskirts Accommodations:Lodgings in Florence ...
www.florence-accommodation.com/florence-outskirts-accommodation/
online **tourist** guide ..... extremely beautiful and full of amazing and **suggestive landscapes** and typical Tuscan sceneries - winding roads, green suggestive hills, ...

Figure 3.9. *Google's results for the query* "suggestive landscapes" – *Italy, from UK pages*

It is only through a process of query refinement that the linguist can invalidate a collocation which a less complex query apparently confirms.

4.4 Phraseology and patterns

Another meaningful option that can be exploited from a linguistic perspective is the search for an unspecified word in a certain position within a phrase. The unspecified word is represented by an asterisk '*', otherwise called a wildcard, in the search string. Unfortunately, this option, referred to as 'fill in the blank' in the advanced search tips provided by Google, is not fully supported by most search engines, including Google itself. Typically, one wildcard in the string should match one word only, so that multiple asterisks could be used as a sort of 'proximity' search option. Google, however, has changed the processing several times over the years, so that one single asterisk does not necessarily match a single word. Despite this lack of precision, the use of wildcards can be helpful for such tasks as checking phraseology and idioms. A search for *a little neglect may * mischief* can, for instance, quickly elicit the missing word in the proverb ('breed'). Lindquist (2009: 190–2) reports instead search results for the phrase *to * one's welcome*, showing how the asterisk in the pattern could be replaced by such verbs as *overstay, outstay, stay beyond* and *outlive.* Similarly, variation in the idiom *a storm in a teacup* is explored by replacing *teacup* with an asterisk in the pattern.

Wildcards can also be used to highlight areas of co-text for a word or phrase which a user may wish to explore also in more general terms. So, a user in doubt over the verb in the pattern *to * a better future* immediately finds suggestions (see Fig. 3.10.).

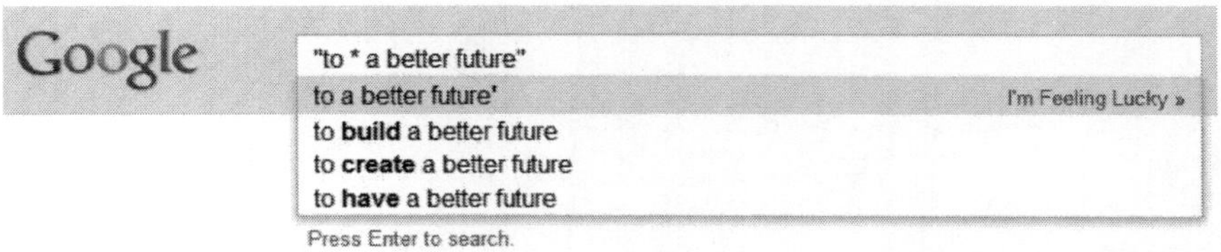

Figure 3.10. *Google's results for the query* "to * a better future"

Wildcards are particularly useful when combined with phrase search to test longer stretches of a text, or patterns. A useful strategy is to divide a long sentence into smaller word blocks and search them within quotation marks. In this way web search is heuristically used to discover how tightly bound a formulaic sequence is, by comparing the number of hits Google generates each time an additional lexical unit is added to a sequence (Shei 2008).

By way of example, a non-native speaker who wants to test the wording '... its clinical behavior cannot be predicted on the basis of histological parameters...' in the context of medical discourse can test the whole sequence by dividing it into smaller chunks; each chunk is then searched for within quotation marks for validation/invalidation (Gatto 2009: 70). In this way, a search for *clinical behavior* can be used to validate this specific collocation, followed by a search for *clinical behaviour * predicted* to test the complete pattern. As the screenshot below (Fig. 3.11.) suggests, the results include highly reliable and relevant matches from international journals and well-known portals for the distribution of medical texts, thus providing useful evidence of attested usage.

Having ascertained that the first part of the sequence is actually used in medical texts, one can go on and test the remaining parts, starting from

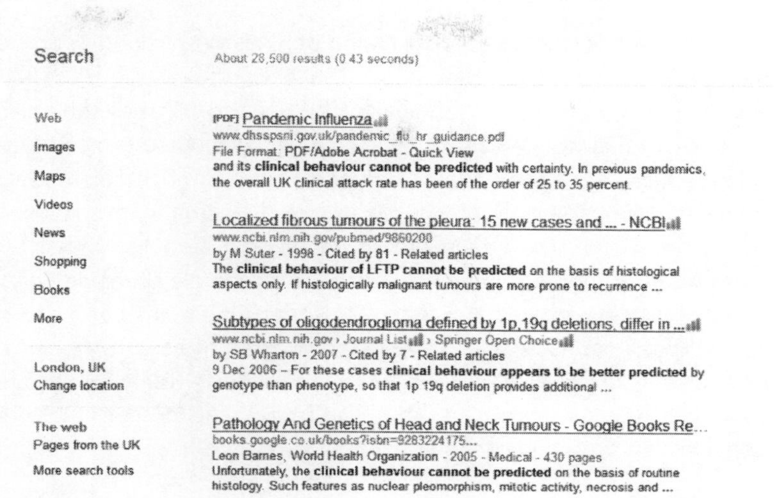

Figure 3.11. *Google's results for the query* "clinical behaviour * predicted"

predicted on the basis of. In this case, another word in the string can be added (e.g. *cancer* or *health*) to enhance the relevance of the results to a specific domain. It is also useful, as will be shown in more detail in the next section, to limit the search to known portals engaged in the distribution of medical journals, to enhance reliability. For example, the query:

cancer "predicted on the basis of" site: www.ncbi.nlm.nih.gov/pubmed

still produces a good number of matches from PubMed, a specialized portal for the distribution of medical articles, finally validating the whole pattern.

4.5 Provenance, site, domain and more: Searching subsections of the web

Options concerning restriction by provenance, site or domain are particularly useful in turning the web into a virtual corpus on demand. While the national top-level domains (such as .it for Italy, .fr for France, .es for Spain, .ie for Ireland and so on) are no more than a 'rough guide to provenance' (Fletcher 2007: 36), they can nonetheless contribute to the exploitation of a regionally differentiated web. A study by Mair (2007) reports very detailed descriptions of experiment to be carried out to investigate variation in present-day English on the basis of regional domain. Telling examples concern the use of prepositions with *different* (*to*, *from* or *than*) or the forms *been being* and *be being*, whose distribution in the national domains of English-speaking countries is reported and commented on (Mair 2007: 233–47).

Restriction to known sites or portals can be used to enhance the reliability of the results. In this way, phraseology in scientific discourse can be validated or invalidated through a web search limited to portals for the distribution of scientific publications (e.g. PubMed, Elsevier, etc.), as seen in Section 4.2.2 above). Similarly a search for academic phraseology would typically profit from validation through attestation of usage in academic domains only. The possibility of starting a paragraph with a rhetorical 'If, as has been argued...' can be, for instance, ascertained by searching the patterns *If, as has been argued* and *If, as it has been argued* both in the whole web and in academic sites only. The results (as seen in Table 3.1.) reveal that the pattern is clearly attested and that omission of the subject is the preferred mode:

Table 3.1 Google results for "If, as has been argued" vs "If, as it has been argued"

	Web	.ac.uk only
If, as it has been argued	37,200	3
If, as has been argued	238,000	1,640

The same search can be performed limiting the results to Google Scholar or to Google Books, with reliable evidence of attested usage which confirms the data reported above.

It is at this stage also worth referring to some recently implemented services aimed at using parts of the web as a corpus, both to gain information concerning language use and as a source of data for the interpretation of cultural dynamics – for instance, online services which exploit the huge amount of printed texts that make up the database of Google Books and treat it as a sort of diachronic corpus. This new Google Books interface (http://ngrams.googlelabs.com) allows linguists the possibility of searching 500 billion words of text to see changes in frequency of words and phrases, by turning a simple query into a complex task in which time span, case-sensitiveness and other detailed criteria contribute to eliciting quick answers to otherwise complex issues. Just consider the data obtained in a matter of seconds on the use of capitalized *Hopefully*, possibly as a sentence initial, by simply querying the Books Ngram Viewer (see Fig. 3.12.).

The graph hardly needs an explanation. It clearly shows the behaviour of capitalized *Hopefully*. Obviously these data require careful controls before

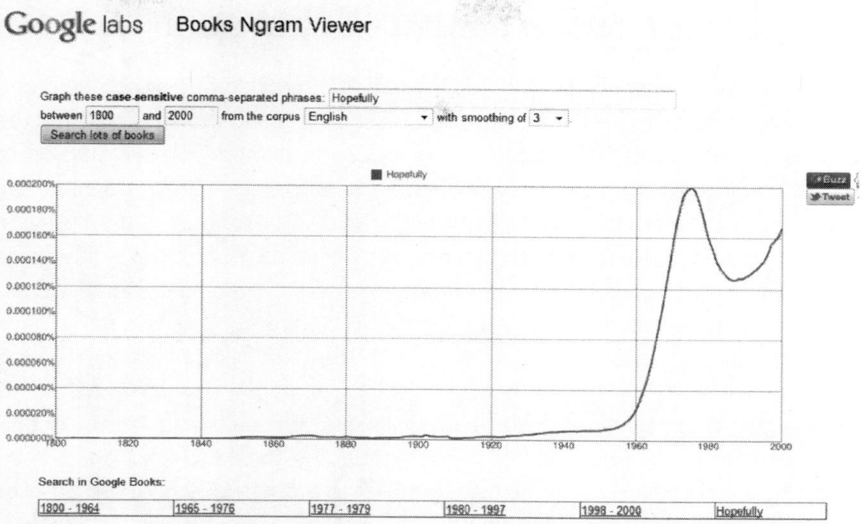

Figure 3.12. *Books Ngram Viewer query for* Hopefully

being used as evidence for scientific purposes, since – as the authors themselves suggests – the greatest challenge lies in their interpretation (Michel et al. 2010). Which books actually make up the database? Which constraints have determined its composition? Which varieties of English are more prominently represented? These are all issues which pertain to the web as corpus as a whole and suggest that all research in this field requires some form of *post-hoc* evaluation of the results.

An even more promising example of the interaction between the immense potential of Google Books and its exploitation from a corpus linguistics perspective is the Google Books interface created for Mark Davies' corpora website. The interface allows for searches in an American English dataset (155 billion words) and in the smaller British and One Million Books datasets. Besides supporting basic queries, such as the frequency of individual words or phrases, the interface allows search for patterns including part-of-speech information and searches for collocates or synonyms. While not immediately relevant to the use of the web as a corpus via ordinary search engines, which is the main focus in this chapter, this system is mentioned here because it reveals the incredibly fertile interaction between Google services and more traditional corpus linguistics.

4.6 Testing translation candidates

Translation is another 'ideal field' (Bernardini 2006) for corpus application, and this is also one of the most interesting areas for exploring uses of the web as corpus via ordinary search engines. If, as argued in Bernardini (2006), browsing monolingual target language corpora throughout the translation process can help reduce the amount of 'shining through' (Teich 2003) of the source language in the target language, browsing the web for instances of attested usage could be a simple – yet not simplistic – way to test translation candidates on the basis of evidence provided from the web. Maniez (2007), among others, provides a number of interesting examples concerning the possibility of using the web in the translation of complex noun phrases in medical research articles. He uses the web to solve such translation tasks as finding a French equivalent for *gluten sensitive enteropathy*. In this case, by querying the web for the pattern *gluten * enteropathie* he was able to retrieve the most frequently used phrases (*entéropathie au gluten, entéropathie d'intolérance au gluten, entéropathie induite par le gluten, entéropathie de sensibilité au gluten*), thus providing a number of alternatives to the literal, and scarcely attested, *entéropathie sensible au gluten*. Even more interesting is his use of search engines count as an aid for the disambiguation of syntactic patterns. This is a typical NLP task, often discussed in the literature (e.g. Volk 2002; Calvo and Gelbukh 2003; Nakov and Hearst 2005), which can be nonetheless reproduced 'manually' by translators when in doubt about a given syntactic pattern. Maniez shows how counts provided by search engines for various word combinations can be used to validate/invalidate dependencies using two examples. The first is the phrase *surgical removal or decompression of cysts*. In this case it is important to know whether *surgical* refers to both *removal* and *decompression*, or only to *removal* (which in languages such as French or Italian would originate different translations). Web search counts returned for the search *surgical decompression* (the author reports over 200,000 matches) indicate that the former is probably the case. The second example refers to the syntactic disambiguation of *adverse events and yields of efficacy*, where a non-native speaker may be uncertain about a possible modification of *yields* by the adjective *adverse*. In this case, again, the results reported by Maniez (less than 30 hits for *adverse yields* and none for *adverse yields of efficacy*) are taken as indicator of no syntactic dependency in this case (Maniez 2007: 165–6).

Other examples are discussed in Gatto (2011), and relate to using the web as an aid in the decision processes relating to the choice between premodification and postmodification of the noun phrase in the translation of the Italian multi-word term *sede di insorgenza*, in the context of a medical text about cancer. Starting from the two translation candidates, *site of onset* and *onset site*, a preliminary exploration simply concerning the frequency of usage was carried out on the basis of data from the web. In this case, mere figures (13,100 matches for *site of onset* vs. 836 matches for *onset site*) seemed to favour postmodification.

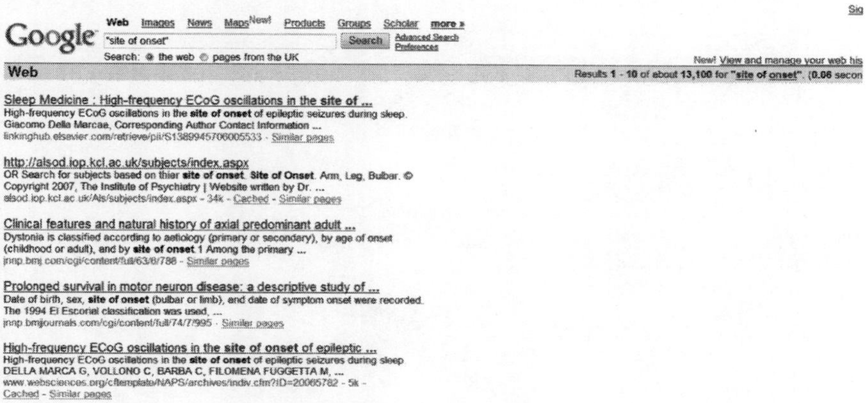

Figure 3.13. *Search results for* "site of onset"

However, these results for *site of onset* did not give sufficiently clear evidence of the relevance of this phrase to the general topic of the text, i.e. cancer. Therefore a Boolean search was used heuristically to refine the query and enhance the possibility of hitting more relevant matches before jumping to conclusions concerning postmodification as the preferred mode to express this concept. Including the word *cancer* in the search string made the search engine return results only from texts having the word *cancer* somewhere on the page, and therefore more likely to be addressing this topic. The new results proved to be more relevant, providing clearer evidence of attested usage for *site of onset* in this context.

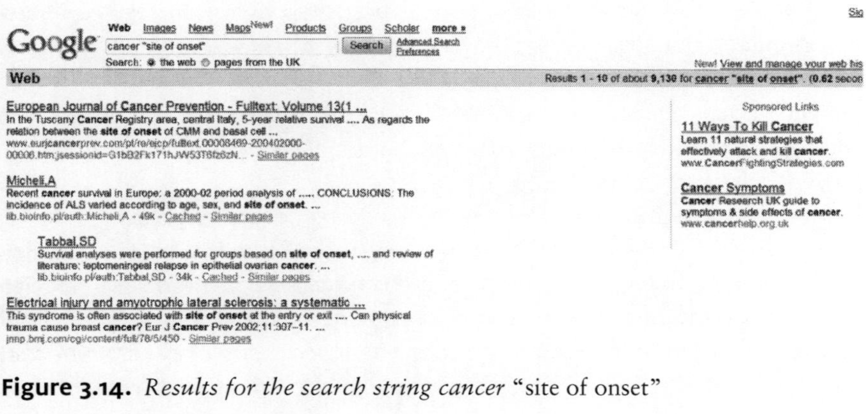

Figure 3.14. *Results for the search string cancer* "site of onset"

As to the alternative *onset site*, the results for the search string including both the word *cancer* and the phrase *onset site* are reported below:

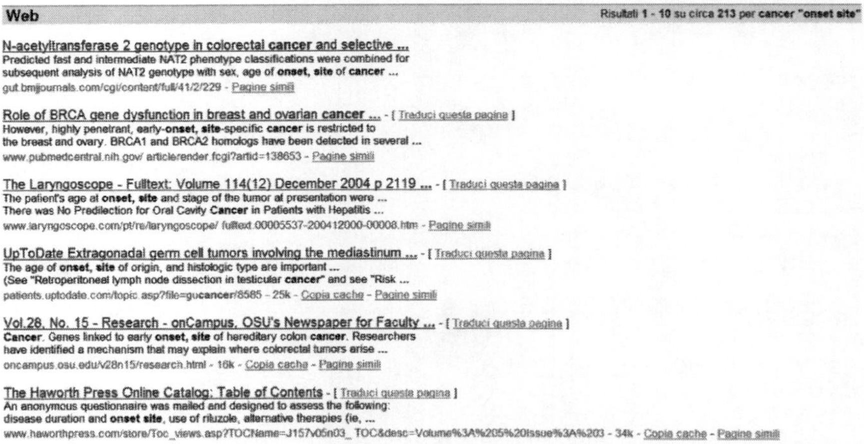
Web Risultati 1 - 10 su circa 213 per cancer "onset site"

N-acetyltransferase 2 genotype in colorectal cancer and selective ...
Predicted fast and intermediate NAT2 phenotype classifications were combined for subsequent analysis of NAT2 genotype with sex, age of **onset, site** of **cancer** ...
gut.bmjjournals.com/cgi/content/full/41/2/229 - Pagine simili

Role of BRCA gene dysfunction in breast and ovarian cancer ... - [Traduci questa pagina]
However, highly penetrant, early-**onset, site**-specific **cancer** is restricted to the breast and ovary. BRCA1 and BRCA2 homologs have been detected in several ...
www.pubmedcentral.nih.gov/ articlerender.fcgi?artid=138653 - Pagine simili

The Laryngoscope - Fulltext: Volume 114(12) December 2004 p 2119 ... - [Traduci questa pagina]
The patient's age at **onset, site** and stage of the tumor at presentation were ...
There was No Predilection for Oral Cavity **Cancer** in Patients with Hepatitis ...
www.laryngoscope.com/pt/re/laryngoscope/ fulltext.00005537-200412000-00008.htm - Pagine simili

UpToDate Extragonadal germ cell tumors involving the mediastinum ... - [Traduci questa pagina]
The age of **onset, site** of origin, and histologic type are important ...
(See "Retroperitoneal lymph node dissection in testicular **cancer**" and see "Risk ...
patients.uptodate.com/topic.asp?file=gu**cancer**/8585 - 25k - Copia cache - Pagine simili

Vol.28, No. 15 - Research - onCampus, OSU's Newspaper for Faculty ... - [Traduci questa pagina]
Cancer. Genes linked to early **onset, site** of hereditary colon **cancer**. Researchers have identified a mechanism that may explain where colorectal tumors arise ...
oncampus.osu.edu/v28n15/research.html - 16k - Copia cache - Pagine simili

The Haworth Press Online Catalog: Table of Contents - [Traduci questa pagina]
An anonymous questionnaire was mailed and designed to assess the following: disease duration and **onset site**, use of riluzole, alternative therapies (ie, ...
www.haworthpress.com/store/Toc_views.asp?TOCName=J157v05n03_TOC&desc=Volume%3A%205%20Issue%3A%203 - 34k - Copia cache - Pagine simili

Figure 3.15. *Results for the search string* cancer "onset site"

The low number of matches (213) seems to suggest that premodification may not be the preferred way to combine the two words. Moreover, it is important to realize that in most of the occurrences reported, the two nouns *onset* and *site* are separated by punctuation marks, generally a comma. By quickly browsing through more result pages, it becomes evident that the majority of hits are for *onset, site* rather than for the noun phrase *onset site*, thus further invalidating any assumptions concerning attestation of usage for *onset site* in this context.

At this stage one could further restrict the query to a known domain such as a portal for the online distribution of scientific journals (e.g. www.elsevier.com) or even to Google Books, to boost the reliability of the results. These would indeed confirm the inappropriateness of *onset site* (featuring, again, *onset, site* rather than *onset site*), whereas an alternative search for *site of onset* produces a significant number of matches, all to be considered relevant and reliable because of the co-occurrence with *cancer* and of the 'controlled' provenance of the results.

This example further highlights the importance of interpreting results. Not only are the number of matches or the provenance of results of key importance, but also their relevance to the required context of use, as well as their reliability, i.e. the degree of precision with which they correspond to the user's query. It is equally important that the user remembers that not all tasks can be performed by search engines equally: engines generally ignore punctuation and consider several variants as one (either by stemming or by ignoring special characters). This is what makes, for instance, a use of web search engines aimed at discriminating between noun+noun constructions and noun+'s+ noun constructions virtually impossible (Lüdeling 2007). It is also worth mentioning that from time to time, the web proves totally unreliable, even utilizing Boolean search protocols. As shown by Vèronis (2005: online), Boolean logic is often defeated by totally absurd results for search strings including more than one item.[3]

A final example reports the evaluation of translation candidates for the Italian phrase *paesaggi aspri*,[4] a phrase taken from a tourist brochure on Sardinia, as discussed in Gatto (2009: 64–6). In this case, the starting point is the dictionary entry for the Italian adjective *aspri* from a bilingual dictionary, which reveals at a glance the problems faced by the translator, even in an apparently trivial case such as this:

> **àspro**, a. 1 (di sapore) sour; tart, bitter [...]; 2 (di suono) harsh; rasping; grating. 3 (Figure duro) harsh; hard; bitter; 4 (ruvido) rough; rugged [...]; 5 (scosceso) steep; 6 (di clima) severe; raw; harsh. • (ling.) [...] (*Dizionario Zanichelli* 2009)

A first selection of translation candidates can be made on intuitive grounds, which makes it quite easy to exclude that the Italian word *aspri* could, in this case, be translated with *sour*, *tart* (relating to taste), or with *rasping* or *grating* (relating to sound). Among the translation equivalents offered by the bilingual dictionary, the only sensible translation candidates would seem to be those relating to points 3, 4 and 5 in the entry. More specifically, *harsh*, *hard*, *rough* and *rugged* seem to be the most plausible candidates. A fifth candidate was obtained by introspection: searching for equivalence of effect, the Italian *aspri* could in this case be replaced with another adjective (e.g. *forti*), thus obtaining *strong* as a new translation candidate for *aspri*. Choosing *landscape* and *scenery* as equivalents of paesaggi, an evaluation of translation candidates for *paesaggi aspri* should therefore consider at least ten competing phrases, resulting from all possible combinations of *hard*, *harsh*, *rough*, *rugged* and *strong* as modifiers with both *landscape* and *scenery*. While all formally possible, the ten combinations may, in fact, not all be actually used, and evidence for this can be drawn from the web.

Table 3.2 (below) shows results for the ten competing alternatives as reported in Gatto (2009: 65). In order to improve the chances of obtaining results that are both relevant and reliable, the query was progressively refined using both Boolean search and geographical restriction. Thus, the ten competing options were searched first through the whole web, and then by choosing only results from UK pages; finally, the words *travel* OR *tourism* were added to the query in order to enhance the possibility of retrieving pages related to the tourism sector. The table also includes comparative data from the BNC and COCA to evaluate the web results.

Table 3.2. Translation candidates for *paesaggi aspri* (Source: Gatto 2009)

	Web	Uk only	travel OR tourism	BNC	COCA
hard landscapes	2180	1440	116	0	0
hard scenery	485	43	2	0	0
harsh landscapes	826	441	193	1	1
harsh scenery	468	30	14	0	0
strong landscapes	507	173	18	1	0
strong scenery	138	6	1	0	0
rugged landscapes	66.300	10900	640	3	7
rugged scenery	51.700	12900	751	1	5
rough landscapes	1400	121	19	0	0
rough scenery	660	32	9	0	0

As Table 3.2 clearly shows, we have positive web results even for the six collocations which are not found in the BNC. By refining the query, however, there is a significant reduction of occurrences, which seems to bring web data closer to BNC and COCA values. The only exception are the collocations *rugged landscapes* and *rugged scenery*, which are actually used in English with increasing frequency, despite their relatively low frequency in such general reference corpora as BNC and COCA. This seems to provide evidence of the capability of the web to capture language use in – as the phrase goes – 'real time'. In terms of the authoritativeness and reliability of the results, a quick glance at some of the web pages ranked higher in the results page shows that there are many edited sources, such as pages from the travel section of popular magazines (e.g. travel.guardian.co.uk) or published travel guides. These results also suggest that evidence of language use obtained by progressively refining the query towards greater complexity can be considered qualitatively reliable and quantitatively significant, provided that one is aware of the relative weight of numbers. As the table makes clear, and the examples provided throughout this chapter have shown, given the large number of pages in English available on the web, any number of matches below 1,000 (a very conservative estimate), for bi-grams like the ones used in this experiment, should count as 0, if evidence of attested usage is not supported by other factors which enhance their reliability (e.g. domain or controlled provenance of the results).

5. Query complexity: Web search from a corpus perspective

As the examples provided have shown, mastering the advanced search options offered by most search engines will probably force the linguist to employ 'workarounds', but can really contribute to making the 'webscape' a less anarchic and less inhospitable space for linguistic research. There seems to be clear evidence that, in spite of its limitations, the web can be used as a reliable source of quantitative and qualitative evidence of usage, provided that a few cautionary procedures are adopted in submitting the query and interpreting the results.

At this stage it might finally be intriguing to explore in more general terms the interface between web search as a pervasive paradigm in our society, a 'universally understood method of navigating our information universe' (Battelle 2005: 4), and the corpus linguistic approach.

The very basic act of searching the web for a single word can indeed be regarded as the instantaneous creation of a temporary finite subcorpus out of the virtually endless and incommensurable web-corpus. Pushing to the extreme Stubbs' idea that each single word or phrase 'creates a mini-world or universe of discourse' (Stubbs 2001: 7), it can be argued that searching a word can be compared to the first step in corpus creation. It is as if, albeit only for a few moments, our virtually endless corpus, the web, complies with finite size, one of the fundamental criteria of corpus design. It will seem now obvious how, for instance, the search for the word *ecoturismo* can create a temporary, virtual subcorpus from the web, all made up of texts written in Italian, someway or other relating to ecotourism. By contrast, a search for the word *cancer* would not necessarily be as precise, and would in fact 'create' a corpus of pages in English dealing with both the disease and the zodiac sign. One should resort to the NOT operator (a minus sign '–' in Google query syntax) to refine the query by excluding references to the horoscope (e.g. cancer –horoscope) or to the disease (e.g. cancer –patients –disease –treatment). Thus, while a search for a single word can be compared to the creation of a sort of subcorpus, the search for two words (or more) can be read in terms of co-occurrence and contributes to the creation of a co-text for each search item, which could be loosely interpreted in terms of field/topic/

domain. Similarly, the search for phrases, combined with the use of wildcards, can represent the search for collocates or patterns. Finally, language, URL and domain restrictions, or search in specific subsections of the web, can indirectly be read in terms of constraints at the level of geographical variation, register and genre.

As highlighted in some of the examples provided in this chapter, it is only through a process of progressive query refinement towards greater complexity that linguists can contribute to improve the quality of the results. Defined as 'the loadstone of search, the runes we toss in our ongoing pursuit of the perfect results' (Batelle 2005: 27), the query is therefore the place where the common practice of web search and the linguist's theoretical approach to the web as a corpus most fruitfully interact. This places an obvious 'burden of care' on the linguist, but ensures that using the web as a corpus can be a rewarding experience.

Conclusion

The issues discussed and the examples reported in this chapter suggest that the web can be used as a 'quick-and-dirty' source of linguistic information, at least for specific tasks, provided that one is well-equipped to face the challenge posed by the web's 'anarchy' and by the limits of ordinary search engines. It is indeed of crucial importance, when accessing the web as a corpus via ordinary search engines, that cautionary procedures are adopted in submitting the query and, even more, in interpreting the results. The complex query thus becomes the place where the corpus linguistics approach and the common practice of web search can significantly interact. It could be argued that it is by virtue of such interaction, and not so much in its own right, that the web can claim the status of a corpus despite so many shortcomings.

Study questions and activities

1 In this exercise you will explore the regional versions of commercial search engines. Go to google.co.uk and submit a query (e.g. shock, bush, terrific scenery, etc.). Now submit the same query to a different regional version of Google (e.g. google.com.au for Australia, or google.ie for Ireland). Do the results differ in some respect? What are the differences and how can they be explained? Now compare results for other countries (France, Germany, Spain, etc.). What do your findings suggest?

2 In this exercise you will use the web to search for evidence of attested usage. Go to http://www.google.com/advanced_search (or to any other search engine's advanced search interface). Use the search engine to compare results for two collocations, to find out which one is apparently more frequent (e.g. 'high temperature' vs 'tall temperature'). What do quantitative data suggest? Which other parameters can be taken into account? How can the query be refined to be more effective in retrieving relevant/reliable results?

3 Now you can devise a complex query to explore the following patterns in academic discourse:
have a ... impact on
a ... increase in

4 Devise a complex query to complete the following idioms:
to eat like a ...
as fit as a ...

5 Using Google, try to explore the occurrences of the *beat about the bush* in the news, or in printed books, or in blogs. Which subsections of the web can you search? Comment on your results.

Suggestions for further reading

Broder, A. (2006), 'From query based Information Retrieval to context driven Information Supply'. *Workshop on The Future of Web Search, Barcelona*, 19-20 May 2006. Videolecture available at http://videolectures.net/fws06_broder_qbirc/ [accessed 1 June 2013].

Geluso, J. (2011), 'Phraseology and frequency of occurrence on the web: native speakers' perceptions of Google-informed second language writing'. *Computer Assisted Language Learning*, 26 (2), 144–57.

Levene, M. (2010), *An Introduction to Search Engines and Web Navigation*. New York: John Wiley & Sons.

Maniez, F. (2007), 'Using the Web and computer corpora as language resources for the translation of complex noun phrases in medical research articles'. *Panace@*, (9), 162–7.

Sha, G. (2010), 'Using Google as a super corpus to drive written language learning: a comparison with the British National Corpus', in *Computer Assisted Language Learning*, 23, 5.

Shei, C. C. (2008), Discovering the hidden treasure on the Internet: using Google to uncover the veil of phraseology. *Computer Assisted Language Learning*, 21(1), 67–85.

Notes

1 According to Broder (2002) an 'informational' need can be defined as the search for information assumed to be available on the web in a static form, so that no further interaction is predicted except reading. A 'navigational' need is represented by the attempt to a reach a particular site that the user has in mind – either because it has been already visited or because the user assumes that such a site exists. A 'transactional' need is the search for a site where further interaction (e.g. booking a hotel or buying a book or downloading a file) can take place.

2 When not otherwise stated, the examples of web search reported in this chapter were carried out in May 2012.

3 For further details on this topic see also the thread Problems with Google Counts in *Corpora List* (2005).

4 This is a typical NLP task using the web as corpus. One of the pioneer studies on the web as a corpus was in fact a study by Grefenstette, who first used the web to improve the performance of example-based Machine Translation (Grefenstette 1999). His case study was based on the evaluation of translation candidates for the French compound *groupe de travail* into English. Starting from five translations of the word *groupe* and three translations of the word *travail* into English, fifteen potential candidates for the translation of the compound were hypothesized. Only one, however, proved to have high corpus frequency (i.e. work group) both in a standard reference corpus and in the web, and this was therefore taken as the best translation candidate.

4

Beyond Ordinary Search Engines: Concordancing the Web

Introduction

This chapter introduces some tools devised to make the web more useful for linguistic research. More specifically, it is focused on those tools that have been developed to make it easier to formulate linguistically appropriate queries to search engines, and that manipulate the results so that the data retrieved are already tailored to linguistic analysis. Despite some limitations, these tools have proved effective in providing linguists with useful data, especially in a teaching context, and in the context of research on phrasal creativity, neologisms, and on rare or obsolete terms (Fletcher 2007; Renouf et al. 2007). Sections 1 and 2 provide background information on the tools and comment on their technical features. Section 3 reports on case studies based on the use of WebCorp and WebAsCorpus, showing how such tools can be used to obtain fresh, ready-made linguistic information otherwise requiring longer and more complex research activities. Sections 4 and 5 finally introduce WebCorp Linguist's Search Engine, a tool specially designed to bypass commercial search engines (Kehoe and Gee 2007), and comment on its use for the investigation of contemporary English.

1. Beyond ordinary search engines: Concordancing the web

As seen in the previous chapter, ordinary search engines provide immediate, but admittedly limited, access to the enormous potential of the web as a ready-made corpus. When accessed through commercial search engines, the web can at best be used as a *reservoir* of authentic language from which evidence of attested usage can be derived. This generally entails the formulation of complex queries and requires a good knowledge of the hidden agenda of commercial search engines, whose priority is by no means to facilitate the use of the web as a linguistic corpus. Even the most rewarding corpus-based linguistic investigation carried out using the web through ordinary search engines may end up forcing the linguist to adopt 'workarounds', leaving him/her miles away from more complete and sophisticated corpus linguistics explorations. It was precisely the awareness of these limitations that prompted in researchers an interest in the development of specific tools and methods aimed at making the web a more hospitable place for linguistic research. To this end, a number of projects have been developed, interpreting in different ways the umbrella phrase 'web as/for corpus', depending on the kind of access they provide to web data, the degree of dependence on existing commercial search engines, the stability and verifiability of results, and the flexibility and variety of the linguistically oriented processing options they offer. In this context, a useful distinction can be drawn between those tools which work as mere 'intermediaries' between the linguists' needs and the information retrieval services already available on the web (pre-/post-processing systems), and tools which try to dispense with ordinary search engines completely, autonomously crawling the web in order to build and index web-derived offline corpora (Lüdeling et al. 2007: 16).

In the attempt to bypass the limited access to the web as corpus provided by ordinary search tools, the first issue to be addressed concerns the possibility of manipulating the format of the results so as to make them immediately amenable to linguistic analysis. One of the earliest attempts in this direction was WebCONC (Hüning 2001, 2002), a linguist-oriented tool whose aim was to allow users to restrict a Google search by language, limiting results to one or more domains. WebCONC basically acted as an interface between users and search engines, allowing the display of search results in a concordance-like format. A similar, though more sophisticated, approach was taken by the WebCorp Project (Kehoe and Renouf 2002) and WebAsCorpus (Fletcher 2007), which are more complex tools that simultaneously treat the web both as a corpus in its own right, and as a temporary offline corpus obtained by operating in a cache mode, i.e. by temporarily storing a copy of the results in a server.

2. WebCorp *Live*

One of the most representative examples in the category of web concordancers is WebCorp, also known as WebCorp *Live*, a suite of tools which runs on top of ordinary search engines and provides contextualized examples of language use from the web in a form already tailored to linguistic analysis. The tool was developed in the context of the WebCorp Project (www.webcorp.org.uk), established in the late 90s 'to test the hypothesis that the web could be used as a large "corpus" of text for linguistic study' (Morley 2006: 283).

Searching a word or phrase using WebCorp is not, in principle, different from searching the web through an ordinary search engine, and the system's user interface is indeed very similar to the interfaces provided by standard web search tools.

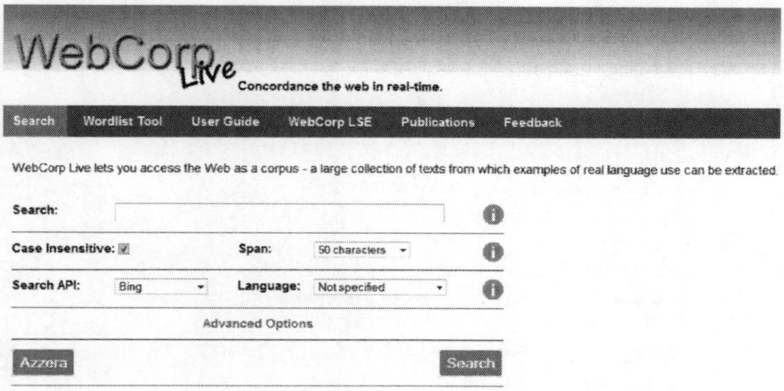

Figure 4.1. *WebCorp* Live *user interface*

The format of the result page is, however, strikingly different. Results are presented to the user in the typical Key-Word-in-Context (KWiC) format familiar to linguists, with the chosen word aligned and highlighted as 'node word' within a co-text of between 10 characters and 10 words, to the left and to the right. Neither the content of the web nor the search engine functions are modified, but only the output format, so that the result page of an ordinary search engine like Google or Bing is transformed into a concordance table that can be immediately used to explore web data from a corpus linguistics perspective (see Fig. 4.2).

```
825:      and a design and art tradition, practised by landscape designers, combining nature and culture. In
826:      nature and culture. In contemporary practice landscape design bridges between landscape architecture
827:         practice landscape design bridges between landscape architecture and garden design.[citation needed]
828:          4 Gardening 5 See also [edit] Design scope Landscape design focuses on both the integrated master
829:      design focuses on both the integrated master landscape planning of a property and the specific garden
830:   of a property and the specific garden design of landscape elements and plants within it. The practical,
831:     environmental sustainability components merit Landscape design inclusion. It is often divided into
832:        into hardscape design and softscape design. Landscape designers often collaborate with related
833:            soils and civil engineering, surveying, landscape contracting, botany, and artisan specialties.
834:         Design project focus can tend towards: in landscape design - artistic composition and artisanship,
835:    from concepts through construction; whereas in landscape architecture - focus of urban planning, city and
836:            and experience of the professional.Both landscape designers and landscape architects practice
837:  of the professional.Both landscape designers and landscape architects practice landscape design.[citation
838:       designers and landscape architects practice landscape design.[citation needed] [edit] Design approach
839:   over time. The up and coming practice of online landscape design allows professional landscapers to
840: s.[citation needed] [edit] Training Historically, landscape designers trained by apprenticing—such as André
841:      in Europe and the Americas went by the name 'Landscape Gardener.' In the 1890s the distinct classificati
842:       In the 1890s the distinct classification of landscape architect was created, with educational and
```

Figure 4.2. *A sample from WebCorp* Live *concordances for* landscape

Unlike ordinary search engines, and simpler web concordancers, WebCorp allows further processing of the search results and the user can set parameters for the concordance span, sort results according to the desired criteria, and compute collocates for the search term. Such functionalities result from a simple architecture that can be represented as in Figure 4.3 below.

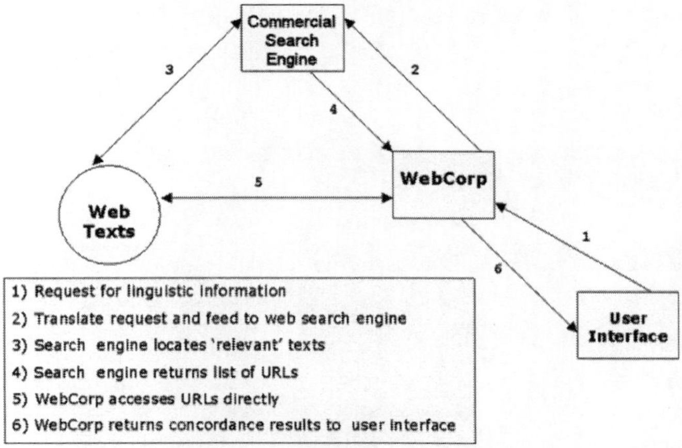

Figure 4.3. *Diagram of the WebCorp architecture (Source: Renouf et al. 2007)*

As the graph clearly shows, the starting point is the WebCorp user interface, which receives the request for linguistic information. The linguist's query is then converted by the system into a format acceptable to the selected search engine, which finds the term through its index and provides a URL for the relevant text. The system temporarily downloads the text, extracts the search term and the appropriate linguistic context, collates it, and presents it to the user in the desired format (Renouf 2003; Renouf et al. 2005).

WebCorp can thus be seen as doing no more than adding 'a layer of refinement to standard web search' (Kehoe and Renouf 2002: online), by framing some of the advanced options of commercial search engines into a new, linguist-friendly environment, pre-processing the user's query before it is submitted to the search engine and then post-processing the results. The advantage of WebCorp lies, therefore, in the possibility it offers for a deeper linguistically oriented exploitation of ordinary web search, which becomes particularly evident when turning to the system's Advanced Search Option interface.

Some of the system's options clearly match, directly or indirectly, the corresponding options offered by ordinary search engines (e.g. domain restriction), whereas other options point to specific functionalities that translate the linguist's query into a complex query submitted to one of the search engines

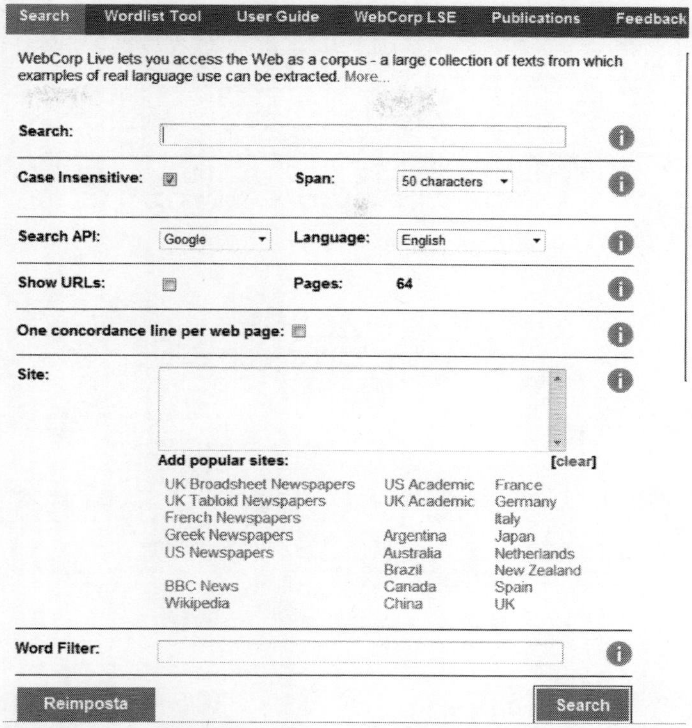

Figure 4.4. *WebCorp* Live *Advanced Search Option Interface*

supported by the tool. Thus, word filters correspond to Boolean search, in that they allow the user to indicate words that should, or should not, appear in the same page as the searched item, whereas search for patterns are transformed by the system into complex queries including wildcards. Then, post-processing functionalities of specific interest to linguists (e.g. KWiC format, computation of collocates, exclusion of stopwords, case sensitiveness) transform the search results into data similar to those obtained through a concordancer from conventional off-line corpora.

It is certainly beyond the scope of the present work to go into further technical details or to survey all the options offered by WebCorp – information that can be easily obtained from the tool's guide and in the growing body of research articles published in the past few years.[1] It is perhaps useful, though, to consider some examples that clearly indicate how WebCorp differs from an ordinary search engine. A WebCorp search makes it possible, for instance, to specify whether the search term should be capitalized or not, thus giving the possibility to discriminate between *Bush*, like the former US President, and *bush*, as in Figures 4.5 and 4.6 overleaf.

```
82: Distinguished Flying Cross for bravery in action. Bush next turned his energies toward completing his
83:  and a member of Phi Beta Kappa. After graduation Bush embarked on a career in the oil industry of West
84:          of West Texas. Like his father, Prescott Bush, who was elected a Senator from Connecticut in
85:       of the Central Intelligence Agency. In 1980 Bush campaigned for the Republican nomination for
86:            mate by Ronald Reagan. As Vice President, Bush had responsibility in several domestic areas,
87:  and visited scores of foreign countries. In 1988 Bush won the Republican nomination for President and,
88:          Michael Dukakis in the general election. Bush faced a dramatically changing world, as the Cold
89:   and reformist President Mikhail Gorbachev, whom Bush had supported, resigned. While Bush hailed the
90:          whom Bush had supported, resigned. While Bush hailed the march of democracy, he insisted on
91:       In other areas of foreign policy, President Bush sent American troops into Panama to overthrow
92:    move into Saudi Arabia. Vowing to free Kuwait, Bush rallied the United Nations, the U. S. people,
93:        from this military and diplomatic triumph, Bush was unable to withstand discontent at home from
94: Association. For more information about President Bush, please visit The George Bush Library and Museum
95:     about President Bush, please visit The George Bush Library and Museum George Bush Presidential
96:   visit The George Bush Library and Museum George Bush Presidential Library Foundation Learn more about
97:  Library Foundation Learn more about George H. W. Bush 's spouse, Barbara Pierce Bush. Did you know?
```

Figure 4.5. *WebCorp* Live *concordance lines for* Bush

```
38: in Australia.[1] In reference to the landscape, "bush" refers to any sparsely inhabited region
39:   inhabited region regardless of vegetation. The bush in this sense was something that was uniquely
40:   Port Hedland (Pop. 14,000) referred to as "The bush" within the media.[2] The bush was revered as a
41:         to as "The bush" within the media.[2] The bush was revered as a source of national ideals by
42:     Lawson and Banjo Paterson. Romanticising the bush in this way was a big step forward for Australian
43:   legacy is a folklore rich in the spirit of the bush. The term bush is also affixed to any number of
44:           rich in the spirit of the bush. The term bush is also affixed to any number of other entities
45:   and Deforestation in New Zealand New Zealand's bush is variable in appearance. Pictured here is the
46:   exotic forests. In contrast to the Australian "bush" it would be impossible to ride a horse through
47:   impossible to ride a horse through New Zealand bush, and foot travel is slow and arduous, except on
48:       cut for purpose. The New Zealand usage of 'bush' probably comes from the word 'bosch', used by
49:        In the North Island, the largest areas of bush cover the main ranges stretching north-northeast
50:           "bushwack[ing]", or "bush-whack[ing]"). bush shirt - a woollen shirt or Swanndri, often worn
51: shirt or Swanndri, often worn by forest workers. bush lawyer - the name of a number of native climbing
52:       or a layman who expounds on legal matters. bush walk - short day walks (hikes) in the bush going
53:       bush walk - short day walks (hikes) in the bush going bush - to live in the bush for an extended
54: walk - short day walks (hikes) in the bush going bush - to live in the bush for an extended period of
55:  (hikes) in the bush going bush - to live in the bush for an extended period of time, which may
56:     [edit] Related terms Icons of the Australian bush: bracken, corrugated iron, banksia, felt hat,
57:           and elastic-side boots. The term "to go bush" has several similar meanings all connected with
58:  all connected with the supposed wildness of the bush. It can mean to revert to a feral nature (or to
```

Figure 4.6. *WebCorp* Live *concordance lines for* bush

The user can also indicate filter words, i.e. words which should be included in the search string, in order to provide a context for the searched item or as a disambiguation method. Thus Renouf et al. (2007: 54) show how a search for *sole* using *fish* as a filter could be useful to discriminate *sole* as a noun from *sole* as an adjective. This is not new in itself, drawing as it does on the principles of Boolean search already discussed in the context of ordinary search engines; however, when combined with the specific affordances of WebCorp as a linguistically oriented tool the results are more rewarding. In Figures 4.7 and 4.8 one can see, for instance, how the collocates computed by the system for the word *volatility* change significantly by effect of the use of *market* and *chemistry* as word filters, and by restriction to a specific domain or genre.

The tool thus really contributes to remove some of the typical obstacles that researchers have to face when using ordinary search engines for linguistic purposes, and provides the user with key features for linguistic investigation that can be summed up as follows:

- the possibility of preselecting a site domain as an indirect way to specify language variety;
- a choice of newspaper site groups (UK broadsheet, UK tabloid, French news, US news, etc.), to allow specification of register;
- a selection of data-subset according to last date of modification;

Collocates

Word	L4	L3	L2	L1	R1	R2	R3	R4	Total
compounds	0	0	0	0	0	0	15	0	15
lipophilicity	0	0	12	0	0	0	0	0	12
organic	0	0	0	0	0	12	0	0	12
stability	0	1	0	0	0	4	4	0	9
low	1	0	0	7	0	0	0	0	8
thermal	0	0	0	0	4	4	0	0	8
AACVD	4	0	0	4	0	0	0	0	8
restrictions	0	0	4	0	0	0	4	0	8
determination	6	0	0	0	0	0	0	0	6
ionic	0	0	0	0	0	3	1	0	4
advantages	0	4	0	0	0	0	0	0	4
stock	0	0	1	0	0	2	1	0	4
measurements	0	3	0	0	1	0	0	0	4
aroma	1	0	0	0	0	3	0	0	4
2010	1	0	0	0	0	0	1	1	3
liquids	0	0	0	0	0	0	3	0	3
Chemistry's	0	3	0	0	0	0	0	0	3
metal	0	2	0	0	0	0	1	0	3
organics	0	0	0	0	3	0	0	0	3
love	0	0	3	0	0	0	0	0	3

Figure 4.7. *WebCorp* Live *collocates for* volatility *(word filter:* chemistry*) domain: ac.uk*

- restriction of the number of instances of an item to one per site, to avoid domination and skewing of results by one author or source;
- sorting left and right co-text;
- use of word filters, to improve precision in search results.

Despite such an extensive range of functions, WebCorp is nonetheless also characterized by inescapable limitations. While ordinary search engines are able to process millions of search string matches, WebCorp can only treat results from a limited number of pages. This means that the proportion of potentially relevant web texts that is actually searched can be too low, and that recall can accordingly be rather poor (Renouf et al. 2007: 57). Moreover, WebCorp also suffers from some of the typical limitations of the search engines from which it depends, such as ranking according to algorithms which the user cannot control; presence of duplicates in results; unreliable word count statistics; limited and/or inconsistent support for wildcard search. Furthermore, experiments carried out with WebCorp are virtually non-reproducible, since the

Collocates

Word	L4	L3	L2	L1	R1	R2	R3	R4	Total
market	0	0	2	73	0	2	3	9	89
price	0	2	1	33	0	0	0	0	36
financial	1	1	9	5	0	7	5	3	31
markets	3	2	1	1	0	1	8	8	24
stock	0	0	10	1	0	2	7	2	22
economic	5	1	0	6	0	1	4	0	17
high	1	5	0	4	2	1	2	2	17
index	1	2	0	0	10	0	0	2	15
excessive	0	4	6	3	0	0	0	0	13
investors	0	2	0	0	0	5	4	1	12
commodity	0	0	10	0	0	0	2	0	12
recent	2	7	1	1	0	1	0	0	12
short-term	0	0	2	8	0	0	0	0	10
said	1	1	2	0	2	2	1	1	10
CBOE	2	2	0	3	0	0	1	2	10
money	2	3	1	0	0	2	1	1	10
extreme	0	2	2	5	0	0	0	0	9
fund	3	0	0	0	0	0	4	2	9
Index	0	0	0	0	7	0	1	1	9
oil	0	0	6	0	0	0	3	0	9

Figure 4.8. *WebCorp* Live *collocates for* volatility *(word filter:* market*) domain: UK broadsheets*

tools output, like the results of ordinary search engines, may vary, even within the same day. On the contrary, as already observed in Chapter 2, the reproducibility of an 'experiment' and the reusability of the data are fundamental aspects of corpus linguistics. The impossibility of reproducing exactly the same search on the same data set is a really serious problem which may impair the scientific validity of results obtained using WebCorp beyond their immediate usefulness for specific tasks or purposes. It should be noted, in any case, that the system's developers have tried to address this problem by storing a copy of the results of each search for seven days.

Notwithstanding its intrinsic limitations, the WebCorp system has been constantly improving and has already proven successful in processing web data for linguistic analysis, especially in a teaching context, where its user-friendliness and ease of access have made it a valuable resource from the start (Kübler 2004). Moreover, specific case studies concerning neologisms and coinages, rare or possibly obsolete terms and constructions, as well as phrasal variability and creativity, have also shown that in many cases the web can be a unique source of linguistic information which a tool like WebCorp can exploit to the full (Renouf et al. 2005, 2007).

By way of example, an analysis of linguistic information obtained through classroom activities is reported below to demonstrate how using the web as a ready-made corpus through WebCorp can immediately improve students' language awareness, and also provide the basis for further explorations.

3. Concordancing the web in the foreign language classroom

There is probably no need to emphasize the interest in corpus linguistics approaches to language teaching (Tognini Bonelli 2001; Sinclair 2004). Drawing on notions such as 'data-driven learning' and 'discovery learning' (Johns 2002; Bernardini 2002), it can be argued that using the web as a ready-made corpus through a simple tool like WebCorp can result in an extremely rewarding learning experience that the students can easily reproduce outside the classroom context. The following pages report on classroom investigations into collocation, neology and phrasal creativity. All examples are from activities carried out with students of English as a Foreign Language, in programmes also including Intercultural Communication and Tourism Studies. The activities had the double aim of enhancing the students' awareness of specific language phenomena (collocation, neologisms, phrasal creativity) and at the same time familiarizing them with the use of the web as a linguistic resource.

3.1 Exploring collocation: The case of *scenery*

To help the students appreciate the special kind of linguistic evidence offered by WebCorp, an activity centred on the collocational profile of a quite common word like *scenery* was proposed. The warm-up phase of this activity consisted in eliciting common collocates for *scenery* through intuition, and commenting on established collocates retrieved from ordinary dictionaries. Students were then introduced to WebCorp and instructed on how to perform a search for the word *scenery* in pages written in English. The words *travel*, *tourism* and *holiday* were added as filters, to elicit results relevant to tourism discourse, and the search was limited to .uk sites to enhance their reliability. The results page includes 200 matches (a limit to the number of occurrences to be processed is imposed by the system to enhance the tool's speed), a sample of which is reported in Figure 4.9 overleaf.

As the sample shows, a number of typical collocates can be identified at a glance (e.g. *breathtaking, dramatic, fantastic, inspiring*). Furthermore,

Left context	Node	Right context
to relax and enjoy taking in the beautiful	scenery	that North America offers whilst experiencing
Scarborough offers some of the most beautiful	scenery	on the Yorkshire Coast. Complete with 2 sandy
whose principal appeal is their beautiful	scenery:	generally former fishing villages which have
overlooked by most visitors. Where is the best	scenery?	One of the most dramatic spots on Corfu's
on Thursday 20 October 2011 The breathaking	scenery	of the Italian Dolomites The Dolomites are
quiet beach coves and some breathtaking	scenery	if you choose a holiday to Zante. The north,
scenic open roads will lead you to breathtaking	scenery,	quaint country towns, hip and happening Toronto
Europe's rich cultural heritage and breathtaking	scenery.	Watch the varied landscapes from the comfort of
As well as offering superb and breathtaking	scenery	whilst driving from one part of Morocco to
Montana offers limitless riding and breathtaking	scenery	CLICK HERE for Montana and USA Horse Riding
horsemanship skills - combined with breathtaking	scenery	and the opportunity to experience cattle drives,
Africa, visitors are assured of breathtaking	scenery,	wildlife and architecture, that captures the
live amidst dramatic mountain and cliff	scenery,	politically tied to Denmark but with the kind
the breathtakingly beautiful beaches, coastal	scenery,	mangroves, savannahs and lush green rainforests
is the best way to enjoy the wonderful coastal	scenery,	wildlife and heritage of this spectacular
o.uk/norfolk For cream teas, Jane Austen, coastal	scenery,	sandy beaches visit Bath. Tourist attractions
mountain pony. There is splendid countryside	scenery	to be enjoyed in the Lampeter area - and
state, offers an intoxicating mix of culture,	scenery	and wildlife, says Martin Dixon. Image 1 of 2
hotel in Aswan, through the spectacular desert	scenery	to the banks of Lake Nasser. During a guided
Europe and Asia, Turkey has enormously diverse	scenery,	with rolling central plains, soaring mountains,
access to some of the region's most dramatic	scenery.	This includes a 287-ft waterfall at Varone, the
into the fjord create some of the most dramatic	scenery	in the world. It is the gateway to Hardangervidda
Bijoux luxury villa, beach and pool, dramatic	scenery	Overview Photos Location Availability Rates
great outdoors, art and folk festivals, dramatic	scenery,	a unique cultural experience or a bit of
off, many more are attracted to the dramatic	scenery,	hot mud baths, and the opportunity to hike up
in La Gomera. Get out and see the fantastic	scenery	the island has to offer either on two wheels or
necessary works done, or just the fantastic	scenery	to name but a few. Scenery The countryside has
availability deals Outdoors With its fantastic	scenery	and wildlife, Scotland has much to offer outdoor
holiday homes in some of Europe's finest	scenery.	At a cost to suit most people. Why book with
networks of transport, Some of Europe finest	scenery,	a fantastic variation in Climate, Hot summers
Aberdeen Forum: short trips from aberdeen (food,	scenery)	Hotels travellers are raving about... Premier
an absolutely brilliant time. The weather, food,	scenery	were magnificent, and the people were so
Tromso Forums Tromso Forum: Best location for	scenery/	aurora photos at ersfjorden Hotels travellers
South Wales has a lot to offer from great	scenery,	good pubs and restaurants, and some excellent
categories. Whether you're interested in history,	scenery,	crafts, shopping, beaches or touring, you'll
Tropea is a seaside resort with impressive	scenery	in the region of Calabria, in the south of
surrounded by beautiful beaches and inspiring	scenery.	It is a destination of surprises. The range of
the coast road, and offers some interesting	scenery	along the way, not least a stunning view across
of the island, James Stewart discovers that its	scenery	is even more impressive in real life The Lonely

Figure 4.9. *Webcorp's output for* scenery *(sample)*

the total number of matches (200) provides a basis of manageable size for further considerations on the linguistic 'behaviour' of the word *scenery*. The concordance table is only a mouse-click away from the original webpage, since each node word is a living hypertextual link to the page itself, which makes it very easy for students to check the original webpage not only for relevance and reliability, but also to appreciate language use in a real-life context.

Beyond mere concordancing, an important property of WebCorp is the possibility of producing a collocational profile for the node word, which is reported immediately after the concordance table. While this utility is easily 'distracted' by redundant web pages, with duplicates and near-duplicates often altering the computation of collocates, the results still remain worth some consideration. In the case of *scenery*, it seemed crystal-clear to students that in texts including the words *travel*, or *tourism*, or *holiday* from .uk sites, the word *scenery* is often accompanied by adjectives such as *beautiful* (22 occurrences), *stunning* (13), *spectacular* (10), *breathtaking* (7), *dramatic* (7), *amazing* (5) and *fantastic* (5), as the sample reporting the top 20 collocates suggests.

These results provided the students with a wide a range of adjectives commonly used in the description of *scenery*, which they could compare with data gained from introspection and with the data from a dictionary of collocations (e.g. *Oxford Collocations Dictionary*). A comparison between the collocates retrieved for *scenery* from more controlled sources like the BNC (see Chapter 1) was in some respects surprising. Given the obvious and notorious limitations of the web as a source of linguistic information, one is really impressed by the similarity of these results, which seem indeed to validate the method used.

All in all, this simple classroom experience apparently suggests that however chaotic and anarchic, the web can provide – at least in specific

Collocates

Word	L4	L3	L2	L1	R1	R2	R3	R4	Total
beautiful	1	3	2	15	0	1	0	0	22
stunning	0	0	0	12	1	0	0	0	13
spectacular	0	0	2	8	0	0	0	0	10
beaches	1	1	3	0	0	2	2	1	10
mountain	0	1	0	8	0	0	0	0	9
wildlife	0	1	2	0	2	3	1	0	9
breathtaking	0	0	0	7	0	0	0	0	7
dramatic	1	1	0	5	0	0	0	0	7
history	2	1	0	1	1	0	0	1	6
holiday	2	1	1	0	0	0	0	2	6
Reviewed	0	0	0	0	3	0	3	0	6
Syvota	0	0	0	0	2	0	2	2	6
amazing	0	0	2	1	1	1	0	0	5
landscapes	0	0	1	0	2	1	0	1	5
see	0	4	1	0	0	0	0	0	5
fantastic	0	0	1	3	0	1	0	0	5
Overview	0	0	0	0	4	0	0	0	4
enjoy	1	2	0	0	0	0	0	1	4
Home	0	0	0	1	0	2	0	1	4
Availability	0	0	0	0	0	0	0	4	4

Figure 4.10. *Collocates for* scenery *from WebCorp (sample)*

situations – linguistic evidence which is comparable to evidence obtained from a conventional reference corpus. These findings enhance confidence in the possibility of moving further into an exploration of collocation, also from a cross-linguistic perspective, since WebCorp can produce concordance lines for words and phrases in any language, thus making it really easy to exploit the implicit nature of the web as a virtual multilingual corpus. An example is reported in Gatto (2009: 93–6), where concordance lines and collocational profiles for such phrases as *paesaggi suggestivi* and *dramatic landscapes* retrieved with WebCorp are compared to explore similarities and differences in their collocational profile.

3.2 Investigating neologisms and phrasal creativity

As seen in the examples reported above, WebCorp represents a step forward in the attempt to exploit the web's potential for linguistic purposes, insofar as it is capable of transforming web data into an object amenable to analysis informed by the corpus linguistic approach. In many cases the results provided are not only immediately useful but also, as has been argued, 'thought-provoking' (Bergh 2005: 38). This is, for instance, the case for neologisms, phrasal creativity and culture-bound words.

One example is the evidence provided by the concordance lines and collocational profile produced for *flexicurity*, a word which appeared in the first decade of the new millennium, and which is often found in newspapers articles and European Union documents. This example was used not only to introduce the meaning of this portmanteau word, unknown to most students, but also as a way to familiarize them with aspects of qualitative analysis for concordance lines, beyond mere collocation. Concordance lines retrieved 'on the spot' with WebCorp only from UK newspapers, UK tabloids, US newspapers and BBC News did not only clarify at a glance the meaning of *flexicurity*, but also indicated the attitudes expressed by the users of the term.

Figure 4.11. *Concordance lines for* flexicurity *(sample)*

As the concordance tables in Figure 4.11 above suggest, *flexicurity* is a word used with a certain degree of caution (almost always in inverted commas). It collocates with such words as *flexibility* (5), *flexible/security* (8); with *social* (8), often in phrases like 'social protection', 'social policy', 'social security', etc. It has a semantic preference for such words as *job* (5)/ *labour* (5), *employment* (5)/*unemployment* (7), and *market*. It often occurs with evaluative adjectives revealing ideological concerns: it is a 'magical mix', but it is also said to be 'controversial', 'a horror', 'a horrible word'. With no previous knowledge of this word the students easily understood its meaning in all its nuances, both in terms of semantic content and in terms of discourse.

Well beyond these simple classroom experiments, a growing body of research articles and book chapters illustrates the possibility of using WebCorp to address more complex research questions, involving grammatical questions (e.g. the use of get/be passives; the distribution of alternative forms like different from/to/than), the analysis of neologisms, and even diachronic investigations that take advantage of the possibility to limit the search to a specified date range or to sort the concordance lines obtained according to date. In this respect, too, the tool provides opportunities for classroom activities.

Profiting from the possibility of limiting the search to a given time span, and focusing on UK newspapers and tabloids, it was possible, for instance, to carry out a classroom experiment aimed at tracking the slow penetration of the word *staycation* in the vocabulary of English holiday habits, starting from the single occurrence retrieved for 2006 and 2007, to the 5 occurrences of 2008 and the 58 occurrences of 2009, to the over 120 occurrences retrieved for 2010, when the word seemed to have definitely entered the English lexicon, to its decline in 2011 when the 60 occurrences of the word in British newspapers apparently signal that the word had partly lost its topicality. On the basis of these data it could be argued that the word had reached a stage of 'stagnation', using the terminology put forward by Renouf to describe a word's life-cycle (Renouf 2007: 71; Renouf 2013).

Finally, WebCorp's performance is incredible when exploring phrasal creativity. As reported in Renouf (2007: 61–89), WebCorp can make it extremely easy to see how a phrase can be changed and transformed by multiple users – a phenomenon which can also be further investigated in terms of a word's life-cycle. One of Renouf's examples concerns variation within the phrase *weapons of mass destruction*, a phrase which became popular in the context of the first Gulf War in the late 80s/early 90s, but actually 'caught the media imagination around 2003' (Renouf 2007: 71). Investigating this pattern could not only show the rise and fall in popularity of the phrase, but also chart the full range of creative alternatives elicited by the patterns *weapons of mass ** and *weapons of * destruction*, which include such phrases as *weapons of mass distraction* or *weapons of class destruction*, as shown in Figure 4.12.

Finally, WebCorp can offer invaluable insights into usage of typical jargon of computer-mediated communication – such as the shortened form *dunno* (meaning 'I don't know'), or acronyms like IMHO (in my humble opinion), and C U (which stands for 'see you'). Using WebCorp, one can take advantage of the possibility of producing concordances in real time for non-standard forms which are thriving in the web. A case in point is the concordance lines produced for the mixed form *l8r* ('later') as used in blogs, which could be quite easily analyzed using WebCorp, by limiting the search to the domain .blogger.com (see Figure 4.13).

As these concordance lines produced in a few seconds suggest, the form is often used in the pattern *I'll + verb + more + l8r* and provides evidence of non-standard spelling in the co-text, as in *ill* for *I'll*, *rite* for *write*, or *C ya'll l8r* for *See you all later*.

Variants of *weapons of mass destruction*, Feb. 20, 2003

weapons of mass * (no destruction)	**weapons of * destruction (no mass)**
weapons of mass distraction	weapons of modest destruction
weapons of mass obstruction	weapons of scant destruction
weapons of mass disruption	weapons of ass destruction
weapons of mass deception	weapons of indiscriminate destruction
weapons of mass discomfort	weapons of ministerial destruction
weapons of mass terror	weapons of market destruction
weapons of mass casualties	weapons of most destruction
weapons of mass entertainment	
	weapons of * (no mass, no destruction)
	weapons of bluff, brinkmanship & bloody-mindedness
	weapons of bumps and bruises
	weapons of nasty scratches

Creativity for *weapons of mass destruction*, Feb. 21, 2003

weapons of mass * (no destruction)	**weapons of * destruction (no mass)**
weapons of mass banalization	weapons of catastrophic destruction
weapons of mass construction	weapons of class destruction
weapons of mass consumption	weapons of complete destruction
weapons of mass deconstruction	weapons of further destruction
weapons of mass distortion	weapons of global destruction
weapons of mass distractions	weapons of godlike destruction
weapons of mass effect (WME)	weapons of great destruction
weapons of mass hysteria	weapons of less destruction
weapons of mass instruction	weapons of local destruction
weapons of mass irritation	weapons of mad destruction
weapons of mass media (WMM)	weapons of massive destruction
weapons of mass partying	weapons of media destruction
weapons of mass protection	weapons of mischievous destruction
weapons of mass repression	weapons of murderous destruction
	weapons of nuclear destruction

Figure 4.12. *Variation and creativity for* weapons of mass destruction *(Source: Renouf 2007)*

```
 good people. Still more 'About me L8r then, hope you will enjoy my blogs.
ive text message like "GR8 meet me L8R" and need help decoding what it mea
kes, if yal wanna know more ask me l8r! Interests softball, guitar, singin
hat B4 history may come back to me L8R in this life (and I'm sure I'll add
hts all i can say... ill rite more l8r... :] Interests i love to dance lik
ht (spelling?) yeah i'll talk more l8r Interests me, horses, my fam, my fr
elie, Real Women Have Curves, more L8r Favourite Music hip hop not played
ss Street by Kenji Jasper, ...more L8R.. Help Centre | Terms of Service |
you wil hear more about angels mum l8r and princess lives with her dad bec
may thnk i'm n introvert.. its nli l8r dat u'l notice d flamboyance in me.
ger. (yea yea, I'll redo this part l8r) Interests Music, Graphic Design, M
in dis nd dat lyke tried philately(l8r gave it 2 ma sis) den a numismatic(
ave comments and i'll do the same. l8r xD Interests Myspace, Blogging, Wat
elf so thats it.. i"ll revise this l8r so I wont seem so weird lol Intere
teen, Ruby's Slippers, ttyl, ttfn, l8r l8r, and Peace Love & Baby Ducks. W
y good looking how u doing ill c u L8R Contact me gillian lauren kc ricky
       The green power ranger (who l8r becomes white) On Blogger since May
 dnt all parents oh well ill write l8r by all who read this Interests Play
 will talk to neone otherwise c ya l8r. Bye GO TROJANS!!! Interests My int
ght I'd put that in there. C ya'll l8r - Ribbit =D Help Centre | Terms of
```

Figure 4.13. *Concordance lines for* l8r *(Domain: blogger.com)*

4. Beyond web concordancing tools: The web as/for corpus

Besides WebCorp, another well-known web concordancing tool is WebAsCorpus, a service accessed through webascorpus.org, a website fully dedicated to the web as corpus offering information, tools and suggestions for web-as-corpus lovers. The service ceased functioning on 1 August 2012 when the Bing API – an Application Programming Interface that enables developers to embed web search into their own tools – was retired. This suggests how tools that 'piggy-back' on search engines, like web concordancers, may not only suffer from typical shortcomings related to the much-discussed limitations of the web as a source of data and of search engines themselves as retrieval tools for linguistic purposes, but – more importantly – leave developers at the mercy of the (commercial) interests of search companies which might decide to drop altogether, or limit access to, a service at any time. In the following pages some examples of research carried out using this concordancer when it was still available (June 2012) will be discussed, not only because of the role that this tool has 'historically' played in the development of the very idea of transforming the web into a ready-made corpus but also because of the special significance of the approach taken which complements mere concordancing with aspects of the 'web for corpus' approach.

More specifically, it might be useful to address the peculiarity of this web concordancer, which lies in its double potential as a web-*as*-corpus and a web-*for*-corpus tool. As a matter of fact, WebAsCorpus simultaneously treats the web as a corpus in its own right, producing results displayed in a typical KWiC format, and as an immediate source of corpora to be further processed for offline linguistic analysis.

By way of example, we can discuss how concordance lines produced for *sustainable tourism* using Fletcher's web concordancer, as shown in the screenshot overleaf (Figure 4.14), offer much more than might appear at first glance. The tool's output is not simply a full page of concordance lines where each string is still the gateway to the original webpage (as was also the case with WebCorp), but it also provides access to a 'real' corpus automatically compiled and available for download in both HTML and .txt format in a matter of seconds. The data obtained can therefore be inspected separately using offline tools, thus overcoming the problem of non-reproducibility raised for most web-as-corpus methodologies. See the tool's output for *sustainable tourism* in Figure 4.14.

These concordance lines are not only a temporary snapshot from the web, as was the case with WebCorp, but the 'visible' part of a corpus already

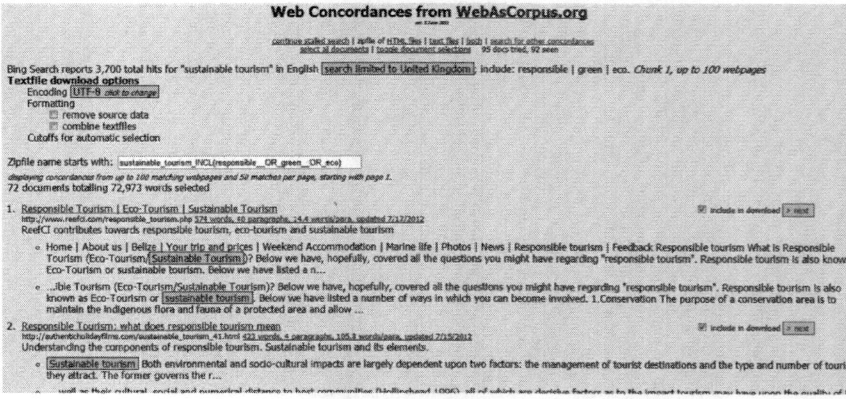

Figure 4.14. *Concordance lines for* sustainable tourism

available for download and for further analysis using typical corpus linguistics investigations (word lists, collocations, etc.) to be carried out – again and again – offline. In this case, the corpus was downloaded and analysed using a free concordancer (AntConc). Exploring the word list obtained from this corpus, attention was focused on the word *local*, in 20th position, for which concordance lines were produced (see Figure 4.15).

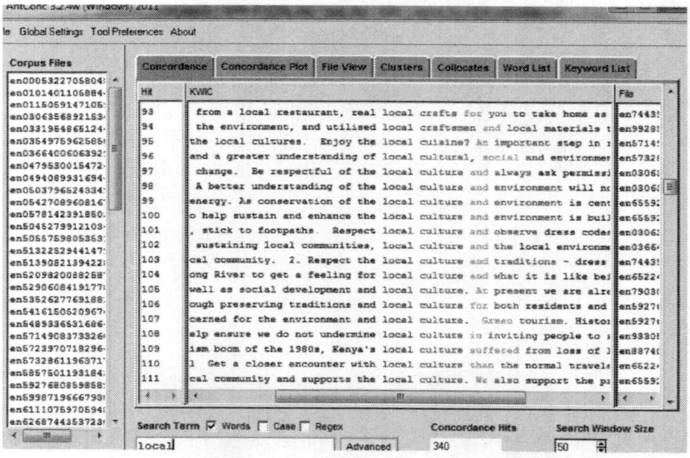

Figure 4.15. *Concordance lines for* local *from the Sustainable Tourism corpus*

The concordance lines appear consistent and well-formed, and provide evidence of patterns of usage for the word *local* in the context of sustainable tourism. But what is really most significant for anyone who has toiled to compile a corpus manually is that so much can be done in a matter of seconds, with 'clean' and reusable results. Despite inescapable limits therefore, web concordancers still represent a significant step in the animated dialogue between the web and the corpus linguistics community which the hybrid umbrella term 'web as/for corpus' so tellingly embodies.

5. Towards a linguist's search engine: The case of WebCorp*LSE*

Systems that rely entirely on commercial search engines, like those described in the previous pages, suffer from serious limitations deriving both from search engines as imperfect corpus query tools and from the nature of the web corpus itself. Though greatly improving on ordinary web search, thanks to the KWiC format and to the possibility of performing some post-processing of the results, such as sorting and computation of collocates, a web concordancer cannot support search for specific parts-of-speech or for specific grammar patterns – unless the corpus temporarily created by the tool is downloaded and compiled for offline analysis. In this case, however, the processing time would be prohibitively long and results could not be realistically offered in real time. Furthermore, the quantitative information obtained could hardly be considered reliable, since it would come in any case from a search with very low recall, as already stressed, and performed on a corpus whose exact size is not known.

This is why the alternative approach of using the web 'for' corpus, rather than directly 'as' a corpus, i.e. the use of online texts to build offline corpora, caught the attention of many developers very soon. The disappointment with search engines as gatekeepers of the 'bounty' of the web grew parallel to the acknowledgment of its potential and prompted the development of tools and resources by researchers who strongly advocated the necessity to dispense with search engines altogether as soon as possible (Kilgarriff and Grefentstette 2003; Baroni and Bernardini 2004; Kehoe and Gee 2007). New tools were developed to facilitate the task of building offline corpora from the web in relatively easy ways. A paradigmatic example in this respect is the 'bootstrapping' approach of tools like BootCaT (Baroni and Bernardini 2004), which will be described in more detail in Chapter 5. This tool was subsequently used as the basis for more sophisticated tools in ambitious projects aimed at building large general reference (BNC-like) corpora from the web for many languages (see Chapter 6).

It should be noted, however, that while the distinction between 'web as corpus' and 'web for corpus' may have been useful to help categorize and discriminate approaches and methods within an emerging research field, the two are obviously contiguous with each other – as we have just seen with webascorpus.org and as we will see in the next chapter discussing BootCaT. As a matter of fact, the very acknowledgement of the need for more stable data sets and more sophisticated query tools – to ensure that high methodological standards can be met also when using the web as a corpus – prompted the same team that developed WebCorp to work on a fully tailored linguistic search engine designed to bypass commercial search engines (Kehoe and Gee 2007). The result of this project is WebCorp Linguist's Search Engine, also known as WebCorp*LSE*, whose key features will be briefly outlined in the following pages.

5.1 *The Web as/for Corpus: From WebCorp* Live *to WebCorp*LSE

As far as WebCorp*LSE* is concerned, the two approaches labelled as 'web as corpus' and 'web for corpus' are not seen as mutually exclusive, and, indeed, the real objective of the team from the start was to devise a solution addressing the limitations and exploiting the potential of both. Rather than simply piggybacking on existing search engines, as with WebCorp *Live*, the approach taken in WebCorp*LSE* entails the development of a large-scale web search engine to give direct access to the textual content of the web. In the words of Kehoe and Gee (2007: online), 'it is in the development of such a search engine that the two hitherto distinct "web as corpus" approaches intertwine'. The approach is represented by the developers as in Figure 4.16 reported below.

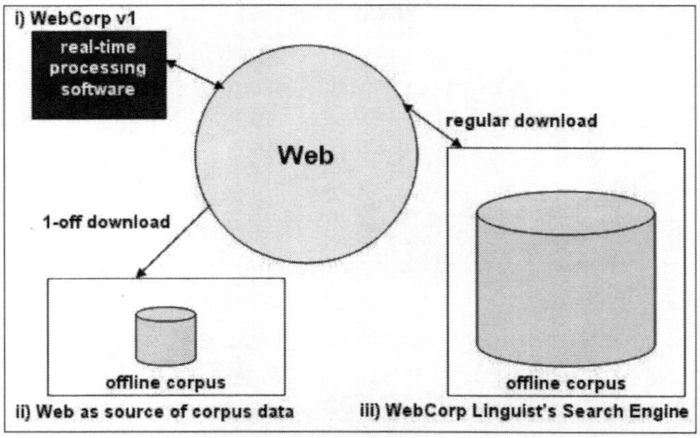

Figure 4.16. *Web as/for corpus approaches in WebCorp* Live *and WebCorp*LSE *(Source: Kehoe and Gee 2007)*

The figure compares/contrasts at a glance the three approaches (web as corpus, web for corpus, web as/for corpus) through the use of unidirectional and bidirectional arrows representing the relationship of each approach to the web. In the specific case of WebCorp Linguist's Search Engine the web is used as a source of data to build an offline corpus, as in the 'web for corpus' approach, but the corpus is constantly fed with new regular downloads from the web, so that it can truly become 'a microcosm of the web itself' (Kehoe and Gee 2009: 255). Like a corpus, this is a body of text of known size and composition, which is available for offline processing and analysis; like the web, it is very large and constantly updated, embodying the 'mega-corpus mini-web approach' in Baroni and Bernardini's (2006: 13) classification. It is, however, important to stress that the developers conceived of this system precisely in terms of a 'search engine' because it actually reproduces – albeit in much smaller scale – the work of a search engine. Like a search engine, the system's architecture includes a web crawler (to download files with textual content from the web and to find links to other files to be downloaded). And as a linguist's search engine, it includes specific linguistically aware processing components which prepare the downloaded documents for proper corpus work.

The whole process involved the creation of a ten-billion-word corpus of English to be searched using a relatively sophisticated corpus query tool. It might be objected that WebCorp*LSE* is not exactly a search engine, because the processing involving web crawling does not take place in real time and because what is finally searched is but a portion of the web. However, as the developers themselves remind us, even when users think they are searching 'the whole web' through an ordinary web search engine like Google or Bing, they are, in fact, searching only Google's or Bing's offline index – which, however large, is still a small proportion of all the data available on the web (if we consider that the so-called 'hidden web' is much larger than even the largest search engine's index). The difference rather lies in the frequency of updating of the data which takes place at an obviously faster pace with commercial search engines.

More technical details on WebCorp*LSE* may not be of interest to readers of this book, and are in any case available elsewhere (Kehoe and Gee 2007, 2009). It is, however, important to reflect briefly on some specific issues (e.g. data cleaning) which concern the texts that finally make up the corpora accessed through WebCorp*LSE*. It is obvious that the creation of a clean data set out of web crawling is crucial to the success of a linguist's search engine. This includes strategies to avoid indiscriminate download in favour of carefully targeted subsections of the web. Furthermore, content of no interest from the linguistic point of view, and of low quality, has to be filtered out to ensure that only proper 'text' is included in the corpus. Kehoe and Gee (2007), describing in detail the strategies adopted, explain that by 'text' they meant:

1 a piece of connected prose

2 written in sentences, delimited by full-stops

3 containing paragraphs

4 complete, cohesive and interpretable within itself

The criteria that have been devised to automatically identify connected prose may vary, and typical strategies include filtering pages on the basis of their size in terms of tokens or bytes, or by considering the number of non-mark-up words (Cavaglià and Kilgarriff 2001; Fletcher 2004b). The specific criteria adopted for WebCorp*LSE* are sentence length, paragraph length, number of paragraphs and frequent lexis. Also fundamental in the creation of large web corpora is the inclusion of components for language detection, date detection, and duplicate/near-duplicate document detection. Finally the project required a thorough process of clean-up to turn the original files (e.g. HTML files or other formats) into text files suitable for analysis with a corpus query tool. Web texts in fact generally contain mark-up tags, scripting languages (e.g. JavaScript), author-defined style sheets, etc. which are to be removed to obtain clean text-only files. Furthermore, even parts included in the sections that should only be reserved to the main textual content of an HTML file (the <BODY> in HTML language) can also contain language that cannot to be classified as 'text' proper (the so-called 'boilerplate' made up of the language used in the structural parts of a webpage, such as header, footer and navigation information). These sections rarely contain connected prose and, while they could be usefully kept in a corpus aiming at studying web language *per se*, become a distraction in a general purpose corpus since they are highly repetitive and would skew statistical information.

Also, in the development of the corpus which makes up the database for WebCorp*LSE*, it appeared desirable that not only HTML web pages, arguably the most accessible, but also other file formats, such as PDF files, Word documents and Postscript files (PDF, PS) were included in the corpus – on the assumption that by including these file formats also the range of registers and genres represented in the corpus would be widened. Indeed, especially PDF files which generally reproduce texts which have not been originally produced for the web, and often reproduce printed and carefully edited material, contribute to the variety of registers as well as to the reliability of the data included in a corpus.

The result of this project was the creation of three corpora built by web crawling and made available for free – upon registration – through the WebCorp*LSE* website. The three corpora are the Synchronic English Web Corpus, a corpus consisting of 467,713,650 words from web-extracted texts covering the period 2000-10; the Diachronic English Web Corpus, consisting of 128,951,238 words covering the period Jan 2000-Dec 2010, with each month containing approximately 1 million words; and the Birmingham Blog Corpus, consisting of 628,558,282 words from blog texts. Some examples of uses of these corpora will be briefly discussed in the next section.

5.2 *Using WebCorpLSE to explore contemporary English*

WebCorp Linguist's Search Engine (http://wse1.webcorp.org.uk/) provides access to the three corpora mentioned at the end of the previous section. These corpora are queried through a user interface which is definitely oriented to the needs of the linguist, though recalling in some respects the user interface of an ordinary search engine. See the access interface for the Synchronic Corpus of English in Figure 4.17 below.

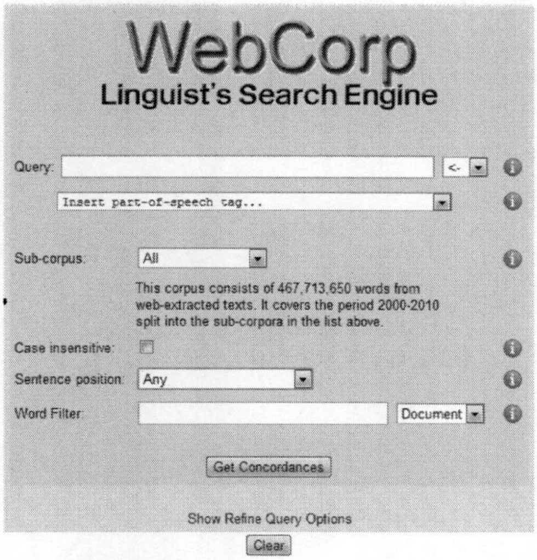

Figure 4.17. *Query interface to the Synchronic Corpus of English*

The query interface immediately highlights the fact that the system supports queries including special characters, part-of-speech tags, as well as other options like case-sensitiveness and position of the searched item in the sentence (initial, middle and final position). Even 'traditional' query refinement through the presence/absence of word filters can be fine-tuned by considering the position of the word filter in the same document or in the same sentence as the search string.

Information available at the click of a mouse right of the query box suggests even more refined search options, also including those that are not generally supported in ordinary web search, such as 'pattern matching' (e.g. search alternative words like *run* or *ran*); 'character wildcards' (e.g. *anti*tion*) or compounds (e.g. *fedup, fed-up* and *fed up*); 'phrase search'; wildcards; and proximity search (using the NEAR operator). These options can obviously be combined to fine-tune the queries so as to allow for a rewarding exploration of the three corpora.

5.2.1 Synchronic English Web Corpus and Diachronic English Web Corpus

When searching the Synchronic English Web Corpus the user can either search the complete corpus or one of the two subcorpora it consists of ('Mini-web Sample' and 'Domains'). The Mini-web Sample is a 339,907,995-word corpus compiled from 100,000 randomly selected webpages to form a sample of the distribution of texts throughout the web. The second subcorpus labelled as 'Domains' includes 127,805,655 words from 56,000 pages selected from 14 domains on the basis of the Open Directory classification of webpages. Each domain consists of 4,000 pages and the number of words for each domain is also given, as reported in Figure 4.18 below.

Arts	7,633,937 words
Business	8,042,995 words
Computers	9,270,736 words
Games	9,236,305 words
Health	10,413,454 words
Home	7,007,868 words
Kids and Teens	9,776,391 words
News	6,792,433 words
Recreation	7,419,495 words
Reference	12,272,054 words
Science	14,919,257 words
Shopping	5,185,703 words
Society	11,231,670 words
Sport	8,603,357 words

Figure 4.18. *Domains in the Synchronic English Web Corpus sub-corpus*

This exploitation of domain categorization of web pages drawing on existing directories might require a word of comment. The existence of directories had indeed initially nourished the hope – as argued in Chapter 2 – that directories themselves could be considered as virtual domain-specific corpora, but this has never proven particularly helpful when working with ordinary search engines. However, this initial frustrating experience is apparently repaid by the performance of WebCorp*LSE*. One only needs to see the difference of collocates computed for the word *spread* from the Business domain and from the Health domain, as reported in Figures 4.19 and 4.20 overleaf, to see how consistent this sub-categorization can be.

As shown in the two figures, the collocational profile of the word *spread* clearly changes in the two domains, according to its completely different meaning in the medical and economic fields. In the medical field its typical collocates are words like *HIV*, *disease*, *prevent*, *cancer*, and so on, whereas in the economic field words like *influence*, *credit*, *excess*, etc. emerge as typical collocates.

It is also important to stress that all concordance lines always come with a link to the plain text and a link to the source URL, and that for each concordance line one can retrieve a cached copy of the original page, in case the link is broken. These features provide a partial solution to the dynamism of the web and are also useful in case the user wants to investigate some of the data further. For instance, the presence of *influence* among the top collocates of *spread* in the Business domain might require double-checking, and this is easily done by activating the link provided (see Figure 4.19 overleaf). In this way access is given to a PDF file containing an article on 'Scalable Influence Maximization in Social Networks under the Linear Threshold Model' distributed through the website Microsoft Research. This is enough to question the relevance to the economic domain of *influence* as a collocate for *spread*, but this is not necessarily a good reason to consider the whole data set as unreliable. On the contrary, this example suggests that all the features that enable an evaluation *ex-post* of the results are not to be seen as mere technical details, but can actually contribute to a more comprehensive investigation of the data set in terms of reliability, relevance, representativeness.

The wide range of options offered by the system to display and summarize the results is also worth mentioning. An example can be the possibility to display results by Domain & Format, whereby a search for *spread* – the same example used earlier – would provide evidence at a glance of the occurrence of this term in different Domains (see Figure 4.22).

Information provided includes also file format (HTML, PDF, etc.) which might be used to derive elements for the description of this web corpus itself, and prompt questions as to the content of the web in more general terms. Information of this kind can also contribute data to investigate the correlation between genres and file format on the web (Mehler et al. 2010: 20).

Display format by date can instead show at a glance patterns of rise and fall in the usage of a word. Figure 4.23 summarizes data for the verb *balkani[z|s]ation* (using the utility which allows to obtain results for alternative spellings).

309 instances of '**spread{N*}**', **health** (0 min 0 sec).

External Collocates

Word	LTotal	L4	L3	L2	L1	Total	R1	R2	R3	R4	RTotal
HIV	1				1	40		38	1		39
disease	7	3	1	1	2	22		6	9		15
prevent	21			16	5	21					
cancer	4		1		3	19		8	6	1	15
virus	2		1		1	15		1	7	5	13
infection	4		2	1	1	13		4	5		9
preventing	12	1	2	9		12					
AIDS						11		5	6		11
risk	9	2	3	4		10				1	1
H5N1	1			1		9			6	2	8
influenza	1				1	9		4	3	1	8
resistance	2	1			1	8		2	4		6
reduce	7			7		7					
flu	2	1	1			7		3	2		5
rapid	6				6	7			1		1
HPAI	1		1			7		5	1		6
resistant	1	1				7		3	1	2	6

Figure 4.19. *Collocates for* spread *from the domain Health (sample)*

511 instances of '**spread{N*}**', **business** (0 min 0 sec).

External Collocates

Word	LTotal	L4	L3	L2	L1	Total	R1	R2	R3	R4	RTotal
influence	102	2		1	99	108		4	2		6
credit	61	3	3	1	54	71		3	2	5	10
excess	26	2			24	28		1		1	2
positive	25	2	1	22		26				1	1
risk	5	3		1	1	21	7	1	2	6	16
CDS	17		1		16	21		1	2	1	4
high	21	6	11	2	2	21					
spread	10	2	6	2		19		4	3	2	9
errors	3	1	1	1		19	13	2		1	16
average	16	1	3	7	5	18	1		1		2
rate	14	1	11	2		18				4	4
yield	15		1		14	17			1	1	2
changes	2	2				16	13		1		14
model	4	2			2	15	4		1	6	11
correlations	2	1	1			13	8		3		11
dynamics						13	12			1	13
q	4	4				13	1	4	1	3	9
correlation	2	1	1			11	4	1	1	3	9
market	6	1	1		4	11		1	3	1	5

Figure 4.20. *Collocates for* spread *from the domain Business (sample)*

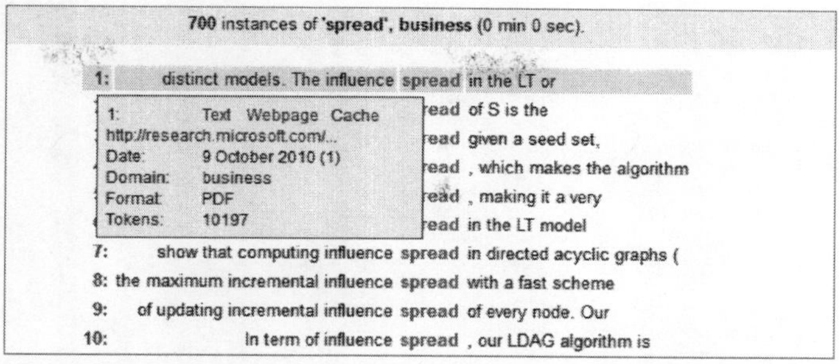

Figure 4.21. *Screenshot from the WebCorpLSE output for the collocation* influence + spread

Breakdown by Domain

Domain	Freq
science	904
health	717
business	700
society	620
kidsteens	572
home	565
games	468
reference	443
sport	429
recreation	351
news	321
arts	316
shopping	309
computers	256

Figure 4.22. *Results for* spread *by Domain*

As the sample reported in Figure 4.23 shows, the word *balkanization/balkanisation* occurs very rarely before 2007 (only once in 2004, three times in 2005, four times in 2006). It becomes more frequent in 2007 and 2008, whereas the number of occurrences drops again to 7 (two of which are irrelevant) in 2009 and 8 in 2010.

Data concerning diachronic phenomena can obviously also be better investigated in the Diachronic Corpus of English included in WebCorp*LSE*, which, however, suffers from being much smaller in size than the Syncronic Corpus. The Diachronic Corpus can be used to provide evidence of the topicality of certain words in given periods in which they appear to be particularly frequent. See Figure 4.24 overleaf reporting a sample of the tool's output summarizing

<table>
<tr><td>1 Jan 2004</td><td>produce (or enhance) ideological</td><td>balkanization</td><td>over time. The preliminary</td></tr>
<tr><td>1 Jan 2005</td><td>author perceived as the</td><td>balkanization</td><td>of campus along the</td></tr>
<tr><td>15 Apr 2005</td><td>to contribute to the</td><td>balkanisation</td><td>of social science, for</td></tr>
<tr><td>13 Jun 2005</td><td>of government 2.7 Budget</td><td>balkanization</td><td>. Autonomous agencies may undermine</td></tr>
<tr><td>16 Jan 2006</td><td>facilitate the fragmentation and</td><td>balkanization</td><td>of Iraq. In the</td></tr>
<tr><td>15 Mar 2006</td><td>issue is a general</td><td>balkanization</td><td>of cultural spheres (the</td></tr>
<tr><td>24 Oct 2006</td><td>economies and end Africa's</td><td>balkanisation</td><td>in order to create</td></tr>
<tr><td>18 Dec 2006</td><td>of the local population,</td><td>balkanization</td><td>. kmymkk | 12.18.06 10:37</td></tr>
<tr><td>12 Feb 2007</td><td>identity. Were the term "</td><td>balkanization</td><td>" not yet in use,</td></tr>
<tr><td>18 Feb 2007</td><td>as desirable, but is</td><td>balkanization</td><td>good for the United</td></tr>
<tr><td>2 Mar 2007</td><td>tribe I see this</td><td>balkanization</td><td>playing at on the</td></tr>
<tr><td>14 Mar 2007</td><td>areas of growth, "domestic</td><td>balkanization</td><td>" occurs (Frey, 1996). Under</td></tr>
<tr><td>14 Mar 2007</td><td>thereby leading to demographic</td><td>balkanization</td><td>(Frey, 1996). How this</td></tr>
<tr><td>27 Jun 2007</td><td>problem and the potential "</td><td>balkanization</td><td>" of the Internet. See,</td></tr>
<tr><td>27 Jun 2007</td><td>problem and the potential</td><td>balkanization</td><td>of the Internet. 1.</td></tr>
<tr><td>27 Jun 2007</td><td>concern about the potential</td><td>balkanization</td><td>of the Internet.363 The</td></tr>
<tr><td>27 Jun 2007</td><td>concerns over the potential</td><td>balkanization</td><td>of the Internet. Tulipane,</td></tr>
<tr><td>12 Sep 2007</td><td>renewable energy capacity. The</td><td>balkanization</td><td>of U.S. energy policy</td></tr>
<tr><td>18 Oct 2007</td><td>conflicts and the eventual</td><td>balkanization</td><td>of the United States.</td></tr>
<tr><td>6 Dec 2007</td><td>immediately after independence The</td><td>balkanization</td><td>of British North America</td></tr>
</table>

Figure 4.23. *Concordance lines for* balkani[z|s]ation

data for the vogue phrase *credit crunch* (this example is discussed using different data sets in Kehoe and Gee 2009). The sample refers to the year 2007 and reports frequency data for the 147 occurrences of the phrase *credit crunch* month per month. The complete output is summed up in Table 4.1.

The data reported in Table 4.1 provide clear evidence of one particular year (2008) in which the phrase *credit crunch* was in vogue, because of its relevance to the financial crisis, showing how its topicality decreased in the subsequent years.

Table 4.1 Summary by date of occurrences of *credit crunch* from WebCorp*LSE* (adapted)

2001	5
2002	2
2003	1
2004	3
2005	3
2006	4
2007	20
2008	61
2009	26
2010	19

1 January 2005	2	2	6
5 March 2005	1	1	
1 September 2005	3	3	
1 January 2006	1	1	4
1 March 2006	1	1	
10 August 2006	1	1	
23 October 2006	1	1	
1 January 2007	1	1	20
6 March 2007	6	6	
9 April 2007	1	1	
1 June 2007	2	2	
1 July 2007	3	3	
17 August 2007	1	1	
1 September 2007	1	3	
19 September 2007	2		
6 November 2007	1	2	
12 November 2007	1		
19 December 2007	1	1	

Figure 4.24. *Occurrences of* credit crunch *in the Diachronic Corpus of English (sample)*

5.2.2 Birmingham Blog Corpus

It is finally important to consider how the data processed by WebCorp*LSE* can also facilitate the investigation of texts representative of web 2.0 genres. A useful resource in this respect is the Birmingham Blog Corpus, which consists of 628,558,282 words from web-extracted blog texts. The corpus is split into sections according to how the texts were discovered and downloaded. See Figure 4.25 overleaf.

In this corpus, the possibility of producing refined searches even for language forms which are non-standard but are increasingly frequent in Computer Mediated Communication can really be rewarding. One example is the use of *kinda* (kind of) commented on below on the basis of information from the 21,818 occurrences of this form in the Birmingham Blog Corpus. As shown in Figure 4.26, *kinda* has a tendency to have verbs like *think, know* or *feel* in its co-text, and co-occurs with such adjectives as *cool, funny,* or *sad* (especially in its right co-text).

Technorati	427,768,219 words
Crawled the top blogs ranked by Technorati.	
Google Blog Search	19,384,429 words
Downloaded new posts daily as identified by Google Blog Search.	
Blogspot and Wordpress	181,405,634 words
Crawled blogs hosted on blogspot.com and wordpress.com. Extracted date information and separated posts from comments.	
posts	94,977,062 words
comments	86,428,572 words

Figure 4.25. *Composition of the Birmingham Blog Corpus*

External Collocates

Word	LTotal	L4	L3	L2	L1	Total	R1	R2	R3	R4	RTotal
----------	538	163	179	179	17	1087	17	258	137	137	549
just	653	74	69	62	448	954	108	30	80	83	301
think	328	69	80	175	4	604	97	6	78	95	276
know	301	63	89	114	35	498	46	22	70	59	197
cool	56	14	11	20	11	489	392	18	9	14	433
funny	55	10	21	15	9	451	367	9	16	4	396
way	143	44	30	36	33	451	183	17	50	58	308
feel	177	7	17	18	135	441	181	12	47	24	264
pm	422	131	124	146	21	422					
really	222	52	54	48	68	406	22	46	57	59	184
thing	131	20	26	49	36	404	190	11	34	38	273
looks	217	20	25	7	165	403	153	4	10	19	186
now	173	38	49	59	27	397		64	114	46	224
sad	15	2	4	6	3	382	347	8	10	2	367
see	75	23	15	35	2	374	56	17	152	74	299
get	146	53	30	27	36	371	68	8	55	94	225
still	269	24	23	30	192	362	15	13	29	36	93
makes	96	10	16	70		331	187	21	16	11	235
sorta	67	1	1		65	325	244	3	7	4	258

Figure 4.26. *Collocates for* kinda *from the Birmingham Blog Corpus*

The frequent collocation of *kinda* with the verb *feel*, especially in the patterns *kinda feel* +ADJ or *feel kinda* + ADJ is reported in Figure 4.27, which provides a sample for the pattern *I kinda feel* + ADJ. In most cases, data from this corpus seem to suggest, the adjective has negative connotations.

Another typical collocate for *kinda* which emerges from the collocational profile reported in Figure 4.26 is *sorta* (sort of). This collocation provides evidence of the pattern *kinda sorta*, often followed by a verb as in the pattern *kinda sorta* + VERB reported in Figure 4.27 below.

21:	Giambi. THANK YOU I	kinda feel bad	about bashing him in
22:	12:41 pm. I	kinda feel bad	for the artist that
23:	looked hungry yesterday. I	kinda feel bad	for Melky, he is
24:	Kim Jong Il. I	kinda feel bad	now for rooting against
25:	32 am. anyone else	kinda feel bad	for the sox? John
26:	4:08 pm. I	kinda feel bad	about breaking up Tony
27:	the recruiting process. i	kinda feel bad	for him. 13. sparty
28:	SO much backlash. I	kinda feel bad	for Danny now, not
29:	let alone WIN. I	kinda feel bad	for tOSU because when
30:	that was asked I	kinda feel bad	for her, i mean
31:	that was asked I	kinda feel bad	for her, i mean
32:	get split up. I	kinda feel bad	for whoever gets Jessica
33:	it actually was! i	kinda feel cheated	. me 03/11/2008
34:	plane looked fake. i	kinda feel cheated	. me 03/11/2008
35:	there's nothin new I	kinda feel disappointed	and a little down
36:	on those days, I	kinda feel free	. Like I can do
37:	childhood, golden times. I	kinda feel guilty	for laughing at your
38:	first video blog I	kinda feel lame	and self-conscious about possibly
39:	and decided, it does	kinda feel old	. I guess I was
40:	in this episode. I	kinda feel sorry	for Saki though, it's

Figure 4.27. *Concordances for the pattern* kinda feel + *ADJ (sample)*

1:	realizing they might be	kinda sorta attracted	to each other, the "
2:	will almost certainly (we	kinda sorta think	) not include quarterback Brett
3:	her money back and	kinda sorta starts	to get her life
4:	at risk. Which would	kinda sorta be	believable if either of
5:	less disco version that	kinda sorta fit	the music. 1976 Do
6:	of causes (as it	kinda sorta does	in Kant) but because
7:	many others that I	kinda/sorta know	. And ... I met many
8:	End on anything. I	kinda sorta knew	that. So, I had
9:	her "dumb nam" by	kinda sorta accusing	Andy of the murders.
10:	saw a building that	kinda, sorta, looked	like an embassy. I
11:	a boy I was	kinda sorta dating	for like a day.
12:	AND that he can	kinda sorta sing	in a way, if
13:	do vote So ... I	kinda sorta yelled	at an old lady
14:	and all, which has	kinda sorta had	a big impact in
15:	there for an hour	kinda sorta listening	to the numbers being
16:	as the Sisterhood, and	kinda sorta know	them.) So ... that pretty
17:	Kentuckiana region again, I "	kinda/sorta" keep	up with the horse-racing
18:	mention Zofran is only	kinda sorta assumed	to be safe .... .greeeeat.
19:	so I think that	kinda/sorta makes	me a roof fiddler.
20:	of drawing someone who	kinda sorta looks	like me P What

Figure 4.28. *Concordances for the pattern* kinda sorta + VERB *(sample)*

These data, like all other data from the three corpora that can be accessed through WebCorp*LSE*, suggest that this is a resource that definitely deserves further exploration by linguists in different research and teaching contexts. The tool combines the user-friendliness of ordinary web search with much more sophisticated linguistically oriented utilities, making it possible to explore new resources that provide useful insight into some characteristics of contemporary English. For these characteristics, WebCorp Linguist's Search Engine is proving particularly interesting in supplementing existing corpus resources in many research areas. A particularly promising field is diachronic corpus linguistics in which these data can be used to complement data from more traditional corpora through a fruitful combined approach (Mair 2012; Renouf and Kehoe 2013).

Conclusion

The examples reported in this chapter only give a faint idea of the immense potential of web data accessed through tools that are tailored for linguistic research. The examples show that linguistic information obtained from web concordancers can be tailored to meet specific needs on the linguist's part, thus proving that the web can be a very useful resource for linguistic analysis. As a tool which requires no specific computer skills, is extremely flexible and relatively quick in providing results, WebCorp *Live* proves particularly good at prompting classroom discussion on specific lexical items and in providing the starting point for data-driven and discovery learning activities. Although not exhaustive, the information obtained from web data in the context of the suggested classroom activities does seem indeed to provide evidence that using WebCorp to produce *ad hoc* concordance lines can really contribute to students' awareness of specific language issues. WebCorp activities can constitute the basis for rewarding learning experiences that students can easily repeat on their own for every language available on the web. Despite such potential, one of the most evident limits of web concordancers is the impossibility to reproduce exactly any experiment, a limitation deriving from the use of search engines on which these systems are exclusively based. This is why approaches combining the web-as-corpus orientation of web concordancers with web-for-corpus approaches can really be seen as an advancement to the mere practice of concordancing the web. These tools offer linguists the possibility of using web data to answer more sophisticate research questions, prompting the move 'from opportunistic to systematic' use of web data recently advocated by Mair (2012: 245–55).

Study questions and activities

- What is the advantage of providing concordance lines from web search results?

- In what research, professional or teaching context do you think tools like the ones described in this chapter would be most useful? Are there any areas of investigation for which these tools might prove totally useless?

- In this exercise you will try to establish the collocational profile of the word *spread* in the economic domain using WebCorp.

  Go to www.webcorp.org.uk and type the word *spread* in the search box. Select 'English' for language, Google (or another search engine if you prefer) for Search API, and set a Span of 50 characters. Then go to the advanced search option interface and include the word *market* as a word filter, before clicking 'Submit'. If the concordance lines you obtain contain many duplicates you can make a new search ticking the box 'One concordance line per web page'.

  Once you have obtained a list of concordance lines for *spread* you can compute its collocates by ticking the box for 'External collocates'. Through the box 'Exclude stopwords' you can also decide whether to include or not function words in the computation of collocates.

  Now refine your results by restricting your query to UK broadsheets and US broadsheets from the advanced options interface. You can also enhance relevance to the economic domain including specialized publications like the *Financial Times* (input the string ft.com in the box reserved for site). How do site restrictions affect the collocational profile you obtain? Compare/contrast the collocational profile you have obtained with the one reported in Figure 4.20.

- Use WebCorp *Live* to explore the pattern *everyone and their * knows*. How do the results you obtain provide evidence of creativity for this idiom?

- Go to WebCorp*LSE* and register as a user (for free). If possible have a look at the slides you can find at WebCorp Linguist's Search Engine Masterclasses (http://wse1.webcorp.org.uk/mc/) before using the tool, and do all the exercises.

- Login to WebCorp*LSE* and search for *rugged* in the subcorpus Mini-web Sample. Open the drop down menu labelled as 'Select a task' and choose 'External collocates' leaving the default parameters. Which words do collocate with *rugged*? Explore the co-text of particularly frequent collocations (e.g. *rugged individualism*). You can also view the cached version of each text to explore the original context.

Suggestions for further reading

Fletcher, W. (2007), 'Concordancing the Web. Promise and problems, tools and techniques'. In M. Hundt et al. (eds), 25–46.

Kehoe, A. and Renouf, A. (2002), 'WebCorp: Applying the Web to Linguistics and Linguistics to the Web'. *WWW2002 Conference*, Honolulu, Hawaii. http://www2002.org/CDROM/poster/67/ [accessed 1 June 2013].

Kehoe A. and Gee, M. (2007), 'New corpora from the web: making web text more 'text-like'. *VariENG,* Vol. 2, http://www.helsinki.fi/varieng/journal/volumes/02/kehoe_gee/ [accessed 1 June 2013].

Mair, C. (2012), 'Using the World-Wide Web to Study Language Change in Progress: From Opportunistic to Systematic Use'. In T. Nevalainen and E. Traugott (eds), *The Oxford Handbook of the History of English.* New York: Oxford University Press, 245-55.

Renouf, A. (2007), 'Tracing lexical productivity in the British Media', in J. Munat (2007) (ed.), *Lexical Creativity, Texts and Contexts.* Amsterdam: John Benjamins, 61–89.

—(2009), 'Corpus Linguistics beyond Google: the WebCorp Linguist's Search Engine'. Digital Studies/Le Champ Numerique, Vol 1, No 1 http://www.digitalstudies.org/ojs/index.php/digital_studies/article/view/147 [accessed 1 June 2013].

Renouf, A. and Keohe, A. (2013) 'Filling the gaps: Using the WebCorp Linguist's Search Engine to supplement existing text resources'. International Journal of Corpus Linguistics, 18: 2, 167–98.

Note

1 The link 'Publications' in WebCorp website is regularly updated with new publications.

5

Building and Using Comparable Web Corpora: Tools and Methods

Introduction

This chapter introduces specific tools and methods devised to create specialized corpora and term-lists from the web in the context of the web-for-corpus approach (Baroni and Bernardini 2004; Baroni et al. 2006). Section 1 describes the basic steps required in the manual creation of small do-it-yourself web corpora and discusses some of the theoretical issues involved. Section 2 describes open-source software that makes the compilation of such corpora a semi-automated process, discussing basic properties of the tools as well as the usefulness of the results when applied to specific terminology and translation tasks. Finally, Section 3 reports on the creation of comparable corpora, showing to what extent the accessibility of recently designed systems and the relatively short time required for corpus compilation can make it extremely easy to create such corpora for work with and across different languages.

1. Building DIY web corpora

Uses of the web as a corpus 'surrogate' (Baroni and Bernardini 2006: 10) through web concordancers, like the ones described in the previous chapter, represent a step forward within the web-as-corpus approach, especially when compared with the use of ordinary search engines. Furthermore, the development of larger resources and *ad-hoc* query tools which combine aspects of both web-as-corpus and web-for-corpus approaches, as is the case with WebCorp Linguist's Search Engine, has enhanced the possibility of exploiting the web's potential from a corpus linguistics perspective. These tools and resources remain anyway quite limited for some specific tasks – such as, for instance, those involving specialized terminology. While the web certainly abounds with examples of specialized terms in context, it is difficult to explore these data using resources like the ones that have been just described. A search with WebCorp would at best produce a good list of collocates, but using this information for an investigation of terminology would require a new web search for each new term; as to WebCorp Linguist's Search Engine, it can be argued that it performs quite well even for specialized single terms, but it cannot provide enough data for multiword terms. An example can be the term *methylation*, for which WebCorp*LSE* finds 252 occurrences in the Synchronic English Web Corpus, but only one instance for the multiworld term *aberrant DNA methylation patterns*. By contrast, an ordinary web search or a search with WebCorp *Live* would provide plenty of examples for terminology of this kind, but the time required to extract linguistic information for each given item using these approaches would be prohibitively long, especially if the data are to be used for a professional task (e.g. a translation) which involves searching for many different words and terms, also in languages other than English.

In this context, the need for *ad hoc* documentation in the form of do-it-yourself, 'quick-and-dirty' disposable corpora (Zanettin 2002; Varantola 2003) – i.e. corpora created from the web for a specific purpose, such as assisting a language professional in some translation task or in the compilation of a terminological database – has long been advocated and has by now become standard practice (Sánchez-Gijón 2009; Zanettin 2012). However, the compilation of a corpus through manual queries and downloads can be an extremely time-consuming process, and a time investment of this kind may appear unjustified, especially when the corpus which results from such effort is meant to be a single-use corpus – as is often the case with corpora created for a specific task – and not for a wider research project (Baroni and Bernardini 2004).

When creating such single-use *ad hoc* corpora, translators generally query an ordinary search engine for a combination of search terms considered relevant to the task at hand, taking as much advantage as possible from the options offered by the engine to focus their query – such as language or domain specification, selection of URLs, Boolean search, etc. (Pearson 2000; Zanettin 2002, 2012). Indeed, the procedures used to assemble web documents for a specialized DIY web corpus are basically the same used to perform queries and evaluate search engine results when using the web as a corpus surrogate through search engines. Increasingly sophisticated web search options (search by date, file format, search within subsections of the web such as Google scholar) have certainly made this process more rewarding, if not quicker, but the results may not always be commensurate with the effort required. It is very often the case, for instance, that after compilation one finds the corpus is still too small to provide enough evidence for less frequent items – a typical consequence of the aforementioned Zipf's Law (see Chapter 1).

Crucial to the success of such corpora is a sound evaluation of the texts retrieved, the relevance and reliability of which need to be assessed by scanning the documents. As suggested in Zanettin (2012: 65), relevance is mostly determined on the basis of the page content, as well as visual clues (titles, layout and images), text type, style and register. The reliability of the texts is, instead, assessed by looking at clues for authoritativeness, for instance by discarding translations and privileging texts produced by recognizable bodies and authorities within the relevant discourse communities (experts, producers, public and private agencies and associations). The texts that are judged suitable for inclusion in the corpus are finally downloaded, cleaned and processed to create a small, highly focused corpus to be explored with a concordancer. Zanettin (2002) illustrates in detail an experiment in which trainee translators had to create a corpus for immediate use during a translation assignment. They were first asked to set up a 'workstation' with all the necessary tools and resources (a concordancing program, internet browser and search engines, word processors, etc.) and then were instructed on how to formulate appropriate queries, evaluate the results, process the selected documents into the corpus and finally analyse the data with a corpus query tool. The corpora created were between 5,000 and 40,000 words each, but proved nonetheless useful for understanding and translating terminology and identifying domain-specific collocations and phraseology. Sánchez-Gijón (2009) also suggests how to develop documentary skills through the creation of a DIY web corpus and suggests protocols to help students formulate queries, evaluate results and process web documents to this purpose.

In the new context created by the emergence of web-as/for-corpus approaches and methods, some of these activities can be automated using BootCaT (Baroni and Bernardini 2004). As its name promises, alluding to the well-known metaphor of 'bootstrapping' in the language of information technology,[1] BootCaT is a suite of programs capable of creating virtually ex-nihilo specialized corpora and term lists from the web in a very short time. It is therefore appropriately categorized under the label 'web for corpus', or web as corpus 'shop', as suggested in Baroni and Bernardini (2006: 10), even though some of its key properties still foreground, as we will see, typical web-as corpus-issues.

2. From words to corpus: The 'bootstrap' process

2.1 Compiling a domain-specific corpus with BootCaT

Originally created as a suite of programs in Perl, mainly for use by computer-savvy operators, BootCaT is now a very user-friendly software, accessible for download through the front-end at http://bootcat.sslmit.unibo.it/. In its underlying philosophy, BootCaT can be seen as the natural development of the above-mentioned practice of building do-it-yourself, 'quick-and-dirty', disposable corpora. With BootCaT, the process of corpus compilation is, in principle, the same as in the manual creation of DIY corpora, but rather than having the linguist first querying the web, then downloading relevant results, and finally performing the necessary format changes and archiving procedures to create his/her corpus, it is the software that performs most of these tasks together in a few minutes. It could be said, therefore, that this system has a bias towards 'customization', in the sense that it is primarily conceived as a tool to help language professionals build the corpus they need, whenever they need it and as quickly as possible. This is a very interesting feature from the point of view of its contribution to the changing face of corpus linguistics. By making the creation of *ad hoc* temporary corpora an easily achievable goal, BootCaT really brings the ideal notion of the web as a sort of virtual multilingual multipurpose corpus *on demand* a bit closer to reality.

The only thing that BootCaT needs to start the process is a number of key words or phrases which the user considers likely to occur in the specialized domain for which a corpus is going to be built. The words chosen to start the process are called 'seeds' and are transformed by the system into a set of automated queries submitted to an ordinary search engine. Thus, if the intention is to create a corpus on alternative forms of tourism based on issues regarding sustainability and responsibility, one can input the words *tourism, sustainable, responsible, green, nature, environment, eco-friendly* and let the software perform the search (see Figure 5.1).

The basic assumption behind this procedure is that, as noted above, any choice of words can indeed be seen as evocative of 'a mini-world or universe of discourse' (Stubbs 2002: 7), and this is probably what triggered, in the authors of the BootCaT system, the idea that a handful of words could be enough to create from scratch – i.e. to bootstrap – a linguistic corpus focused on whatever domain is required. The key role played by the choice of seeds is anyway far from trivial, and requires careful considerations which border on important issues in Information Retrieval. Some of these aspects have been discussed in Gabrielatos (2007) in the attempt at identifying a measure, termed as 'relative query term relevance' (RQTR), to strike the balance

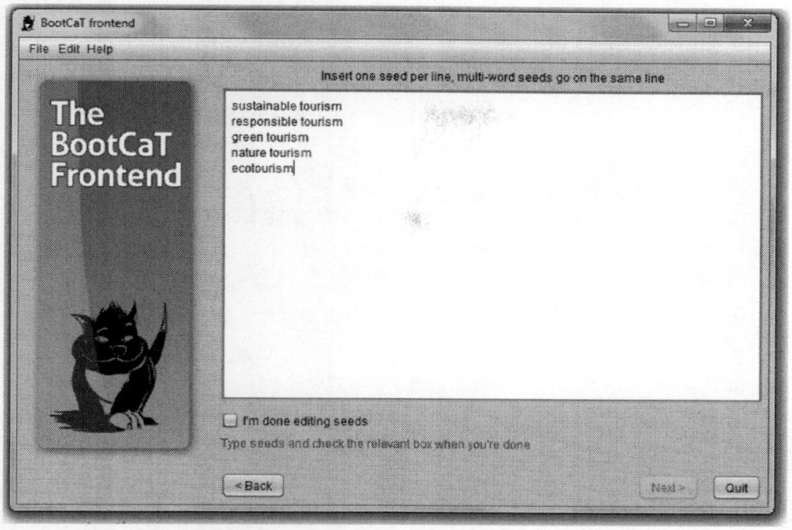

Figure 5.1. *BootCaT user interface*

between precision and recall in creating corpora from the World Wide Web. In the words of Gabrielatos:

> When compiling a specialised corpus from a text database by use of a query, there is a trade-off between precision and recall (e.g. Chowdhury 2004: 170). That is, there is a tension between, on the one hand, creating a corpus in which all the texts are relevant, but which does not contain all relevant texts available in the database, and, on the other, creating a corpus which does contain all available relevant texts, albeit at the expense of irrelevant texts also being included. (Gabrielatos 2007: 6)

The issues addressed are complex, and would require more extensive treatment than is feasible within the limits of this book section. What is important to stress here is that corpus compilation will always entail this trade-off 'between a corpus that can be deemed incomplete, and one which contains noise (i.e. irrelevant texts)' (Gabrielatos 2007: 6), which means that some terms and/or concepts may be missing or under-represented in the corpus and that statistical results may be skewed. This is why extreme care is required in choosing the input seeds and why it is always necessary to assess the relevance of both the query terms and the documents retrieved by reading (a sample of) the documents returned.

Starting from the input 'seeds', the system automatically downloads the top pages returned by a search engine for each query (ten by default), post-processes them, and finally produces a corpus which is immediately available for analysis offline using a concordancer (e.g. Wordsmith Tools, AntConc, etc.). This first nucleus can be used to extract new seeds using an offline corpus tool, either by choosing new seeds from items in the frequency word list produced from the corpus, or by extracting its keywords (by comparing the frequency of occurrence of words in this corpus with their frequency of occurrence in a reference corpus, as seen in Chapter 1). This recursive procedure can be repeated several times, until the corpus reaches the desired size (Baroni and Bernardini 2004).

A key feature of BootCaT is that, although mainly automated, the process of corpus creation is clearly divided into different phases, allowing the user to interact with the system throughout the process. At each phase the user can, in fact, control several important parameters, such as the number of queries issued for each iteration, the number of seeds used in a single query, the number of pages to be retrieved. It is also possible to limit the search to specific domains and exclude others – for example, the user can limit the crawl to British or American academic sites (.ac.uk or .edu) and at the same time exclude pages from Wikipedia and from .com sites, as shown in Figure 5.2 below.

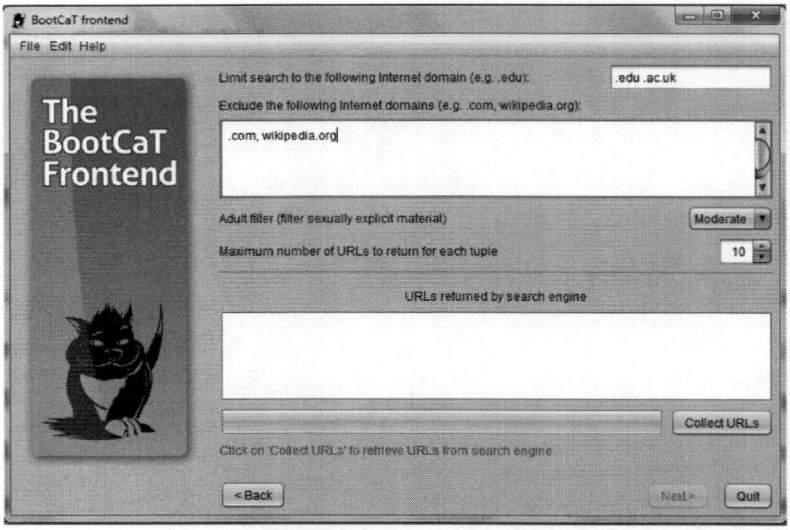

Figure 5.2. *BootCaT user interface*

On the basis of the specific parameters set by the user, the system collects a number of URLs that can be visited before they are included in the corpus, preventing undesired pages from being further processed. This is a particularly important option because it contributes to enhancing the relevance/reliability of the pages which finally make up the corpus. In order to obtain a more focused text collection, one might for instance decide to discard URLs that link to social networks or to commercial services.

Using the procedure so far discussed, it is very easy to compile corpora for highly specialized domains. We might consider, for instance, the case of a corpus on the subject of epigenetics, a branch of biology that studies 'heritable changes in gene expression or cellular phenotype caused by mechanisms other than changes in the underlying DNA sequence' (Wikipedia). The seeds used to trigger the 'bootstrap' process for this task were taken from the keywords section of a research article on epigenetics, assuming that these keywords were representative of the domain of interest (e.g. cytochrome, enzyme system, genetics, metabolism, DNA methylation, etc.) and were used by the system to produce the tuples, i.e. groups of two or three seed words to be submitted as queries to a search engine, as shown in Figure 5.3 below.

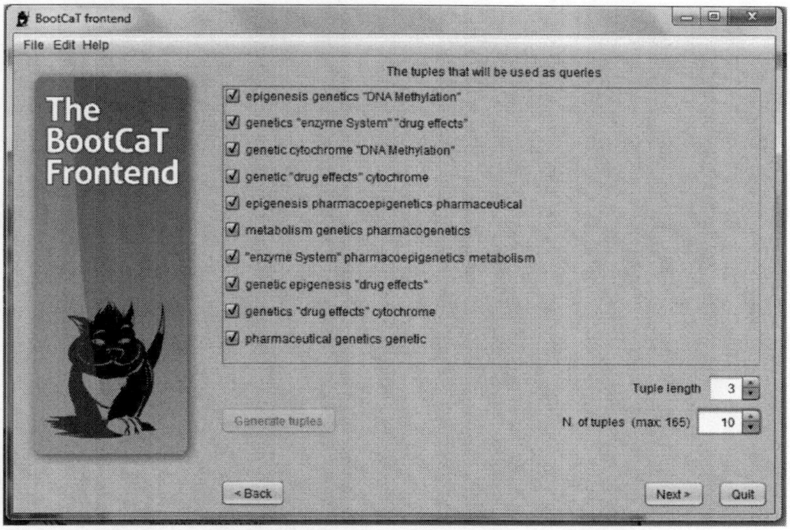

Figure 5.3. *Queries sent to Bing search engine through BootCaT*

Using the queries randomly generated by the system, the automated process was launched to retrieve a number of relevant pages for immediate download (see Figure 5.4 overleaf).

It is certainly not the purpose of the present study to go into further technical detail concerning the pre/post-processing work 'going on behind the scenes'. It is perhaps useful, though, to consider how an automated

Figure 5.4. *List of URLs available for download through BootCaT*

procedure can replace much of the work that should otherwise have been done manually by the linguist, thus making the act of corpus compilation similar to a slightly more complex web search. As already seen, the system takes in the seed words suggested by the user (i.e. the words a user would normally input into a search engine to retrieve pages to be included in a DIY corpus) and turns them into a number of queries simultaneously sent to a search engine, each containing a randomly selected triple of the seed terms. Each query returns up to 100 hits, the top ten of which – the most relevant and reliable according to the search engine's proprietary algorithm – are taken by the system. To make sure that only webpages made of consistent texts are included in the corpus, the system also filters out very short (less than 5kB) and very long (over 2MB) web pages, on the assumption that these rarely contain useful samples of language. Finally, duplicate and near-duplicate webpages are deleted, while the remaining pages are further processed to filter out the so-called boilerplate (HTML mark-up, javascript, navigation bars, etc.), again a work that should otherwise be performed manually. Last, but definitely not least, the data collected are saved locally to one's own computer in a single directory, including the cleaned-up corpus in .txt format, the seeds used to start the process, the tuples used as queries, and the URLs selected.

The decisive importance of these pre/post-processing tasks performed by the system can hardly be overemphasized, and will be readily acknowledged by anyone who has attempted to use the web as a corpus either through ordinary search engines or through a simpler tool like WebCorp. By allowing simultaneous queries to a search engine, by filtering out duplicates and near-duplicates, by excluding pages which, on the basis of size alone, can be assumed to contain little genuine text (Fletcher 2004b), by automatically removing the so-called boilerplate, and by making the necessary format changes to transform the results of a query to a search engine into a corpus ready for use with a concordancer, the system does more, if not better, than the linguist can manually do, and all this in a much shorter time. The result is a relatively clean text collection available to the user in a few minutes. The table below reports a list of the first 30 content words from a 153,000-token corpus on Epigenetics created in a few minutes using BootCaT.

Table 5.1. Content words from the Epigenetics corpus (sample)

10	1168	CYP
16	884	DNA
17	806	methylation
20	732	gene
21	667	drug
27	595	expression
31	512	cells
32	506	genes
37	410	cancer
49	338	human
54	256	cell
58	248	CpG
61	245	metabolism
62	243	genetic
63	235	patients
64	232	treatment
65	230	epigenetic
69	226	response
70	225	protein
71	224	cytochrome
72	224	drugs
74	212	associated
75	209	enzyme
76	209	promoter
79	202	enzymes
84	194	histone
85	190	clinical
86	187	activity
91	178	regulation
93	175	effects

These terms can all be considered relevant to the domain under analysis, and can be used to identify new seed terms to run the process a second time. As to the information that can be retrieved from the analysis of a few concordance lines, this also seems to be immediately useful. By way of example, we can consider a sample of the concordance lines for the 857 occurrences of the word *methylation* in the corpus, as reported in Figure 5.5.

```
integrity, are frequently silenced by aberrant methylation [ 123 ]. MLH1 encodes a DNA mismatch repair prote
model of schizophrenia. 99 A role for aberrant methylation mediated by folate levels has been suggested as a
ocortical carcinoma, which often have aberrant methylation status ( Gao et al. 2002 ). Steroidogenesis in ad
an genetic mutations [ 99 , 100 ]. If aberrant methylation of CpG sites in noncancer tissues is associated w
Kawahara, K, Hiyama, K, Nishiyama, M. Aberrant methylation of DPYD promoter, DPYD expression, and cellular s
ism in TSG inactivation. The cause of aberrant methylation in cancers is the major question in cancer epigen
 a clinical study of drug resistance, aberrant methylation patterns were observed for 9 of 14 genes examined
 L929 mouse fibroblast cells leads to aberrant methylation of the CpG island in the promoter of the Dnmt1 ge
drug resistant breast tumors. Moreover, absent methylation of the ABCB1 promoter correlated with disease pro
in cancer cells: correlation of accessibility, methylation, MeCP2 binding, and acetylation. Nucleic Acids Re
ations of the histone proteins by acetylation, methylation, SUMOylation or phosphorylation. DNA methylation
s occur at multiple sites through acetylation, methylation and phosphorylation. DNA methylation occurs at 5-
nomic states. Recent strategies for addressing methylation in large genomes include enzyme directed reduced
o observed that DNMT3b knockout did not affect methylation of any of the examined genes but only caused deme
d ( Kouzarides, 2007 ; Bártová et al., 2008 ). Methylation at histone 3 lysine 27 (H3K27me3 and H3K27me2) is
n different histones ( Bártová et al., 2008 ). Methylation at H3K4 normally results in an open chromatin con
e â?µ Anttila S, Hakkola J, Tuominen P, et al. Methylation of cytochrome P4501A1 promoter in the lung is ass
Medline 37. Chim CS, Kwong YL, Fung TK, et al. Methylation profiling in multiple myeloma. Leuk Res 2004 ; 28
reased density of CpG methylation. All allelic methylation patterns were variegated, which is consistent wit
es and that the induction of silencing allowed methylation to spread towards and eventually into the promote
ancer drugs. Genome-wide approaches to analyze methylation involve comparative microarray hybridization foll
CRC, histone marks of aberrant acetylation and methylation levels on specific residues have been revealed, a
91 For example, shifts in both acetylation and methylation are required to coordinate DNA accessibility and
stic patterns of site-specific acetylation and methylation on histone tails (the ?histone code') are involve
is issue, we investigated the distribution and methylation status of CpG dinucleotides in the mouse Tact1/Ac
on of 2 methylated tumour suppressor genes and methylation of an oncogene. Similarly, small molecules such a
```

Figure 5.5. *Concordance lines for* methylation *from the Epigenetics Corpus (sample)*

Even at first glance, the screenshot from the output obtained using a simple, free concordancer (AntConc) provides immediate evidence of the kind of information made available to users. It is not our purpose here to analyse these lines in detail, but to emphasize how these well-formed concordances clearly suggest a profile for *methylation* in terms of collocates and patterns that could be profitably explored from a corpus linguistics perspective for terminological purposes. What is more important to stress here is that all this information comes from a corpus automatically created from the web in less than five minutes through a process contiguous with ordinary web search, albeit significantly enhanced by the specific web-as/for-corpus methodology adopted.

Given the relevance of tools like BootCaT in the context of what can be labelled as 'translation-driven corpora' (Zanettin 2012), it is hardly surprising that methods and techniques used to 'bootstrap' corpora from the web are increasingly discussed and described in the translation studies literature. Zanettin (2012: 66–7) reports in detail the compilation of a small specialized corpus on 'human geography' starting from a list of keywords extracted from the entry 'Human Geography' in Wikipedia as seeds. First a word list was obtained from the Wikipedia entry using a concordancer, then a list of keywords was obtained by using the BNC frequency word list as a reference corpus (as seen in Chapter 1, Section 3.2.1). From the resulting word list only ten content words were selected and used as seeds for a BootCaT run. The search was limited to PDF files from the British academic domain (.ac.uk), and to the first ten hits for each of ten queries. Further settings suggested by the author included file size between 5 and 2000 kB (given by default in the system) and the number of words in each file (between 300 and 10,000 words). The search returned about 80 pages, of which only a half were finally selected and downloaded. This resulted in a corpus of about 200,000 words, and it took about 20 minutes before the corpus was ready for analysis and use for translation purposes. Examples of quick-and-dirty disposable web corpora which proved useful to assist in a specific translation task or project are also reported in Ferraresi (2009). Other uses of corpora compiled with BootCaT for descriptive translation studies are exemplified by a study by Bernardini et al. (2010) on institutional academic English in Europe. In this study examples of native and non-native usage of English are compared on the basis of corpora of English texts from Italian and English academic websites obtained through the procedure of corpus compilation so far discussed.

2.2 Compiling specialized corpora with WebBootCaT

Besides being available to users as a stand-alone software, BootCaT can also be accessed as a web service through the Sketch Engine website (www.sketchengine.co.uk), a service which will be discussed in more detail in the next chapter. When accessing WebBootCaT through the Sketch Engine, the user no longer needs to download or install any software, but relies on the program installed on a remote server. The same server also keeps a copy of the corpus created by the user, which can be loaded into a specific corpus query tool, i.e. the Sketch Engine (Kilgarriff et al. 2004), or downloaded in .txt format to one's own personal computer for offline analysis with any other tools (e.g. Wordsmith Tools or AntConc). In Gatto (2009: 103–28), the procedure used to compile two comparable corpora of medical texts using WebBootCaT is reported and their usefulness for translation tasks is assessed. Here, the cyclical process required to rapidly produce a nearly 500,000-word corpus on Renewable Energies will be briefly summarized.

The Renewable Energies corpus was compiled through a semi-automated iterative process like the one described in the previous paragraph, this time with the help of WebBootCaT. As with the stand-alone version, all the linguist has to do with WebBootCaT is to key in seed terms, which are then randomly combined by the system and turned into query strings. The system downloads the top pages returned for each query to make up the first nucleus of the corpus. Choosing the seed terms is a particularly sensitive area in the case of corpus compilation using BooTCaT and WebBootCaT, for reasons that have been briefly commented on earlier in this chapter with reference to the 'trade off between precision and recall' (Gabrielatos 2007). For this reason it is important not to rely simply on intuition when choosing the seeds, and search for alternative ways to make sure that seed terms are not arbitrarily chosen. One solution is to compile a small 'pilot' corpus from which keywords and/or clusters can be extracted as seeds for the corpus; in this way the limitation of a subjective identification of key words and terms for a specific domain can be reduced. An alternative is the extraction of keywords from a Wikipedia article, when available, on the specific domain for which a corpus is going to be built – as seen in the example from Zanettin (2012: 66–7) reported in the previous section. With WebBootCaT the extraction of seed terms from Wikipedia has become a standard practice and this possibility is implemented in the system (Figure 5.6). In this way, relatively reliable seeds are almost effortlessly obtained and the process can start.

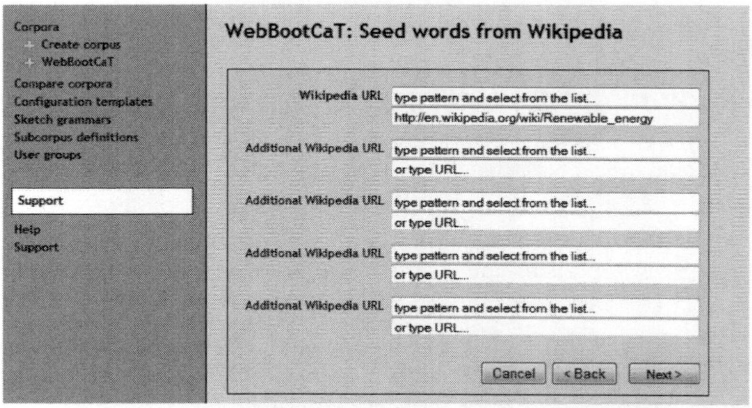

Figure 5.6. *Seed selection using Wikipedia*

Following this model, a list of potential seed terms was extracted (see Figure 5.7), from which some terms (e.g. proper names) were deleted since they were not considered good seeds.

Using the seeds retrieved from the entry for 'Renewable Energies' in Wikipedia, the system collected a number of URLs from which texts were automatically downloaded for inclusion in the corpus. Again, as with the stand-alone version, the automated process is clearly divided into distinct phases, allowing the user to interact with the system throughout the process.

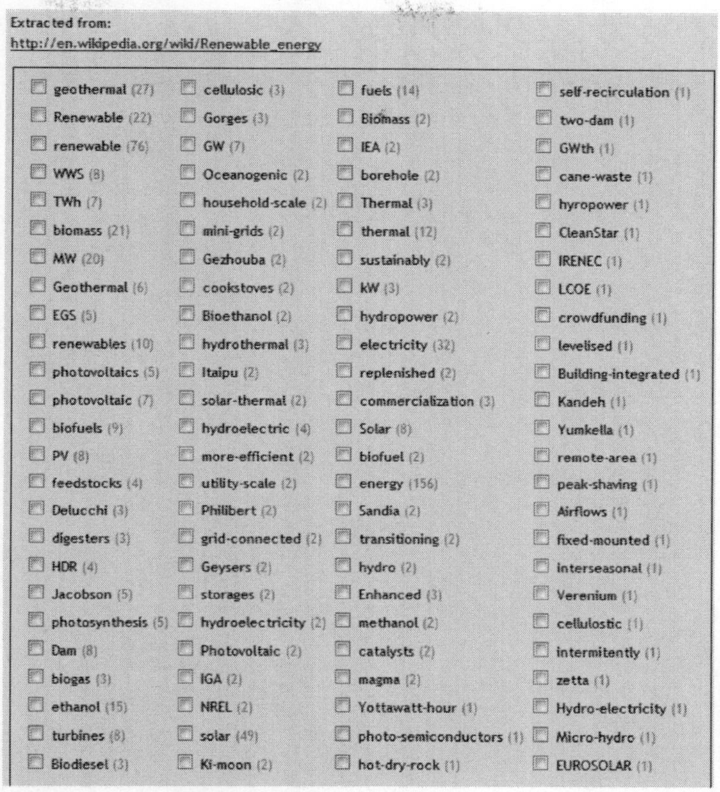

Figure 5.7. *Seeds selected using Wikipedia*

This is a particularly important option because it not only contributes to enhancing the relevance/reliability of the pages which finally make up the corpus, but also – and more crucially – involves the user in a decision-making process comparable, to some extent, with the one underlying the creation and compilation of corpora using more traditional methods. As mentioned above, it is especially important to evaluate the texts by considering information inferred from website addresses or by actually visiting the webpage. In the case of our Renewable Energies corpus for instance, it was necessary to deselect URLs that did not seem to be reliable or useful in the corpus, as in the case of a number of URLs pointing to online shopping or videos.

Having inspected and selected or deselected the URLs, the system can run to compile the first nucleus of the corpus. From this nucleus new seed terms can be automatically extracted by comparing the frequency of occurrence of words in the corpus with their frequency of occurrence in a reference corpus; the keywords extracted can then be turned into new seeds. This crucial step concerning keyword extraction is also automated in

WebBootCaT, since a list of key-terms can be extracted in a matter of seconds by simply activating the relevant option in the user interface and choosing one of the reference corpora available. In this process, the keywords themselves will appear as 'semi-processed' items that can be inspected in the form of concordance lines even while the process of corpus compilation is still in progress. Each key-term is indeed 'already' and 'not yet' part of the corpus under compilation and can be investigated as part of the corpus *before* being used as a new seed, as if it were in a liminal space between the living textual body of the web (to which it still belongs) and the offline corpus towards which it is moving. In this way the user can evaluate both concordance lines and collocates for each key-term in order to decide whether that term should be used as a new seed for the iterative process of corpus compilation, or if it should be removed (see Figure 5.8 below and Figure 5.9 overleaf).

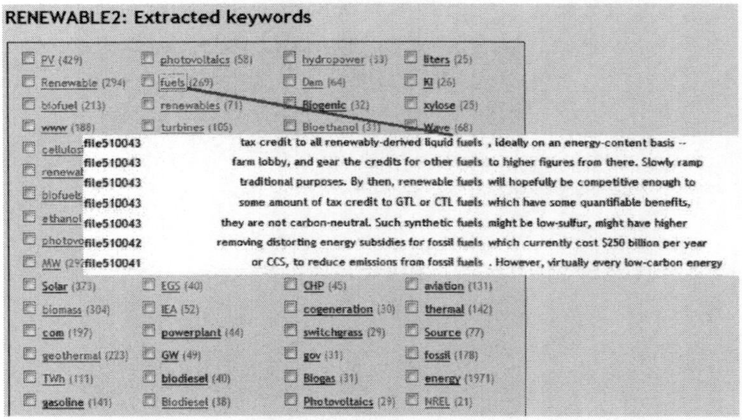

Figure 5.8. *Concordance lines for the key-term* fuel

It is also important to stress how the system computes not only single keywords but also key multiword terms. A sample is reported in Figure 5.10 below.

The possibility of inspecting concordance lines and collocates for each keyword and multiword term while the process is still in progress greatly contributes to the creation of a corpus potentially made only of relevant and reliable texts. Furthermore, each concordance line is itself still in a mid-way position between the web of texts it is part of and the offline corpus that is being compiled. This is made evident by the link to the doc.id on the left of each concordance line, which gives the user the possibility of both inspecting the original webpage once again and of editing – if necessary – the text-only file which has been obtained from that same webpage, using the two links provided (see Figure 5.11).

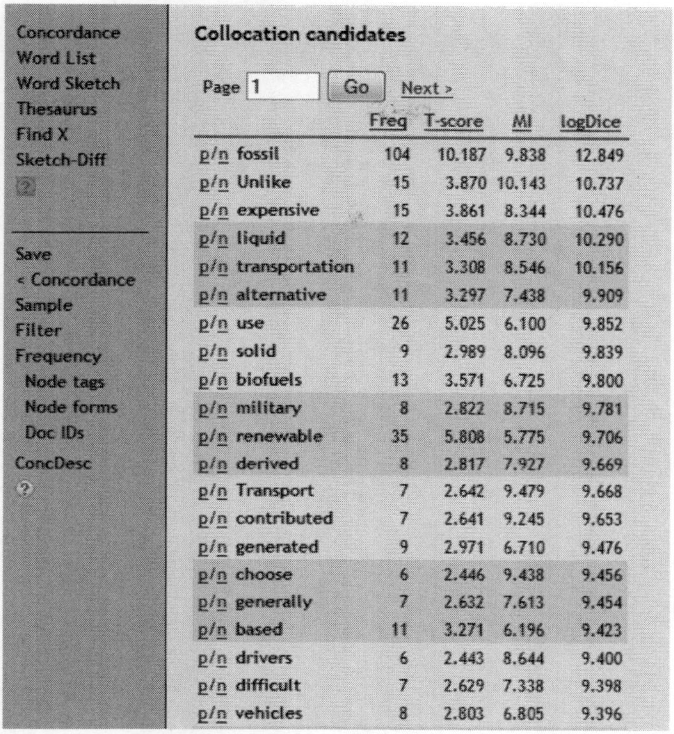

Figure 5.9. *Collocations for the key-term* fuel

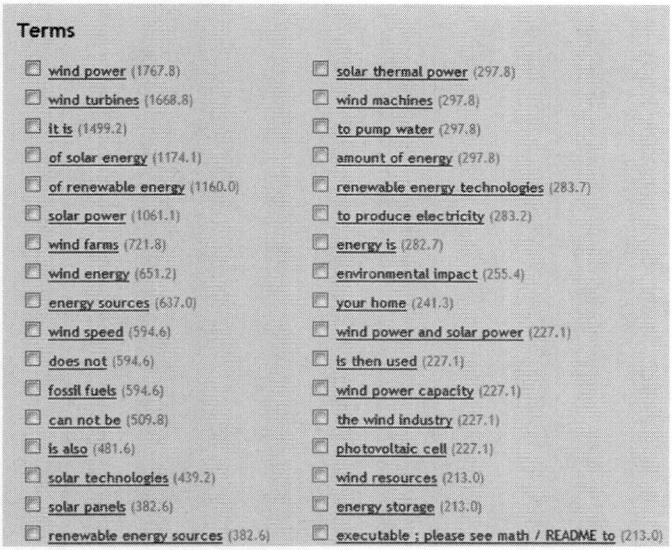

Figure 5.10. *Multiword terms from the Renewable Energies corpus (sample)*

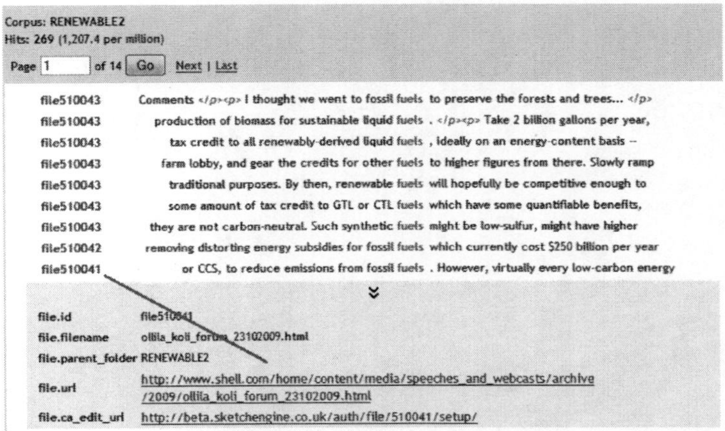

Figure 5.11. *Concordances for* fuel *with links to the URL and to the editable plain text version*

This suggests that building a web corpus using a semi-automated procedure like the one made possible by WebBootCaT by no means relieves the linguist of care and theoretically informed concerns. The main difference between compiling a corpus manually and performing the same task semi-automatically, is that part of the energy that was previously spent in the design and preparation of the corpus before it was compiled with more traditional methods is now spent while the process is still in progress, and sometimes even after the process is finished. This, for instance, was the case of an Italian corpus of medical texts in which some shortcomings were highlighted, due to insufficient care taken during the preliminary inspection of candidate websites. In this corpus, one of the first key-terms appeared to be *Ricategorizza*, a term which seemed to require further investigation. Indeed, the concordance lines produced for this term suggested that it referred to the 'categorization' of posts in a website named it.answers.com. Since the corpus was meant to be representative of medical discourse at a specialized level, this website was considered to be neither relevant nor reliable. Having identified the file name from the doc.id and after visiting the corresponding URL, the file was removed from the corpus, with the consequent reduction of the corpus in tokens, and the disappearance of *Ricategorizza* from the key-terms lists. A similar problem was faced with the English Renewable Energies corpus. The list of multiword terms included the string *executable; please see Math /README to* (see Figure 5.10). The corresponding file was identified and removed from the corpus, with the consequent disappearance of the cluster from the key-term list.

Once key-terms have been inspected and selected or deselected as new seeds and the candidate URLs have been checked for relevance and reliability, the system can run once again to compile a larger corpus, through an iterative process that can be repeated several times (three or four are generally enough).

The result of this recursive procedure is a web corpus that comes to the user in a few minutes, combining the orientation of the web towards freshness, topicality and being up-to-date with aspects of 'good practice' in corpus work. In this respect, the possibility given by the system, both in the offline and online version, to inspect pages before (and after) the download, as well as the possibility of limiting the crawl to a few pre-selected websites or domains, can be seen as an indirect and relatively effective way to control aspects of corpus compilation which are related to the key issues of relevance, reliability and representativeness.

As seen in Chapters 2 and 3, some aspects related to the reliability of the texts retrieved and to their genre and register can also be taken into account regarding the format of files. Most web corpora tend in fact to contain only HTML pages, originally produced for the web, which are more easily turned into plain text, but it is known that some other file types (e.g. PDF) are frequently used for publications, such as books or articles, which originate outside the web; the possibility of restricting the crawl to these file-types may have a significant impact on the resulting corpus at the level of register. The compilation of a corpus using WebBootCaT can, for instance, be limited only to PDF files for the sake of greater reliability. The screenshot in Figure 5.12 comes from a corpus on Cultural Anthropology compiled out of PDF files only.

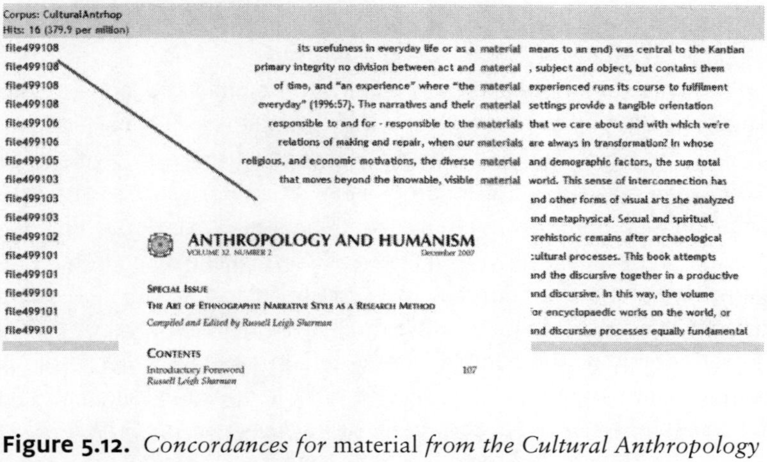

Figure 5.12. *Concordances for* material *from the Cultural Anthropology corpus*

As the image shows, the corpus contains carefully edited sources, thus reducing the commonsense impression that using web data, especially through automated processes, might imply harvesting predominantly low-quality data.

The question of (pre-)determining the genre of the texts retrieved without having to actually read them remains nonetheless open, as observed in McEnery and Hardie (2012: 58). In the case of BootCaT, success in this respect crucially depends on the user ability to select terms that are not only associated to a specific topic but also, if necessary, to a specific genre. The necessity of going beyond mere content and implement a genre-driven approach to complement the already successful topic-driven approach in BootCaT is clearly a priority (Bernardini and Ferraresi 2013: 8).

3. Building and using comparable web corpora for translation practice

On the basis of the characteristics so far described, we can now see to what extent tools like BootCaT and WebBootCaT can be used to facilitate the compilation of comparable corpora. By repeating the same procedure using seed terms from different languages, corpora for many languages can be compiled, virtually for any language available on the web. Research work is actually underway to build on these tools and create new tools even more specifically devoted to the compilation of comparable corpora (Kilgarriff et al. 2011). In the meantime, the whole set of procedure has been used for the creation of large general reference corpora for many languages (Sharoff 2006; Kilgarriff et al. 2010), as we will see in the following chapter.

As seen in Chapter 1, comparable corpora are those consisting of two or more collections of texts similar in respect of genre, topic, time span and communicative function. These corpora are becoming increasingly popular resources, especially in Translation Studies and Natural Language Processing. In Translation Studies they are extensively used to find translation equivalents in examples of authentic language usage by native speakers, or for cross-linguistic discoveries and comparison. In NLP the automatic creation of comparable corpora has been in recent years the main focus as a way to make up for the scarcity of parallel corpora (i.e. multilingual corpora including translated texts and their source texts) in providing data to train statistical machine translation systems or to build terminology databanks.

The very notion of comparable corpora in some way or other foregrounds the related notion of comparability for corpora, a question which pertains to monolingual and multilingual corpora alike. It is beyond the limited scope of this section to go into further detail concerning issues of comparability for corpora, which have been extensively debated especially in the context of corpus-based translation studies (Laviosa 1997; Ohlan 2004). It is, however, important at least to acknowledge that comparability between corpora in different languages is not simply related to the 'content' of a corpus but should be ensured by similarity of sampling techniques, balance and representativeness, and that comparability shares with balance and representativeness the status of a controversial issue. For the purpose of the present section, however, a looser view of comparability in terms of 'different languages but similar content' (Kilgarriff et al. 2011: 123) will be adopted, assuming that by reproducing a semi-automated process on the basis of similar criteria, starting from 'comparable' seeds in different languages, the corpora created can with good approximation be considered as largely comparable.[2]

This section reports on the compilation of a corpus on 'renewable energies', this time composed of Italian texts. The Italian Energie Rinnovabili Corpus was compiled using the same criteria as those followed for the English Renewable Energies corpus described in the previous section, with the aim of creating two ideally 'comparable' corpora. As already stressed, the focus will be not on theoretical issues concerning the comparability of the corpora, but rather on an evaluation of the data retrieved and on the feasibility of tasks involving the compilation of comparable corpora even in the limited time-investment justified by a translation task, be it in the context of a translation workshop or in the professional setting.

The Energie Rinnovabili corpus is a 414,422-word corpus obtained using – again – keywords from Wikipedia as initial seeds. It was compiled by going through the same steps described for the creation of the English Renewable Energies corpus. In the process, many similarities between the two corpora emerged, especially concerning key-terms. These similarities were confirmed at the end of the process when word lists obtained from the two corpora using AntConc were compared. By way of example, Table 5.2 below reports the first 25 content words in each list (numbers to left and right refer to the position in the frequency list and to the number of occurrences respectively).

In Table 5.2 it is possible to notice that over half of the words in one list have their equivalent in the other list (e.g. *energy/energia*; *power/potenza*; *impianti/plants* and so on). Closer inspection of the complete lists in both languages confirms that they are fairly consistent with each other, even though equivalent words occupy different positions in the two lists, depending on their relative frequency and on grammar differences between the two languages (e.g. the English word *wind* corresponds to both *vento* [noun] and *eolico* [adjective] in Italian).

The similarity of the two word lists seems to foster a certain confidence in the comparability in content between the two corpora, suggesting that they could well be used as the basis for an exploration of phraseology in the two

Table 5.2. Sample from the wordlists extracted from the Renewable Energies and Energie Rinnovabili corpora

11	**energy**	2876	**11**	**energia**	3788
16	**power**	2167	**30**	**elettrica**	1309
26	**electricity**	1321	**32**	**impianti**	1256
28	**solar**	1220	**33**	**produzione**	1180
30	**renewable**	1108	**43**	fonti	937
33	**Energy**	903	**44**	**impianto**	888
34	**system**	896	**46**	**solare**	831
39	**wind**	765	**49**	**acqua**	799
40	capacity	747	**50**	**potenza**	791
41	**Generation**	747	**51**	**Rinnovabili**	774
42	**production**	738	**62**	Centrali	587
54	**PV**	640	**64**	**Sistema**	570
55	geothermal	625	**67**	**MW**	543
56	**systems**	619	**70**	nucleare	522
58	MW	598	**74**	calore	494
59	**cost**	590	**75**	centrale	479
62	Fuel	558	**76**	**gas**	478
63	**Plant**	542	**84**	**fotovoltaico**	440
69	**Power**	506	**88**	rete	434
70	**costs**	504	**93**	energetico	421
71	**gas**	498	**94**	vento	395
75	**water**	487	**97**	**prodotta**	393
77	**plants**	480	**99**	**sistemi**	387
85	development	428	**11**	**energetica**	382
			30	**costo**	370

languages, possibly leading to the creation of a specific glossary and/or phraseological dictionary. In this respect we can consider information retrieved about the English term *emissions* and the Italian *emissioni*. By exploring concordance lines for *emissions* in the English Renewable Energies corpus it is easy to notice typical patterns in which *emissions* is preceded by *carbon dioxide*, *CO_2*, *greenhouse gas*, *GHG* whereas *emissioni* in the Italian corpus is accompanied by the equivalent terms *anidride carbonica*, *CO_2*, *gas serra* (see Figure 5.13).

Similarly, an analysis of the collocational profile for such terms as *plants*, *photovoltaic/ PV*, *fuel*, *biomass* and their Italian equivalents *impianti*, *fotovoltaico/ FV*, *combustibile*, *biomasse* provides insight into typical collocations and patterns, highlighting similarities and differences in usage (see Figure 5.14).

hydroelectricity is beneficial to reduce carbon dioxide emissions , it causes other environmental impacts
power plants to offset their carbon dioxide emissions . </p><p> Those sorts of carbon credits -
wider range of plants and release fewer emissions than traditional biofuels like ethanol.
calls for a reduction in greenhouse gas emissions to prevent "dangerous anthropogenic interference
also recommended a tax on greenhouse gas emissions to promote research and fuels with low
manner would also reduce greenhouse gas emissions , he said. Fewer pollutants are released
reducing transportation-related greenhouse gas emissions . First round program allocations amounted
2022—enough to reduce U.S. greenhouse gas emissions equivalent to 20 coal-fired electricity
are fully implemented and the total EU GHG emissions in 1990 some additional measures are taken
newly announced plan to regulate hazardous emissions from coal-burning power plants: </p><p> "
futures and found a 30 per cent reduction in emissions by 2030 will add up to $40 billion in electricity
do not directly account for the indirect emissions of electricity and could create an incentive
and reduce the resulting pollution. Low emissions and environmentally friendly energy sources

ambientale positivo, rappresentato dalle evitate emissioni di anidride carbonica per l'utilizzo di
dell'Università degli Studi di Perugia(8) le emissioni di anidride carbonica di una centrale eolica
del mondo; sicura e completamente a zero emissioni di carbonio, può essere immagazzinata e
ibride, di automobili a benzina con basse emissioni di CO2, di GPL. Nell'attesa dell'idrogeno
ciclo di produzione ad impatto nullo sulle emissioni di CO2. Il motore Stirling può diventare
pari al 20% dei consumi e di tagliare le emissioni di CO2 di un eguale 20% entro il 2020 (
dell'ambiente • Come ridurre o compensare le emissioni di CO2 • Quali sono le procedure per accedere
eliminerebbero (se si esclude il gas naturale) le emissioni di CO2. Inoltre sviluppare queste soluzioni
problema del riscaldamento globale e delle emissioni di CO2: una definizione parallela di energie
metano.[21] L'obiettivo di minimizzare le emissioni di diossine contrasta in parte con il recupero
proiezioni al 2020 </p><p> b) riduzione delle emissioni di gas a effetto serra del 13 % rispetto
clamorosi: l'energia nucleare non solo produce emissioni di gas serra, ma esse sono superiori a
stabilisce tempi ed entità della riduzione delle emissioni di gas serra e individua esplicitamente
uso di nuove fonti • incentivareridurre le emissioni di metano dalle discariche di rifiuti e

Figure 5.13. *Concordances for* emissions *and* emission *from the Renewable Energies and Energie Rinnnovabili comparable corpora*

While apparently trivial, these examples show how the tools described made both the compilation of the two comparable corpora and their exploration feasible, even in the limited time span of a translation workshop or for a quick translation task. The corpora proved to be both a valuable source of information, contributing to a clearer understanding of contrasting lexicogrammar patterns in the specific domain under analysis, and a source of data to be exploited through long-term activities, such as the compilation of a bilingual glossary or phraseological dictionary. Some examples that illustrate the potential usage of the corpora for these purposes will be briefly commented on.

The information made available by the two corpora was used to find translation equivalents for the English *installed capacity* and for the Italian *impianto eolico*. For the English *installed capacity* (occurring 104 times in the English corpus) a translation with *capacità installata* seemed to be inappropriate, as suggested by the low number of occurrences (only 6) for

harvest maximum wind energy. A series of wind *farms* installed for supplying electricity
30,000 to $40,000 every year. Managers of wind *farms* in the U.S. earn between $70,000
produces electricity. Every year, more and more wind *farms* come to life. In fact, a lot of states
also affected. The best places to put up wind *farms* are those of high altitudes, onshore
Ireland.[65] These are some of the largest wind *farms* in the world, as of December 2011
industry-utility partnerships. The first wind *farms* in India were established in the
was centred on the demonstration effect of wind *farms* , which were supported largely by
due to the reactive power requirements of wind *farms* . The reactive power requirements
power producers. The incentive is limited to wind *farms* with a maximum aggregate installed
</p><p> I think we should keep putting up wind *farms* as fast as we can until we run out
want to investigate the CF of California wind *farms* and the environmental impact. </p>
changing weather patterns. When placed in high wind locations, wind *farms* can capture great
patterns. When placed in high wind locations, wind *farms* can capture great quantities of energy
changing weather patterns. When placed in high wind locations, wind *farms* can capture great
patterns. When placed in high wind locations, wind *farms* can capture great quantities of energy
he said. </p><p> From the sky </p><p> Turbine wind *farms* produce renewable electricity, which
said, citing the need for development of wind *farms* and transmission infrastructure. </p>
infrastructure. </p><p> Haynes proposes developing wind *farms* to not only provide energy for use
altitude sites, are preferred locations for wind *farms* . Typical capacity factors are 20
to the visual and other impacts of some wind *farms* , with local residents sometimes

Figure 5.14. *Concordances lines for* wind

this phrase in the Italian corpus. An analysis of the collocation profile for the lemma INSTALLARE revealed instead *potenza* as the first collocate in order of frequency, and an inspection of the concordance lines immediately revealed *potenza installata* (97 occurrences) as an appropriate translation equivalent. Similarly, in the search for a translation equivalent for *impianti eolici*, where the literal translation *wind plants* could find very scarce evidence in the corpus (only 3 occurrences), an investigation of the co-text of *wind* clearly suggested *farm* as the typical collocation in English (see Figure 5.14), pointing to *wind farm* as a translation equivalent for *impianto eolico*.

The examples provided are largely representative of the basic use of comparable corpora by translators and terminologists. Once again, however, what is being stressed here is not the role of corpora for translation or terminological purposes in itself, which is not new, but the fact that the information retrieved comes from comparable corpora created in a few minutes from the web, using tools and methods which exploit to the full the potential of the web as a virtually inexhaustible source for multilingual corpora *on demand*.

Conclusion

On the basis of the examples reported so far it can be argued that, despite some obvious limitations, BootCaT and WebBootCaT perform well for several tasks, especially when the time spent in creating the corpora and the immediate usefulness of the information that can be retrieved are considered. The data retrieved are mostly consistent and well-formed and the possibility for the linguist to interact with the system throughout the process greatly enhances the quality of the final results. Furthermore, as far as WebBootCaT in particular is concerned, the fact that the process of corpus compilation takes place on a remote server and that corpus data can be analysed both online, using the corpus query tool (Sketch Engine) installed on the same server, and offline, by downloading it on one's own computer, really makes WebBootCaT a useful example of how some aspects of corpus work have been changing under the impact of the web, bringing the exploitation of the web as a virtual multilingual corpus on demand a little closer to reality.

Study questions and activities

1 Discuss possible uses for small DIY web corpora (both monolingual and comparable). In which contexts do you think they might prove particularly useful? Why?

2 Describe the aim of a research project involving the creation of a specialized corpus. Provide an outline of the corpus (or corpora) involved in your project. What type(s) of texts would you include?

3 In this activity you will experience first-hand some aspects of corpus compilation.

- Decide a subject field/topic for a specialized corpus (e.g. sustainable tourism, geology, cultural anthropology).
- Carry out a web search to identify relevant and reliable texts to be included in your corpus engine. You can also decide to download text from one specific source or database (e.g. texts on tourism can be downloaded from the Travel section of newspapers like the *Guardian*, *The Times* or the *Independent*).
- Evaluate the results of each web search, and decide whether to include the resulting documents or not. Create a folder with subfolders to save the texts you choose both as a complete webpages and as text (.txt), keeping record of as many details as possible (at least file name and URL).
- See how much you can do in half an hour and make projections about how long would it take to compile a 100,000-word corpus.

4 Now reproduce the same task using BootCaT and consider similarities and differences in the approach.

- Go to http://bootcat.sslmit.unibo.it/ and download BootCaT front-end graphical interface. To run the program you might need a search API. You can obtain one from https://datamarket.azure.com/ following the guided procedure from the BootCaT front end.
- Select a topic/subject for your corpus. You can choose the same subject/topic of your manual DIY corpus. Possible projects are also suggested in Zanettin (2012) and include Cosmology, Retinopathy, the European Monetary Union.
- Launch BootCaT. From the Edit menu select Options, and specify a working directory in your computer where you will store the corpora. Then click on Next. Provide a name for the corpus, select a language, and type in the 'seeds' you have chosen for your subject/topic.
- Set parameters for Tuple length and Number tuples (e.g. if you input 3 for 'tuple length' and 10 for 'number of tuples' the system will retrieve only documents which contain at least 3 random combinations of the seed words, and will generate 10 queries at each run). Set the number of pages per query (e.g. 10), then click on Collect URLs. Once presented with the results, tick relevant links on the basis of the URL address, if this is sufficient, or by inspecting pages. Then click on 'Build the corpus'. The corpus will be automatically saved to your computer in a directory which includes the cleaned-up corpus (in .txt format), the seeds used to start the process, the tuples used as queries, and the URLs selected).

5 Finally you can familiarize with WebBootCaT through the Sketch Engine web site.

- Go to www.sketchengine.co.uk and register for a free one-month trial. Click on WebBootCaT and create a corpus following the guided procedure. You will be presented with steps similar to the ones of the stand-alone version. If necessary, watch the online tutorial 'Creating a corpus by crawling the internet using WebBootCaT' (http://www.youtube.com/watch?v=SOEkK3_VOBI)

6 Reflect on the exercises you have done. How did you select your seed terms? Have you tried to change seeds? How did changes affect the results? Which other criteria have you used? With what effect? Have you found duplicates or near-duplicates in the results? Which strategies have you used to enhance the relevance, reliability and representativeness of your corpus? How would you rate the resulting corpus in view of its possible uses?

Suggestions for further reading

Baroni, M. and Bernardini, S. (2004), 'BootCaT: Bootstrapping corpora and terms from the web', in *Proceedings of LREC 2004*. Lisbon: ELDA, 1313–1316. Available at http://sslmit.unibo.it/~baroni/publications/lrec2004/bootcat_lrec_2004.pdf [accessed 1 June 2013].

Bernardini, S. and Ferraresi, A. (2013). 'Old needs, new solutions. Comparable corpora for language professionals', in S. Sharoff, R. Rapp, P. Zweigenbaum and P. Fung (eds), *BUCC: Building and using comparable corpora.* Dordrecht: Springer.

Bernardini, S., Ferraresi A. and Gaspari, F. (2010), 'Institutional academic English in the European context: a web-as-corpus approach to comparing native and non-native language', in A. L. López and R. C. Jiménez, *English in the European Context*, Bern: Peter Lang.

Ferraresi, Adriano (2009), 'Google and beyond: web as corpus methodologies or translators', *Revista Tradumàtica* 7, http://webs2002.uab.es/tradumatica/revista/num7/articles/04/04.pdf [accessed 1 June 2013].

Zanettin, F. (2012), *Translation-Driven Corpora.* Manchester: St Jerome.

Notes

1 A bootstrap is a leather or fabric loop on the back or side of a boot to help pull it on. By extension bootstrap means 'self-reliant and self-sustaining: relying solely on somebody's own efforts and resources' and 'starting business from scratch: the building of a business from nothing, with minimum outside capital'. In information technology the word synonymous with start up procedure (MSN Encarta 2007: online).

2 This is the view espressed in the introduction to BUCC (Buliding and Using Comparable Corpora) Workshops, a series of events held annually since 2008 (see http://comparable.limsi.fr/bucc2013/bucc-workshop.html)

6

Sketches of Language and Culture from Large Web Corpora

Introduction

This chapter investigates and evaluates the scenario opened up in corpus linguistics by the possibility of creating and exploring large general purpose web corpora. The case studies reported show how some of the tools and data sets developed in the context of research on the web as corpus can be used to obtain not only information about language use, but also fresh insights into discourse and society. Sections 1 and 2 introduce large general purpose web corpora as a new 'object' possessing both web-derived and corpus-like features (Baroni and Bernardini 2006), with a specific focus on the two-billion-word corpus of English called ukWaC. Section 3 describes the Sketch Engine as a web-based corpus query tool through which a large number of general reference web corpora for many languages can be accessed and explored. Finally, Section 4 illustrates 'sketches' for the word *culture* from ukWaC. The data are discussed through comparison with evidence from the British National Corpus in order to describe similarities and differences between data from a web-derived corpus and more traditional resources.

1. From web as corpus to corpus as web: Introducing large general purpose web corpora

In the second chapter of the present book the most typical ways of understanding the phrase 'web as/for corpus' were introduced, following Baroni and Bernardini (2006). So far, two main aspects have been dealt with in detail.

The first is access to the web as a ready-made corpus, or 'web as corpus surrogate', either through ordinary search engines (Chapter 3) or through the use of pre/post processing tools which help the user obtain web search results in a format suitable for linguistic analysis (Chapter 4). The second is the use of software tools that transform the compilation of small DIY corpora from the web into a semi-automated task (Chapter 5), an approach also labelled as the 'web as corpus shop'. If we exclude attention to the web as a corpus 'proper' – i.e. using the web as a corpus representative of web language, which is not the focus of the present book – one more meaning of the phrase 'web as/for corpus' that still needs to be discussed is the category labelled as 'mega-corpus mini-web'. This category is, according to Baroni and Bernardini (2006: 13), 'the most radical way of understanding the expression Web-as-Corpus', and refers to the creation of 'a new object, a sort of mini-Web (or mega-corpus) adapted to language research'. The specific contribution of this new object to the web-as-corpus scenario is that it is characterized by both web-derived and corpus-derived features: 'Like the Web, it would be very large, (relatively) up-to-date, it would contain text material from crawled Web sites and it would provide a fast Web-based interface to access the data. Like a corpus, it would be annotated, it would allow sophisticated queries, and would be (relatively) stable' (Baroni and Bernardini 2006: 13–14).

By combining web- and corpus-like features, this new kind of corpus is meant to answer the widely felt need for resources that keep all the potential for size, variety and topicality offered by the web, while ensuring some of the standards (reliability, reproducibility, stability) of conventional corpora and allowing for analysis with more sophisticated corpus query tools than commercial search engines. To some extent, this represents the stage at which linguists have finally come to terms with the limitations of the web as a linguistic resource, but have come to view such limitations as a sort of 'necessary evil' to be addressed if one is determined to exploit to the full the otherwise enormous potential of the web. More specifically, it could be argued that some of the typical disadvantages of web corpora are accepted (e.g. reduced control over content; noise; imbalance; over-representation of some groups, such as younger speakers, males, techno-savvy people), assuming that none of these disadvantages are specific to web corpora *per se*. Rather, they are simply 'foregrounded' by such corpora, while they are in fact common to all 'large corpora built in a short time and with little resources', as suggested by Baroni and Ueyama (2006),

> If one collected a Web corpus of about 100M words spending the same amount of time and resources that were invested in the creation of the BNC, there is no reason to think that the resulting corpus would be less clean, its contents less controlled or its copyright status less clear than in

> the case of the BNC. Vice versa, collecting a 1 billion word multi-source corpus from non-Web sources in a few days is probably not possible, but, if it were possible, the resulting corpus would almost certainly have exactly the same problems of noise, control over the corpus contents and copyright that we listed above [...]. Thus, we would like to stress that it is not correct to refer to the problems above as 'problems of Web corpora'; rather, they are problems of large corpora built in a short time and with little resources, and they emerge clearly with Web corpora, since the Web makes it possible to build 'quick and dirty' large corpora. (Baroni and Ueyama 2006: 32)

Apart from the obvious advantages of size and timeliness, a fundamental advantage of the creation of large general purpose corpora from the web is that this has made available to the research community a good number of web corpora for many languages. Much work has indeed been done in the context of research on the web as corpus to create not only new resources for English, but also to create resources for languages for which no standard reference corpus, such as the BNC, was available before. Such languages, Baroni and Ueyama (2006) observed at the beginning of this exciting enterprise, do not simply include so-called 'minority languages', but also well-studied European languages, such as German, Italian or French. A good example is the collection of BNC-sized corpora (around 100M tokens) developed by Sharoff (2006), freely available as the Leeds Collection of Internet Corpora (http://corpus.leeds.ac.uk/internet.html). This collection currently provides corpora for English, Chinese, Finnish, Arabic, French, German, Greek, Italian, Japanese, Polish, Portuguese, Russian and Spanish, all to be queried via an online interface. These corpora were developed with a methodology based on the use of automated search engine queries – a large-scale version of the procedure described in the previous chapter – which has become a standard in this context. The approach is similar to the one any ordinary user could experience first-hand using BootCaT, and indeed the tools used to create these corpora include customized versions of BootCaT itself, as reported both in Sharoff (2006) and in the Leeds Collection of Internet Corpora website.

As the screenshot in Figure 6.1 suggests, with the Leeds Collection of Internet Corpora we are really seeing a serious attempt to exploit the potential of the web as a multilingual reference corpus without renouncing typical standards of corpus research. All the corpora are POS-tagged and collocates can be ranked with reference to typical statistics for the computation of collocates (see Chapter 1) such as MI-score, *t*-score and Log-likelihood.

A similar approach is behind WebCorp Linguist's Search Engine, developed by the same research team that developed WebCorp (see Chapter 4). The

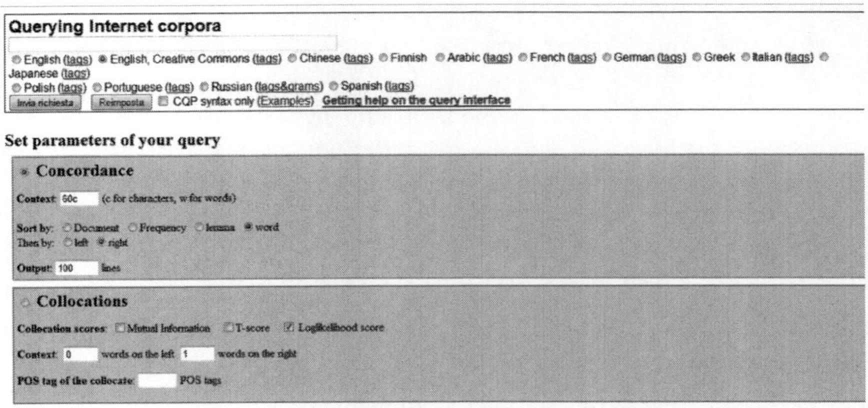

Figure 6.1. *Leeds Collection of Internet Corpora query interface (Source: http:// corpus.leeds.ac.uk/internet.html)*

project has made available to the research community three large corpora of English, all built by crawling the web, which allow for sophisticated queries, including pattern matching, wildcards and parts-of-speech. The corpora support post-search analyses, including time series, collocation tables, sorting and summaries of meta-data from the matched web pages. Further examples and a comprehensive introduction to the main issues relating to 'web corpus construction' are provided in a study by Schäfer and Bildhauer (2013).

The most representative example of the category is perhaps the collection of corpora compiled in the context of the WaCky project (Web as Corpus Kool Ynitiative). These corpora represent the 'mega-corpus mini-web' category and include corpora for English, Italian, German and French. Among these, ukWaC will be described in more detail in the following pages.

More recently, new projects have been launched in the same line, with the aim of producing larger and larger resources. One is the so-called 'TenTen' collection, whose name designates the target size of the corpora, which is set at 10^{10} (10 billion) words (Jakubíček et al. 2013). The corpora developed so far include zhTenTen (Chinese, Simplified), enTenTen (English), deTenTen (German), itTenTen (Italian), noTenTen (Norwegian), ptTenTen (Portuguese), skTenTen (Slovak), esTenTen (Spanish), esAmTenTen (American Spanish), arTenTen (Arabic), czTenTen2 (Czech), frTenTen (French), jpTenTen (Japanese), and ruTenTen (Russian). The development of these corpora can be tracked on the Sketch Engine website.

Finally it is important to mention the development of a large Corpus of Global Web-Based English (GloWbE) by Mark Davies (2013) at Brigham Young University. The corpus is composed of 1.9 billion words from 340,000 websites in 20 different English-speaking countries and was released in April 2013.

2. Mega-corpus, mini-web: The case of ukWaC

Among the large web corpora for English created using the 'mega-corpus mini-web' approach, ukWaC, a two-billion-word corpus of English developed between 2005 and 2007 as part of the WaCky project, deserves particular attention. The aim of the WaCky collection was to offer new corpus resources characterized by a compromise between a very large size and thorough post-processing for linguistic purposes. Ideally, these resources were to be similar to traditional general language reference corpora, containing a wide range of text types and topics, which means that they were to include both pre-web texts of a varied nature (like recipes, short stories, transcripts of spoken texts) and texts representing more typical web genres, like personal pages, blogs, or postings in forums (Baroni et al. 2009: 212).

As can be easily imagined, a crucial aspect in this approach to the web as corpus is the necessity to dispense with commercial search engines and perform an autonomous crawl of the web, which obviously requires considerable computational skills and resources. Following this, there is the equally fundamental problem of cleaning the data produced by the crawl (removing undesired pages, discarding duplicates, removing mark-up language and other features typically associated with web documents). Finally, the resulting corpus being a very large one, the data need to be annotated so as to allow for analysis with specific corpus query tools. The basic steps involved in the compilation (and evaluation) of these large general purpose corpora from the web via automated crawling are described in Sharoff (2006), Baroni and Kilgarriff (2006) and – as far as ukWaC in particular is concerned – in Ferraresi (2007), Baroni et al. (2009) and Jakubíček et al. (2013). The process of web corpus construction can be seen as being divided into different phases. The first phase concerns the selection of 'seeds' or 'seed URLs' to start the web crawling, followed by post-crawl cleaning of the data, removal of duplicates and near-duplicates, and annotation of the resulting corpus.

2.1 *Selecting 'seed URLs' and crawling*

The compilation of a large general corpus requires a number of pre-selected URLs (or crawl seeds) from which to start, using a procedure not dissimilar in principle to the one described in the previous chapter for the semi-automated compilation of DIY corpora from the web. As for ukWaC, the first step consisted in identifying different sets of seed URLs to ensure variety in terms of content and genre (Baroni et al. 2009). This is the step most closely related to problems of representativeness. Here, the fact that the question of representativeness is far from being settled further complicates matters on both a practical and theoretical level. On the one hand, it seems that for web corpora the problem of representativeness can only be addressed on applicative grounds, trying to devise methods for crawling web pages that loosely correspond to certain criteria (e.g. crawling pages only from a specific regional domain, like .uk, or only from academic or government sites, like .ac.uk or .gov.uk and so on). On the other hand, no detailed design of the corpus is really possible and in this context *post-hoc* methods to evaluate the composition of corpora have emerged as crucial new concerns (Baroni and Ueyama 2006: 32; Ferraresi 2007: 43; Sharoff 2007; Jakubíček 2007: 85–109), to complement the notion of design based on the definition of *a priori* criteria, which was of paramount importance for traditional corpora. Accordingly, the totalizing concept of representativeness is addressed – and to some extent replaced – through the related (and relative) concepts of 'balance' and 'unbiasedness' (Kilgarriff and Grefenstette 2003; Ciaramita and Baroni 2006).

To perform the crawling for the creation of ukWaC, random pairs of selected content words were submitted to a search engine. The developers explain their option for bigrams, i.e. sets of two words, by the fact that single-word queries tend to yield potentially undesirable documents (e.g. dictionary definitions, or the top pages of companies with the relevant word in their name), whereas more than two words might tend to retrieve pages with lists of words, rather than connected text. Also crucial was the strategy adopted to ensure variety in terms of content and genre. Drawing from research on the effects of seed selection upon the resulting web corpus (Ueyama 2006), it was found that using seed words sampled from traditional written sources, such as newspapers, or from existing reference corpus material tended to yield 'public sphere' documents, such as academic and journalistic texts addressing socio-political issues and the like, whereas queries with words sampled from a basic vocabulary list, such as a learner's dictionary, tended to produce corpora featuring 'personal interest' pages, like blogs or bulletin boards. Since it was desirable that ukWaC contained both kinds of documents, relevant sources were chosen accordingly. As Ferraresi (2007) explains, the BNC was used as a primary source, from which 2000 mid-frequency content words were picked and paired randomly before being submitted as queries to a search engine. Two other lists of tuples were then taken from the demographically sampled spoken section of the BNC (namely the section containing samples from informal conversation, rich in basic vocabulary) and from a vocabulary list for learners of English as a foreign language, containing more formal or even academic words. By way of example, the table in Figure 6.2 reports a sample of the seeds used, taken from Ferraresi (2007: 35).

The crawl was limited to pages in the .uk domain, as a simple heuristic device to retrieve the largest possible number of pages supposedly representative of

BNC SEEDS	BNC DEMOGRAPHIC SEEDS	ESL SEEDS
aspects file	cooking ground	populate fist
sensitive presumably	cool police	statewide pliant
pilot consumption	general damn	reasonable frustrated
radio lots	smaller leaving	abhor colorful
johnson reduce	keen bedroom	snow visage
acceptable self	houses otherwise	attach elevator
guidance williams	thrown carrots	petal phlegmatic
yorkshire leaves	tapes double	sniff chum
session desk	chip fairly	ankle tabloid
beer scale	certain happy	lieutenant overhand
surprised raise	young given	secretarial validity
arranged eventually	beer pieces	prom overcame
dependent regulations	sink massive	deprived overhaul
gain silence	living council	ad-lib scraps
everywhere sentence	gate stuart	incompetent fanciful
ireland phase	shame shower	integral feat
ancient definition	particular poor	jargon incidentally
carefully discipline	joking bags	foible whole-wheat
bell frame	doubt prices	aerospace gender
thousands contemporary	months salad	dynamo thermos

Figure 6.2. *Randomly selected bigrams used as seeds for the crawl in the compilation of ukWaC (Source: Ferraresi 2007)*

language use in the United Kingdom, and excluded non-HTML data, i.e. web pages containing files in such formats as PDF, .jpg, etc.

2.2 Post-crawl cleaning and annotation

Once the crawl is over, the linguist is presented with a vast set of HTML documents which have to be post-processed and cleaned before being converted into a linguistic corpus. Aspects of clean-up have been already dealt with in Chapter 4 with reference to the WebCorp Linguist's Search Engine. In the case of ukWaC, the first step entailed identifying and discarding potentially irrelevant documents on the basis of size, i.e. both small documents (below 5kB) and large documents (over 200kB). These files were removed on the assumption that they tend to contain little genuine text (Fletcher 2004). Then, removal of duplicates was performed. In this phase, not only the duplicates of a given document are removed, but also the document itself, since it is an overt policy in the compilation of web corpora to privilege precision over recall – a strategy which can be adopted owing to the vastness of the web (Baroni and Kilgarriff 2006). In the case of ukWaC, besides removing documents with their duplicates, which were rather easy to identify, the cleaning process also included removal of near-duplicates, i.e. documents that differed only in minor details, such as a date or a header.

After this phase, the 'noise' of non-linguistic material was removed from the documents. This generally means separating genuine language text from HTML code and from the so-called boilerplate, i.e. all the linguistically uninteresting material, such as navigation information, copyright notices, advertisements, link lists, fixed notices and other sections lacking in human-produced connected text (Baroni and Kilgarriff 2006). As pointed out by Baroni and Bernardini (2006: 20), it is highly unlikely that one wants the bigram *click here* to come up as the most frequent bigram in a corpus of English, unless the aim of the corpus is precisely the study of the linguistic characteristics of webpages *per se*.

The last step is to filter the data for pornography. The importance of removing pages containing pornography is generally acknowledged and stressed not 'out of prudery', as Baroni and Kilgarriff (2006: 88) argue, but because these pages tend to contain low-quality, randomly generated text and other linguistically problematic elements like long keyword lists.

Finally the corpus needs to undergo lemmatization and part-of-speech (POS) annotation. Given the size of ukWaC and similar large web corpora, this task has to be performed through automated machine-learning techniques. In the case of ukWaC, POS tagging was performed with the widely used TreeTagger.

Using the procedure described above, a good number of very large general purpose corpora from the web were compiled in a relatively short time. While in many respects these corpora share some of the limitations of web corpora, they also display key characteristics of traditional corpora, such as an attempt at being based on some sort of design, and finite – though enormous – size.

A direct consequence of size has been the creation of adequate tools for all linguists to access and query such corpora. Not all linguists can be expected to have the necessary technical skills to manage huge amounts of data, and the risk was envisaged that the corpora could remain inaccessible to novice or non-technical users. Furthermore, the compilers were constrained by copyright problems from publicly distributing the corpora for offline analysis. This suggested the opportunity of adopting a user-friendly web interface allowing users to do actual research on the corpora, while allowing the compilers to make the corpus available through their servers (Baroni and Kilgarriff 2006: 89). Significantly, this is one of the key features which most obviously connects with web search as the major paradigm underlying all web-as-corpus tools and approaches. As Baroni and Bernardini (2006: 37) state,

> The enormous popularity that Google enjoys among linguists can only in part be explained by the fact that it makes an unprecedented amount of

> language data available. We believe that an equally important role is played by the fact that Google search is easy to use and can be accessed through a familiar user interface, presents results in a clear and tidy way, and that no installation procedure is necessary.

In other words, the new corpora obtained by web crawling could only reach a wider community if integrated with a similar user-friendly 'intuitive and familiar' interface; the corpus tools specifically designed for such large web corpora had to make corpus search more similar to web search. As the developers themselves would argue, 'we should not only use the Web as a corpus, but also present the corpus as Web, i.e. provide access to Web corpora in the style of a Web search engine' (Baroni and Bernardini 2006: 37). It is perhaps worth emphasizing that the authors are not simply advocating the development of new corpus tools, but are clearly indicating a shift in user expectations, as a consequence of a growing and widespread familiarity with ordinary web search. This seems to point to a metamorphosis in our way of conceiving corpora and corpus tools under the impact of the web, which in turn brings about interesting changes as far as the basic activities of accessing, distributing and querying corpora are concerned. Some of these changes will be described in the following pages.

3. Exploring large web corpora: Tools and resources

The compilation of web corpora by semi-automated crawling has not only turned the ideal concept of a hybrid object, combining web-derived and corpus-like features, into a reality, but has also triggered research on novel ways to access and retrieve corpus data. The typical scenario where the linguist 'downloads the corpus to his machine, installs a program to analyse it, then tweaks the program and/or the corpus mark-up to get the program and the corpus to work together, and finally performs the analysis' (Wynne 2002: 1205) seems to coexist with – or seems to be increasingly replaced by – a new model based on a 'distributed architecture' in which the researcher works from any computer on data and query tools located on a remote server, so that it becomes redundant to replicate the digital data (the corpus) in a local copy and to install a local copy of the software, since all the processing can be done directly online. In this new context, corpora and corpus tools have undergone a process of transformation that seems to be related to similar changes taking place in society at large as far as the distribution of goods and resources, including linguistic resources, are concerned. While corpora like the BNC or tools such as the Wordsmith Tools could be considered as finite 'products' in a conventional way, in the sense that they are goods reproduced in multiple copies which can be sold and purchased, this is no longer the case with some of the recently compiled large web corpora and web-based corpus query tools, for which it would be more correct to talk about 'services' (Kilgarriff 2010).

This changing scenario is evident in the so-called fourth generation concordancers (McEnery and Hardie 2012) which display the tendency to make traditional corpora available and searchable through online interfaces (see Chapters 1 and 2), as is the case of the corpora distributed and accessed through Mark Davies' website (Davies 2005) or the BNCWeb (Hoffman 2008). What all these services have in common is that they all provide telling examples of a different way of conceiving the basic activities of accessing, distributing and querying corpora. Corpus analysis can now be performed using a web-based corpus query tool, which often contributes to the exploration of concordance lines by supporting complex queries and providing sophisticated statistics related to collocational profiles, clusters, and the phraseological patterns in which each word in the corpus participates. In this scenario, a particularly interesting example of the changing face of corpus linguistics, especially as far as very large corpora are concerned, is the Sketch Engine.

3.1 The Sketch Engine: From concordance lines to word sketches

As corpora become larger, they require more sophisticated corpus query tools, capable of assisting the linguist in interpreting the data. In the new context in which corpus research involves investigating a huge amount of data, even the basic act of reading, interpreting and drawing conclusions from concordance lines can become a problem. However refined and detailed, mere concordancing and statistics related to collocates, clusters or patterns may no longer be enough when dealing with corpora where words can have thousands of occurrences, and the plethora of data with which the linguist is likely to work runs the risk of becoming overwhelming. In this respect, a significant improvement in the analysis of corpus data is represented by the possibility of supporting the linguist's investigation with a tool providing synthetic statistics related to the lexical and grammatical relations in which each word in the corpus participates, as offered by the Sketch Engine.

The Sketch Engine works on a number of pre-loaded POS-tagged corpora for several languages, including the BNC, ukWaC, the British Academic Spoken English Corpus (BASE), the British Academic Written English Corpus

(BAWE), along with a large number of other corpora, for over 40 languages. It also provides access to parallel corpora, such as the EUROPARL 5 and OPUS parallel corpora, and new utilities have recently been implemented that allow users to upload their own monolingual, comparable and parallel corpora. As the table shows (see Figure 6.3), the first step for the user is therefore to select one of the many corpora made available by the service.

Corpora

Corpus name	Language	Tokens	Words
British National Corpus	English	112,181,015	96,048,950
Brown	English	1,175,675	1,007,299
enTenTen08	English	3,268,798,627	2,759,340,513
EUROPARL5, English-Italian	English	45,856,570	40,885,291
ukWaC	English	1,565,274,190	1,318,612,719
frWaC v1.0 old	French	1,628,667,738	1,330,564,200
deWaC	German	1,627,169,557	1,348,188,416
itWaC	Italian	1,909,535,703	1,591,491,087

Show less corpora

Corpus name	Language	Tokens	Words
Arabic web corpus	Arabic	174,239,600	407,005
arTenTen	Arabic	6,637,387,738	5,794,161,583
CHILDES Afrikaans Corpus	Arabic	33,134	26,020
BengaliWaC	Bengali	13,719,158	11,761,881
BulgarianNC	Bulgarian	26,518,884	20,974,953
BulgarianNC2 nonweb	Bulgarian	27,721,533	22,398,409
BulgarianNC2 web	Bulgarian	545,637,740	419,509,472
BulgarianNC2 web 10M	Bulgarian	9,478,549	7,693,929
CHILDES Catalan Corpus	Catalan	277,816	209,525
Chinese GigaWord 2 Corpus: Mainland, simplified	Chinese, Simplified	250,124,230	205,031,379
Internet-ZH	Chinese, Simplified	277,931,664	198,205,344
zhTenTen	Chinese, Simplified	2,106,661,021	1,729,867,455
zhTenTen (10M)	Chinese, Simplified	11,028,308	9,012,125

Figure 6.3. *Corpora available from the Sketch Engine user interface (sample)*

As with any other corpus query tool, the main task performed by the Sketch Engine is to report word lists and provide concordances in a clear KWiC format. The tool also features a number of buttons to allow further exploration, such as 'Sample', 'Sort', 'Filter' and 'Collocation', and the advanced options of 'Word Sketch' and 'Sketch Difference'.

The 'Concordance' button immediately displays concordance lines for any word in the corpus, also – if required – limited to a specific word class. In Figure 6.4 below we can see the concordance lines produced from ukWaC for the noun *risk*.

maintained that detention places Begum at	risk	of self-harm and suicide. The Immigration
are doing it but it puts them at further	risk	. Begum's supporters are very worried about
condition. If this happens she will be at	risk	of self harm and suicide. Begum recently
should be considered as part of an overall	risk	assessment. Compliance with any guidance
the major online DVD rental sites offering	risk	free trials in the UK. Read our opinions
at most. DVD Rental Trials They all have	risk	free DVD rental trials! Pick from the rental
off-site pages or other sites is at your own	risk	. General Provisions Pinocchio's of Comrie
a labelled format statement reduces the	risk	of introducing inconsistencies between
war on terror have made us all more at	risk	of terrorist attack. Iraqi civilians face
I am very very short sighted and at high	risk	of retinal detachment. Two years ago i
observations of CMEs in the inner heliosphere	Risk	There is a possibility of a launch delay
snake can be captured and/or killed without	risk	of anyone else being bitten, take it to
and Confused, Don't Look Now and at the	risk	of destroying any hint of credibility
financial support for groups at particular	risk	of poverty, such as child benefit and the
together. To be able to deploy this at minimum	risk	"Rapid Application Development" techniques
that you are taking also increases your	risk	of developing cancers. Testicular cancer
to Japan and Korea in the Far East. The	risk	of infection is greatest in long term visitors
long term visitors to rural areas, and the	risk	to short term visitors and visitors to
workers, farmers, etc. are potentially at	risk	of infection by contact with the infected
the disease is endemic you can reduce the	risk	of becoming infected with the virus by

Figure 6.4. *Concordance lines for* risk *(noun) from ukWaC*

Using the 'Collocation' button the system generates a list of collocates for the node word, which can be sorted according to different statistics, such as Raw Frequency, MI-Score, *t*-Score and logDice.

Collocation candidates

Page 1 Go Next >

	Freq	T-score	MI	logDice
p/n assessment	13684	116.768	9.118	10.132
p/n reduce	8033	89.407	8.673	9.486
p/n factors	7336	85.469	8.880	9.466
p/n management	11665	107.483	7.694	9.294
p/n increased	6792	82.138	8.223	9.167
p/n cancer	5415	73.402	8.635	9.084
p/n disease	5749	75.545	8.094	8.969
p/n assessments	3757	61.227	9.837	8.864
p/n risk	5879	76.204	7.349	8.663
p/n high	8610	91.972	6.826	8.578
p/n developing	4031	63.088	7.304	8.348
p/n heart	3827	61.401	7.066	8.203
p/n minimise	2180	46.627	9.530	8.122
p/n factor	2557	50.372	8.017	8.115
p/n increase	3843	61.447	6.831	8.097
p/n infection	2247	47.272	8.500	8.049
p/n associated	3099	55.261	7.094	8.036
p/n health	5474	73.015	6.251	7.978
p/n greater	2921	53.593	6.896	7.906
p/n increases	2107	45.733	8.086	7.904
p/n injury	2148	46.123	7.696	7.848

Figure 6.5. *Collocates of* risk *(noun) from ukWaC*

For each collocate the system also allows immediate visualization of recurring patterns. By way of example, Figure 6.6 shows patterns for the collocation *risk* (noun) + *associated* from ukWaC.

) were significantly *associated* with the	risk	of developing PAD. The association between
baseline were *associated* with an increased	risk	(95% confidence interval) of myocardial
non-significant RR 1.06 (0.91, 1.23). The	risk	of disease *associated* with raised lipoprotein
pressure, were *associated* with an increased	risk	of femoral plaque, independent of age and
were significantly *associated* with lower	risk	. In conclusion, therefore, atherosclerotic
there is now increasing interest in the	risk	factors *associated* with abnormal fat distribution
E. and Mech, L. D. (1991) Wolf predation	risk	*associated* with white-tailed deer movements
upfront capital outlay plus the *associated*	risk	. It is initially most prevalent in HR and
used, in particular the uncertainty and	risk	*associated* with predictions, is essential
partnerships that eventually fail are at	risk	of being most strongly *associated* with
alone are not *associated* with a diminished	risk	of dementia and that the more mentally
appeared to be *associated* with a reduced	risk	of developing dementia? Dr Vergehese offered
products are also *associated* with increased	risk	of TD. In the UK, we drink water straight
by women is *associated* with an increased	risk	of harm (Royal College of Psychiatrists
associated with a considerably increased	risk	of harm. The government has recently made
risk reduction/harm minimisation advice	risk	*associated* with providing services in the
Background-Physical activity is *associated* with lower	risk	of cardiovascular disease, but the mechanisms
stimulant drugs is *associated* with: injecting	risk	behaviours for blood-borne diseases (Hunter
discovery of variants *associated* with increased	risk	in prostate cancer in four separate populations
information exists about the overall health	risk	*associated* with silicone gel breast implants

Figure 6.6. *Pattern for the collocates* risk *(noun)* + associated *from ukWaC*

Information about the source-text of a particular concordance line can be obtained by clicking the document-id code at the left-hand end of the relevant line, even though – it is important to stress – the volatility of the internet often makes it difficult to retrieve the original page. In any case, the text can be inspected in its entirety by expanding the co-text for the node word, as in Figure 6.7 below.

exposure of yourself?" ' "There is little	risk	," said Tyrrel. "You can bear witness of
effective way of trying something out without	risk	of corrupting anything else in memory.
impossible unless we are willing to accept some	risk	of this kind. But if those who market the
of their time and energy and running the	risk	of death. That, say the Zahavis in The
were it not, it would lose face and be at	risk	of a coup d'état . In short, 'conspicuous
wayside because people are scared to take a	risk	buying something new and different when
20, and at £20 you're prepared to take a	risk	and buy a film that you've heard is good
gives some theory-making a bad name. The	risk	of selectively borrowing pieces of theories
parliamentary scrutiny. That cannot make sense. No	risk	is posed to national security by allowing
will not accept any amendment that would	risk	reducing the protection. Let us consider
epidemiology as well as evaluation design,	risk	assessment, health protection and health
seat in the House of Commons. To avoid the	risk	of an uprising in Ireland, the British
, nervous travellers had also to run the	risk	of encountering The Hound of Hell - for
a pump is operating: a. Overloading. One	risk	of overloading is the danger of excess
displacement pump. Excess speed also runs a	risk	of damage from cavitation. c. Cavitation
provide Granger's team with project planning,	risk	analysis and management, cost modelling
revenue concerned. There is also a very high	risk	of avoidance where the person or body running
also recognise that if there is a serious	risk	that it would become a substitute for

expand
matters of public expenditure within that building, such as tenders for furniture and services, maintenance costs, and the number of people on full-time contracts, are outwith parliamentary scrutiny. That cannot make sense. No *risk* is posed to national security by allowing a degree of scrutiny of innocuous matters--scrutiny that is carefully controlled through a prejudice test that would filter out questions that might prejudice our security, which is something that no Member of
expand

Figure 6.7. *Concordance lines for* risk *expanded*

Besides producing concordances and providing information on the collocational profile of a word, in a way not dissimilar from other typical corpus tools, the Sketch Engine also supports more complex queries formulated using regular expressions. So a search for the sequence verb + indefinite article + adjective + *risk* could be expressed as in Figure 6.8 below.

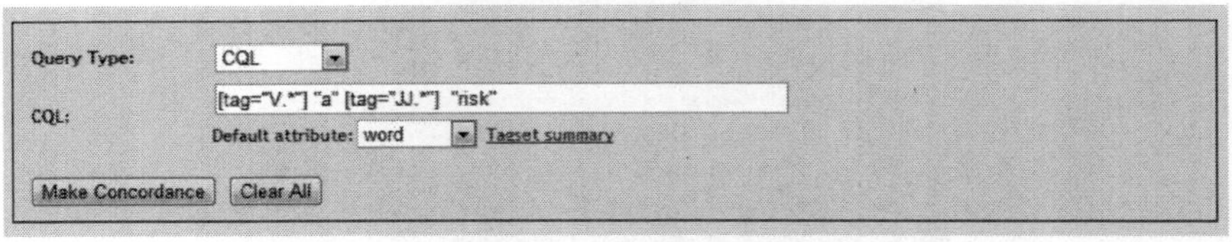

Figure 6.8. *A Sketch Engine query using regular expressions*

This query retrieves all the examples of *risk* being preceded by the sequence verb + indefinite article + adjective, as shown in Figure 6.9.

management, we must also recognise that it there	is a serious risk	that it would become a substitute for,
Write anything less than ecstatic and there	's a slight risk	you might turn a good friend into an enemy
are worsened by illicit drug use, there	is a potential risk	to the safety of staff, other patients
to the unborn child. However, where there	is a significant risk	of exposure (e.g. yellow fever) the need
Psychologically, he may then be prepared to	take a bigger risk	in passing you than he would if he thought
block aggressively, or no 2 is going to	take a terrible risk	) then hang back a little and defend your
regulations restricting a practice if there	is a reasonable risk	that harm would be done otherwise. References
open to inspection and review so that there	is a greater risk	of them contravening the duty to promote
freedoms. But this lack of structure also	brings a high risk	of wasting time, especially for the less
tripped up by bad luck" - Bowker realises he's	taking a huge risk	with Blackpool. Not only does it dip its
scheme Factors of interest Hypertension	is a major risk	factor for stroke and ischaemic heart disease
E. Owen MSS. 7266-7. 49 Clearly Rowlands	was a bad risk	, for see Wilkins' evidence to bank of England
was fined £15,000. A company who failed to	provide a detailed risk	assessment was criticised for failing to
fingerscans. The wireless travel ID plan	contains a significant risk	of unauthorized access. Although DHS states
concluded that, in this respect, Bt11 "does not	present a greater risk	to human health or the environment than
director Antonio Maria Costa says: "There	is a palpable risk	that Afghanistan will again turn into a
/04/2006: Blue Loon 20/04/2006: Hospital	is a financial risk	to NHS 14/04/2006: Links 13/04/2006: Body
that liability for economic damage will	create a financial risk	that some German universities, research
participants to different interventions. There	is a greater risk	of selection bias in quasi-random trials
data support the view that GM soya does not	represent a significant risk	to human health through gene transfer,"

Figure 6.9. *Concordance lines for the sequence verb + indefinite article + adjective* + risk

Besides offering the same service as an ordinary concordancer, the Sketch Engine is specifically designed to offer the linguist 'word sketches', i.e. 'one-page automatic, corpus-based summaries of a word's grammatical and collocational behaviour' (Kilgarriff et al. 2004). More precisely, a word sketch reports a list of collocates for each grammatical pattern so that, for each collocate, the user can see the corpus contexts in which the node word and its collocate co-occur. By way of example, Figure 6.10 reports a sample from the word sketch for the noun *nature* from ukWaC.

nature *(noun)* ukWaC freq = 217685 (139.1 per million)

object_of	42982	1.7	subject_of	16077	1.1	adj_subject_of	2773	1.3	modifier	76661	1.4	modifies	20001	0.4
understand	2012	7.66	endow	46	6.19	unaided	8	5.9	very	3360	9.27	reserve	4924	10.75
reflect	1054	7.32	reclaim	59	6.19	incapable	10	4.81	human	5087	8.8	conservation	2102	9.46
change	2302	7.22	inspire	148	6.01	cruel	13	4.74	exact	755	7.78	trail	1010	8.83
explore	768	6.89	abhor	31	5.89	unpredictable	10	4.67	true	1986	7.73	lover	481	8.02
emphasise	278	6.83	dictate	56	5.78	uniform	12	4.6	divine	596	7.65	walk	272	5.98
examine	559	6.73	trail	40	5.75	prone	10	4.31	precise	542	7.35	designation	50	5.63
determine	621	6.71	intend	103	5.01	susceptible	9	4.29	sensitive	490	6.85	conservationist	34	5.59
explain	587	6.54	complicate	28	4.77	infinite	9	4.22	dynamic	444	6.82	photography	78	5.17
misunderstand	126	6.39	constrain	24	4.75	conservative	10	4.0	sinful	270	6.77	extent	113	5.09
clarify	162	6.3	determine	134	4.71	inherent	10	3.99	confidential	325	6.69	conservancy	20	4.99
reveal	395	6.23	arise	69	4.5	subjective	8	3.94	interdisciplinary	255	6.56	ramble	21	4.98
investigate	319	6.07	tend	53	4.46	capable	29	3.7	complex	606	6.49	spirit	156	4.89
highlight	292	6.03	conspire	12	4.46	unknown	17	3.47	diverse	388	6.48	importance	152	4.84
illustrate	233	5.95	preserve	48	4.46	superior	10	3.28	sexual	283	6.17	enthusiast	43	4.71
stress	141	5.94	influence	65	4.25	evident	11	3.12	spiritual	296	6.11	scope	61	4.58
alter	182	5.94	compound	13	4.18	distinct	10	2.84	general	744	6.03	documentary	37	4.57
concern	480	5.89	walk	91	4.09	beneficial	8	2.76	cyclical	151	5.96	photographer	45	4.55
appreciate	208	5.89	fortify	11	4.05	dangerous	16	2.73	fundamental	266	5.95	hike	20	4.52
grasp	100	5.81	bestow	10	3.96	weak	10	2.52	second	832	5.89	warden	24	4.51
describe	516	5.73	decree	8	3.88	dependent	9	2.35	unpredictable	157	5.89	sanctuary	22	4.45
question	134	5.73	compel	10	3.87	wonderful	16	2.34	journal	352	5.88	park	149	4.35
transform	144	5.71	exacerbate	11	3.83	unlikely	11	2.34	dual	178	5.86	detective	22	4.35
emphasize	87	5.68	fascinate	10	3.82	rare	13	2.23	serious	425	5.83	watching	16	4.32
indicate	297	5.66	abound	9	3.73	likely	45	2.19	technical	386	5.8	diary	40	4.18
recognise	335	5.65	obey	11	3.71	sensitive	9	2.18	essential	420	5.72	Struct	11	4.16

Figure 6.10. *A sample from the word sketch for* nature

As the table makes clear at a glance, *nature* occurs 273,784 times in ukWaC. The sketch reported by the Sketch Engine shows that the word tends to occur as the object of verbs of mental process, such as *understand, reflect, explore, examine, reveal, investigate* (see the 'object of' pattern in the 1st column), which seem to point to a high level of abstraction for the meaning of the word *nature*. The pattern labelled as 'modifier' (4th column) in the 'sketch' is characterized by such adjectives as *human, true, divine*, all pointing to the spiritual/philosophical meaning of the word *nature*. Collocates which point instead to a meaning of the word connected with the idea of landscape are those in which *nature* pre-modifies such words as *reserve, protection, trail, walk* (5th column), thus resulting in such patterns as *nature reserve* (apparently the most frequent collocation) or *nature trail, nature lover*, etc. As discussed elsewhere (Gatto 2009: 145–9), a comparison of the word sketch for *nature* in English with the sketch for *natura* in the Italian itWaC corpus was enough to provide an explanation of important differences in the use of these two apparently equivalent words in the two languages, which seem to be deeply rooted in cultural differences (Manca 2004).

It is also important to notice that the software can also check which words occur with the same collocates as other words, and generates a 'distributional thesaurus' on the basis of these data. (Sketch Engine Help), i.e. an automatically produced 'thesaurus' which finds words that tend to occur in similar contexts as the target word. By way of example, one can see how the 'abstract' profile so far discussed for *nature* is confirmed by the list of candidate synonyms for *nature* retrieved with the Thesaurus function, which includes such abstract nouns as aspect, kind, concept, etc.

nature *(noun)* ukWaC freq = 217685 (139.1 per million)

Lemma	Score	Freq
aspect	0.467	206464
kind	0.421	244923
concept	0.403	135228
history	0.4	438898
structure	0.399	238867
character	0.398	227178
form	0.391	589563
quality	0.382	412213
element	0.378	188709
understanding	0.377	165540
knowledge	0.374	276273
culture	0.372	164112
sense	0.37	214518
power	0.369	403968
development	0.369	699563
idea	0.368	411451
experience	0.367	531602
principle	0.366	158836
type	0.362	409884
context	0.362	145903
reality	0.36	102708
state	0.36	354855
fact	0.36	405897
value	0.355	407202
process	0.355	527541
effect	0.354	389099
situation	0.353	214341
relationship	0.352	225868
pattern	0.35	122187
theory	0.35	154248

Figure 6.11. *Candidate synonyms for* nature *computed with Thesaurus (sample)*

In the case of Word Sketches the information provided by the system is therefore different from information obtained from any ordinary concordancer. A system that can provide such a summary of a word's behaviour is an appropriate answer not only to the need for processing large amounts of data, as in the case of large web corpora, but also matches the desire to exploit the inclusiveness, variety and accessibility of web data, without renouncing high standards of linguistic investigation. Furthermore, the very fact that both the corpus query tool and the corpora made available for analysis are offered as an integrated web-based service seems to make the Sketch Engine a good example of what it might mean to present the corpus as web, rather than simply using the web as a corpus.

3.2 The Sketch Difference function

Besides producing word sketches for individual words, the Sketch Engine has a specific function to compare sketches for two words. The patterns and combinations shared by the two items are highlighted, while patterns and combinations typical of one or the other are contrasted. Figure 6.12 reports a comparison between *scenery* and *landscape* from ukWaC.

Common patterns

landscape	6.0	4.0	2.0	0	-2.0	-4.0	-6.0	scenery

object_of	15012	3849	1.7	1.4
admire	24	178	4.6	8.0
enjoy	127	653	3.8	6.2
boast	17	49	3.7	5.6
appreciate	24	55	3.2	4.6
absorb	11	15	3.0	3.8
view	62	66	3.8	4.0
spoil	21	12	4.6	4.5
experience	60	51	3.5	3.3
vary	65	40	4.2	3.7
overlook	24	11	3.9	3.1
discover	56	27	3.9	3.0
contrast	79	24	6.3	5.2
describe	99	36	3.5	2.1
undulate	72	8	7.0	5.2
shift	50	10	5.1	3.2
capture	48	11	4.2	2.3
explore	262	66	5.6	3.6
surround	542	120	7.0	4.9
paint	216	35	6.9	4.6
reveal	80	11	4.2	1.4
change	878	91	5.9	2.7
design	244	18	4.7	1.0
create	403	30	4.5	0.6
dominate	381	22	7.5	3.6
enhance	203	8	5.7	1.1

adj_subject_of	1423	1241	1.9	5.2
stunning	8	85	2.7	6.1
spectacular	11	115	3.2	6.6
breathtaking	14	72	5.2	7.6
wonderful	7	28	1.2	3.2
beautiful	28	78	2.7	4.2
impressive	7	14	1.7	2.7
worth	7	11	0.6	1.2
wild	10	13	2.5	2.8
interesting	7	9	0.1	0.5
similar	13	9	0.6	0.1

modifier	33772	13606	1.7	2.2
splendid	13	78	3.1	6.4
breathtaking	140	667	6.7	9.8
awe-inspiring	10	35	3.2	6.2
spectacular	227	1295	6.7	9.7
stunning	219	1023	6.6	9.3
glorious	26	103	4.0	6.7
magnificent	103	414	5.8	8.3
alpine	19	50	4.0	6.5
majestic	28	57	4.6	6.7
mountain	192	638	5.6	7.5
coastal	156	395	6.3	8.1
wonderful	105	304	4.7	6.4
limestone	59	79	5.3	6.4
beautiful	715	1336	7.1	8.1
dramatic	283	436	6.9	7.9
picturesque	115	105	6.3	7.0
unspoilt	115	69	6.6	6.9
rugged	179	100	7.1	7.2
mountainous	98	33	6.4	5.9
varied	251	108	6.9	6.2
desert	172	51	6.6	5.5
volcanic	107	25	6.4	5.2
lush	123	28	6.6	5.4
wooded	93	7	6.2	3.5
rural	631	48	7.4	3.9

modifies	16539	1625	0.8	0.3
beach	18	44	2.1	3.5
coastline	8	12	2.9	4.3
lighting	7	10	1.5	2.3
village	18	26	1.3	1.9
	11	11	1.9	2.1
town	19	21	0.7	0.9
mountain	12	11	1.8	1.8
landscape	19	11	2.2	1.6
flora	29	10	4.9	4.2
bird	12	7	0.9	0.2
	16	8	1.7	0.9
culture	33	17	1.8	0.9
wildlife	156	57	6.1	5.0
change	279	67	3.5	1.5
view	90	20	2.2	0.1
construction	34	7	2.7	0.5
history	252	32	3.8	0.9
heritage	104	7	5.3	1.7
architecture	243	10	6.3	1.9
painting	538	7	7.1	1.0

Figure 6.12. *A sample from the Sketch Difference for* scenery *and* landscape

As this sample from the Sketch Engine report shows, collocates for which the two lemmas share patterns and combinations are sorted according to salience scores and coloured according to difference between the scores, so as to emphasize preference for one or other lemma. Thus, from the 'modifier' column one can deduce a preference for adjectives such as *splendid, breathtaking, awe-inspiring, spectacular, stunning* and *glorious* to modify *scenery* more often than *landscape*, which in turn is more typically modified by such adjectives as *wooded* or *rural*.

Patterns or combinations that can be considered unique to the one or other lemma are reported in separate columns. In Figures 6.13 and 6.14 overleaf, we can see the '*scenery* only' and '*landscape* only' patterns given by the Sketch Engine.

"landscape" only patterns

and/or	15900	1.9
seascape	201	8.5
portrait	328	7.7
townscape	95	7.5
biodiversity	146	6.9
portraiture	50	6.5
cityscape	44	6.4
scenery	119	6.2
archaeology	92	6.1
ecology	66	6.0
conservation	135	5.6
amenity	60	5.5
recreation	43	5.2

subject_of	8362	1.7
sketch	10	4.8
fascinate	11	4.5
evolve	31	4.4
evoke	12	4.3
soften	7	4.0
stretch	16	3.6
encompass	12	3.6
characterise	12	3.5
feature	57	3.4
influence	29	3.2
undergo	17	3.1
contrast	7	3.1

adj_subject_of	1423	1.9
barren	14	6.2
desolate	7	5.7
hilly	7	5.6
untouched	9	5.5
devoid	8	5.4
reminiscent	12	5.4
bleak	10	5.1
rugged	8	4.8
lush	8	4.7
rich	55	4.0
flat	22	3.4
diverse	15	2.9

object_of	15012	1.7
dot	160	7.6
shape	223	6.8
transform	205	6.8
litter	67	6.7
farm	78	6.7
conserve	68	6.3
scar	43	6.3
alter	121	5.8
blight	31	5.8
populate	42	5.8
inhabit	45	5.6
evoke	39	5.6

modifier	33772	1.7
urban	698	7.7
historic	582	7.6
prehistoric	180	7.1
lunar	148	7.0
barren	147	7.0
agricultural	227	6.6
rolling	125	6.5
cultural	513	6.5
sacred	142	6.5
scenic	100	6.2
bleak	96	6.2
arid	80	6.2

modifies	16539	0.8
architect	730	8.5
gardener	282	8.1
painter	288	7.9
archaeology	178	7.0
seascape	63	6.8
gardening	101	6.6
photographer	167	6.5
ecology	93	6.5
designation	77	6.4
photography	141	6.1
designer	228	6.0
characterisation	52	5.9

Figure 6.13. *A sample from the* landscape *only patterns*

"scenery" only patterns

and/or	6464	2.4
prop	109	7.8
costume	178	7.2
birdlife	9	5.3
tranquility	10	5.2
cove	13	4.9
lochs	10	4.9
sunshine	26	4.8
walking	26	4.7
hospitality	23	4.5
loch	8	4.5
seabird	7	4.4
solitude	7	4.4

object_of	3849	1.4
savour	16	6.4
chew	24	6.1
enliven	7	5.1
guarantee	7	1.8
store	7	1.5
miss	9	1.0
mention	7	0.6

subject_of	2981	1.9
chew	14	5.4
abound	10	5.2
impress	10	2.9
overlook	9	2.8
pass	11	0.7
improve	13	0.0

modifies	1625	0.3
prop	19	5.7
costume	25	4.6
waterfall	9	4.5
cliff	8	3.0
castle	11	2.7
close	9	2.2
lake	9	2.2
plenty	8	2.0
weather	16	1.8
store	16	1.8
walk	9	1.3
interaction	7	1.1

adj_subject_of	1241	5.2
destructible	9	7.6
imaginable	17	7.0
diversified	10	6.6
magnificent	41	5.5
picturesque	11	4.6
superb	32	4.2
lovely	37	4.1
awesome	9	4.1
dramatic	25	4.1
fabulous	10	4.1
amazing	33	4.0
grand	14	3.8

modifier	13606	2.2
breath-taking	47	6.7
cliff	76	5.8
costume	38	4.8
unsurpassed	11	4.5
stupendous	8	4.1
Andean	8	4.1
sylvan	7	4.1
destructible	7	4.1
topside	7	4.0
fjord	7	3.9
sensational	8	3.9
captivating	7	3.8

Figure 6.14. *A sample from the* scenery *only patterns*

Again, the qualitative difference from information that can be obtained just by exploring concordance lines is self-evident, especially if one considers that these data were obtained by summarizing (in a matter of seconds) information relating to the 25,445 occurrences of *scenery* and the 110,908 occurrences of *landscape* from ukWaC.

These examples not only testify to the rich potential for linguistic information stored in the interaction between large web corpora and sophisticated web-based corpus query tools, but also indicate the great potential that lies in the possibility of processing more data when the tools performing the analysis can contribute information of this kind. However, it is always necessary to be aware of the peculiar nature of these data sets and tools. Though much more reliable than the web itself, both qualitatively and quantitatively, the data from corpora created via semi-automated crawling of the web still have limitations due to their exclusive provenance from websites downloaded over a specific time span. Moreover, the tools may often fail to identify specific language categories and provide misleading results. By way of example, one could consider the information gained from a word sketch for the adjective *light*, as in Figure 6.14.

In the 'adj_subject column, the sketch ranks *cigarette* as the most significant collocate for the adjective *light*, but as soon as concordance lines are inspected, one becomes aware of a systemic mistake whereby the noun *lighter* has been included in the computation, because it is an omograph of the comparative of the adjective *light* (see Figure 6.14). As for the attributive position of the adjective (3rd column), the highest ranks are again for a mistaken interpretation of *light*. In the collocation *light bulb*, *light* is a noun modifier, not an adjective, whereas collocation with *refreshment* correctly entails the adjective. This suggests that these data need to be handled with care. Nonetheless, provided that care is taken, the exploration of these large web corpora using the Sketch Engine can be extremely rewarding.

light *(adjective)* ukWaC freq = 102598 (65.5 per million)

adj_subject	5663	5.8	modifier	8097	0.3	modifies	72657	2.8	and/or	30302	2.8	adj_comp_of	8706	4.9
cigarette	247	7.97	enough	220	6.76	bulb	2212	9.51	airy	1252	10.16	shed	199	7.61
shed	92	7.82	surprisingly	66	6.75	refreshment	1091	8.54	brown	593	8.08	emit	39	5.87
Zippo	31	7.41	comparatively	48	6.69	fitting	698	7.75	spacious	401	7.99	polarise	20	5.8
cigar	30	6.36	relatively	248	6.57	touch	1027	7.64	coloured	397	7.89	throw	97	4.93
steering	49	6.22	wonderfully	42	6.25	snack	525	7.49	dark	958	7.86	polarize	7	4.46
kg	44	5.94	fairly	153	6.18	lunch	853	7.47	blue	786	7.8	radiate	9	4.45
kilo	14	5.8	exceptionally	40	6.16	pollution	650	7.37	fluffy	151	7.17	travel	60	3.98
clutch	22	5.56	amazingly	26	6.12	switch	579	7.33	leaded	138	7.14	cast	21	3.83
wind	179	5.44	remarkably	37	6.06	rain	730	7.31	bright	430	7.01	shine	14	3.81
burden	60	5.27	incredibly	53	6.05	intensity	520	7.29	grey	223	6.95	reflect	76	3.78

Figure 6.15. *Word sketch for* light *(adjective) (sample)*

Goodman (Bryan Coleman) hands in a	*cigarette* lighter	found at the murder site - a lighter which
Goodman, the farm owner, finds a	*cigarette* lighter	belonging to Morris. 4 TX : 2nd March 1959
apparent bite. "It felt like a	*cigarette* lighter	from a car put on that area and then just
plenty of 12v male / female '	*cigarette* lighter	' extensions. Tuck under the trim, the curly
With two flicks from a green	*cigarette* lighter	he turned himself into a human torch. The
which he had attacked with a	*cigarette* lighter	to good effect. The Dutch fly tying equipment
matches and keep them dry, or a	*cigarette* lighter	, for the candles. April 2 - Monteverde
This cooler operates from a 12 V	*cigarette* lighter	. A built-in battery control system protects
(CFC free). Power Source: 12V	*cigarette* lighter	or 230V mains supply via an adapter (sold
useless. Non-smokers would find a	*cigarette* lighter	useful for leeches. We drank gallons of
avoid charging from my car's	*cigarette* lighter	, as it is an older car, and I am not sure
with censure if you get your	*cigarette* lighter	out to see what the awful stuff is on your
, would set him alight with a	*cigarette* lighter	, then put the fire out, then set him alight
pathetic comfort in the heavy silver	*cigarette* lighter	that he could feel in his pocket as he
it out with a wet shirt and a	*cigarette* lighter	! Finally I got in touch with Lou and arranged
carried on aircraft. A single	*cigarette* lighter	can be carried on the person but must not
they want it to refill their	*cigarette* lighter	. This law covers the whole of the UK. Some
hood which, powered by the car's	*cigarette* lighter	, gives you privacy. The fan which inflates
sealed with Lucifer by applying a	*cigarette* lighter	so realistically to his bleeding arm that

Figure 6.16. *Concordance lines for the collocation* light + cigarette *(sample)*

4. Case study: Sketches of *culture* from the BNC to the web

The brief overview of the Sketch Engine functions in the previous sections can only suggest the scope and variety of information that can be gained at a lexico-grammar level by exploring mega-corpora from the web using a tool capable of summarizing data in a way that is meaningful for the linguist. The potential of these tools and resources can also be exploited at a higher level of analysis insofar as they can also yield evidence – and objective data – of discourses taking place in society at large. An example of this will be provided in the present section by using the Sketch Engine to investigate the behaviour of a notoriously 'difficult' word: *culture*. Samples and suggestions from the sketch obtained for *culture* from ukWaC will be discussed and, when possible, related to and/or complemented with information drawn from other sources.

The background for this case study can be found in a growing body of work in which the corpus linguistics approach has been profitably used to attain a deeper understanding of discourse and society, starting from Stubbs 2001 to the research by Hoey *et al.* 2007, to mention just a few contributions in this field. It is also important to mention the growing body of studies which integrate discourse analysis and corpus linguistics (e.g. Baker 2006). While recent research in corpus linguistics is now meeting the challenge of tackling issues related to discourse and society, embodying what Teubert would consider corpus linguistics' inherently sociolinguistic perspective (Stubbs 2002; Teubert 2007), it seems important to explore the specific potential – and limitations – of the tools and resources revolving around the notion of the web as corpus. In this respect special attention deserve also studies that have been carried using the Sketch Engine, such as Pearce (2008) or Wild et al. (2013).

4.1 A very difficult word ...

The choice of the word *culture* as a case study for the present chapter perhaps needs a word or two of explanation, since it was provoked by Raymond Williams' famous statement that culture is 'one of the two or three most complicated words in the English language'. Culture, as Williams reminds us (1985: 87–93), in all its early uses, was a noun of process: the tending of something, basically crops or animals. This meaning provided a basis for the important next stage, when the tending of natural growth was metaphorically extended to a process of human development so that the word *culture* came to be taken in absolute terms as signifying a process of refinement. After tracing the key moments in the development of this word, Williams distinguishes three categories in modern usage:

1 the noun which describes a process of intellectual, spiritual and aesthetic refinement; e.g. a man of culture.

2 the noun which describes the products of intellectual and especially artistic activity; e.g. Ministry of Culture.

3 the noun which indicates a particular way of life, whether of a people, a period, a group, or humanity in general; e.g. Jewish culture.

We are not concerned here with the results of research by Williams and his followers, who consistently engaged in discussing the evolution of *culture*, and similar key words, thereby contributing to the rise of what is now known as cultural studies. Indeed, what seems to be more relevant to the use that can be made of corpus tools and resources like the ones under analysis in the present chapter is rather the methodology. As a matter of fact, in his introduction to *Culture and Society*, Williams states that his enquiry into the development of this word should be carried out by examining 'not a series of abstracted problems, but a series of statements by individuals' (1966: xvii). Furthermore, as recently argued by the authors of *New Keywords*, Williams explored 'not only the meanings of words, but also the ways people group or "bond" them together, making implicit or explicit connections that help to initiate new ways of seeing their world [...] So that readers might follow and reflect on the interactions, discontinuities and uncertainties of association that shape what Williams called "particular formations of meaning"' (Bennet et al. 2005: xix).

It is this similarity which suggests that sketches for *culture* from a contemporary corpus of English – even a web corpus obtained by web crawling, such as ukWaC – could provide interesting insights into such a complex word. However, before moving on to investigate the sketch obtained for *culture* from ukWaC, a preliminary analysis of data from the more traditional BNC has been carried out, as a benchmark for the data obtained from this investigation and for the sake of comparison between the two data sets.

4.2 Sketches of culture from the British National Corpus

In the 100,000,000-word BNC, *culture* occurs 10,107 times, with a normalized frequency of 90.1 per million. This is clearly a number of occurrences which could not have been explored without a tool contributing to the automatic extraction of linguistic information, and it is certainly impossible – given the limited scope of a sub-chapter in a book – to provide an exhaustive exploration here of the data made available by the tool under analysis. What is rewarding is the possibility of gaining an overview of the information retrieved and suggesting topics for further discussion. In Figure 6.17 below, a sample from the sketch of *culture* is reported. The sketch is here limited to five patterns.

object_of	1270	1.1	subject_of	770	1.2	modifier	5837	1.7	modifies	865	0.3	and/or	2728	1.8
create	45	5.29	become	17	2.6	popular	190	8.49	shock	41	7.63	language	162	7.14
develop	34	4.85	seem	14	2.65	different	169	6.69	medium	37	7.83	history	97	6.42
change	31	4.95	provide	13	2.18	political	162	6.96	minister	29	3.99	society	88	5.71
see	27	1.94	come	13	1.67	other	132	4.85	industry	23	3.99	education	75	5.7
understand	23	4.88	exist	11	5.02	western	125	7.91	club	22	4.23	art	68	6.05
reflect	20	5.04	grow	10	3.95	youth	91	7.52	dish	21	6.77	religion	56	7.54
use	20	1.96	remain	10	3.23	national	87	5.86	study	18	3.32	culture	48	6.19
promote	17	5.59	develop	9	2.95	new	76	4.26	supernatant	16	8.87	tradition	39	6.36
base	16	3.57	produce	9	2.49	british	72	5.74	system	14	1.74	politics	34	6.24
share	14	4.72	begin	9	2.36	dominant	68	7.93	plate	13	5.18	people	33	2.47
absorb	11	6.02	influence	8	4.47	tissue	67	7.62	media	11	4.85	communication	30	5.76
influence	11	4.87	determine	8	3.49	european	66	6.21	change	10	2.25	life	27	2.94
define	11	4.45	affect	8	3.35	american	64	6.41	vulture	9	7.85	race	26	5.62
establish	11	3.53	change	8	3.02	human	62	6.31	clash	8	5.88	structure	26	4.38
find	11	1.25	flourish	7	7.01	material	60	5.53	conflict	7	4.21	information	23	3.51
represent	10	3.51	include	7	2.03	enterprise	59	6.87	health	7	2.56	value	21	3.83
pop	9	6.56	mean	7	1.9	cell	55	5.98	contact	6	3.69	literature	20	5.81
bring	9	2.2	consist	6	4.35	common	53	6.07	technique	6	3.19	identity	18	5.78
foster	8	6.48	emerge	6	4.34	contemporary	51	7.23	experiment	5	3.99	science	18	4.72
adopt	8	4.0	represent	6	2.8	high	51	5.19	condition	5	1.88	nature	18	4.15
describe	8	2.75	show	6	1.02	modern	50	6.28	period	5	1.73	sport	17	5.16
require	8	2.23	define	5	3.35	english	48	6.13				system	16	1.91
call	8	1.63	create	5	2.14	local	46	4.79				way	16	1.78
transmit	7	5.96	suggest	5	2.04	mass	40	7.08				heritage	15	6.19
constitute	7	4.9	help	5	1.76	traditional	39	6.21				knowledge	15	4.1

Figure 6.17. *A sample from the word sketch for* culture *from the BNC*

According to data computed by the Sketch Engine, in the BNC the world *culture* shows a tendency to occur as the object of such verbs as *create, develop, change, see, understand, reflect* (see the 1st column on the left). It is frequently used as the subject of verbs like *become, seem, provide*. It is modified by such adjectives as *popular, different, political, other*, and modifies words like *shock, medium, minister,* etc. Finally it tends to co-occur with such terms as *language, history, society, education* in the patterns *language and culture, culture and society*, etc.

A look at concordance lines for *create*, as shown in Figure 6.18 below, suggests a frequent co-occurrence of *culture* with words relating to a socio-economic domain, such as *staff, enterprise, job, work*, etc:

</p><p> But it has also begun to *create* a corporate culture	where some companies have become a kind of economic
to the extent that it not only *created* a dependency culture	by reducing the incentive to work, but put a premium
amusement. </p><p> `These awful events *create* a drug culture	which can never be a part of our culture, and they
community of the feudal nobility *created* a national culture	; the peasants did not participate because their membership
pointed out on Thursday, PR has *created* a political culture	of backstairs deals and perpetual campaigning. Take
the English in the age of Bede *created* a vigorous culture	whose ripples were to be felt across Western Europe
casual labour system]. </p><p> This *created* a workplace culture	very different from that characteristic of many other
is seen as the main drive to *create* an enterprise culture	that will hopefully lead to an increase in the numbers
Mrs Thatcher's strategy of *creating* an enterprise culture	, which massively rewards those at the top while penalizing
benefits with the expressed aim of *creating* an enterprise culture	has also affected those who would want to become
incentives and initiative, thereby *creating* an enterprise culture	in which the benefits of growth will ultimately spread
Government has attempted to *create* an incentive-based culture	. On the income side, this aim has been pursued by
disempower people. You can *create* an organisation culture	that says never take chances, always cover your back
flicker before countless millions *creating* a common mass culture	, the presentation of sport on British television
entrepreneurs. It has *created* a cost-conscious business culture	, and rooted out many of the more outrageous make-work
Fairweather. </p><p> `What we have to do is *create* a culture	in which appointing women to senior jobs is easier
abound in the enterprise. As it is, they *create* a culture	that compensates for life at work; a myth system

Figure 6.18. *A sample from the concordance lines for the collocation* create + culture

It is easy to see how *culture* in this context has partially lost its original meaning of a process/product of refinement, as in the famous Arnoldian sense of 'a pursuit of our total perfection, by means of getting to know, on all the matters which most concern us, the best which has been thought and said in the world' (Arnold 1869: viii). Culture here rather concerns a set of ideas/behaviours relating to a specific group in a specific context, like a workplace, company or organization – a new restricted meaning of culture.

If collocates are ranked in order of salience, some other interesting verbs seem to gain prominence. Some of these verbs are: *assimilate, absorb, transmit, respect, modify, change, understand, influence, share, dominate*. It is not possible to investigate them all in detail, but it might perhaps be interesting to stress that these verbs suggest power relations, as shown in concordance lines for *assimilate* in Figure 6.19 overleaf.

the West and its adherents slower to *assimilate* the	culture	of their pagan contemporaries. </p><p> By the 430s
gone a long way towards *assimilating* the dominant	culture	of pagan Romans. An easy symbiosis had come into
already far advanced along the road of *assimilating* the	culture	and the religion of their Roman subjects at the time
youth-hostel-cum-doss-house. Once the experience of local life and	culture	has been *assimilated* , the traveller moves on, a
folk-life, while attempting to *assimilate* Polish szlachta	culture	and cultural values for themselves. </p><p> After the
reflect the great American ability to *assimilate* other	cultures	, turning them into something uniquely their own.

Figure 6.19. *A sample from the concordance lines for the collocation* assimilate + culture

Power relations are also evoked when considering the adjectives preceding the noun *culture* in the 'Modifier' pattern (3rd column), which features, in terms of raw frequency, such words as *popular* and *different*, whereas in order of saliency the most common collocates are *popular, dominant* and *western*. Here, a quick look at concordances for *dominant* immediately highlights notions of opposition and conflict, with repeated reference to patterns of marginalization, resistance and, again, assimilation, as shown in Figure 6.20 below.

dilution and commercial exploitation) the	*dominant* culture	of a succeeding metropolitan and paranational period
gone a long way towards assimilating the	*dominant* culture	of pagan Romans. An easy symbiosis had come into
this subgroup is then likely to become the	*dominant* culture	in the greater society. When any dominant group asserts
Teen age, of the love affair between the	*dominant* culture	and youth. No longer would youth and its culture
well-upholstered `dissenting' niches from both the	*dominant* culture	and traditional opposition to it. Too much is at
, cast as out-groups, as bogeymen by the	*dominant* culture	, but attempting to fashion their own, necessarily
where the terms of discourse are set by the	*dominant* culture	, but in private space. Hence the failure of most
North America who are marginalised by the	*dominant* culture	and to provide access for their participation in
so firmly delineated as `private' by the	*dominant* culture	and woe betide those who, like politicians in sex
subject to peer group pressure from the	*dominant* culture	in the 16-24 age group.' </p> Hunt for missing mother
Irish catholics were represented in the	*dominant* culture	as an inferior race, ridiculed, and considered incompetent
by a type of music that had been in the	*dominant* culture	throughout Punk rock - black disco music. `The Afro-American
Warning against forced assimilation into the	*dominant* culture	, it advocated the right to national and ethnic self-identity
than as a tool for assimilation into the	*dominant* culture	and access to their arts. They may, then, easily
expect; it is one of the hallmarks of the	*dominant* culture	, after all, that it is about thirty to fifty years
society, brought within the norms of the	*dominant* culture	, and protected from deviant modes of thought and
media. </p><p> Despite the opposition of the	*dominant* culture	, the music of those within the culture but not of
less. Hearing people are members of the	*dominant* culture	, who usually wish to preserve their hearing status
of the `private' out of the hands of the	*dominant* culture	; it is this fact, just as much as the actual physical
internalized the structures and values of the	*dominant* culture	? Are they not paradoxically reproducing the laws

Figure 6.20. *A sample from the concordance lines for the collocation* dominant + culture

As for the list of nouns modified by *culture*, this is opened, in order of frequency, by *shock*, a collocation which relates to a distinctively modern experience defined as *culture shock*, 'the feelings of isolation, rejection, etc., experienced when one culture is brought into sudden contact with another, as when a primitive tribe is confronted by modern civilization' (*Collins Cobuild*

Dictionary). When ranked in order of saliency, the list of nouns modified by *culture* is instead significantly led by *supernatant*, a word which, like *tissue* in the list of modifiers, relates *culture* to its scientific meaning as the process of 'a group of bacteria or cells which are grown, usually in a laboratory, as part of an experiment' (*Collins Cobuild Dictionary*). Similarly, *medium, dish, plate, media* and *experiment* all refer to the use of the term *culture* in its scientific sense, with results mostly coming from the subcorpus of scientific academic texts from the BNC.

More consistent with the meaning of *culture* as a process and product of intellectual refinement is the tendency of culture to co-occur with such words as *language*, *history*, *society*, *education*, *art*, *religion*, *tradition*, in the patterns '*culture* and/or NOUN'.

4.3 Sketches of culture *from ukWaC*

A preliminary survey of information on the word culture derived from the BNC served as a basis and background for the exploration of the sketch for *culture* offered by ukWaC. The data certainly deserve further exploration; nevertheless, the insight they offer into the behaviour of such a complex word has intriguing implications. So it will be a challenge to see whether or not the 'experiment' carried out using the BNC can be replicated with a less controlled and much larger resource like ukWaC.

In the ukWaC corpus, *culture* occurs 161,537 times with a normalized frequency of 104.8 per million. This means that, roughly speaking, the two data sets are quantitatively comparable with reference to the position of the word *culture* in each corpus, even though ukWaC provides a number of occurrences of *culture* which is nearly sixteen times greater than the number of occurrences found in the BNC. These occurrences include both those in which *culture* is a scientific term and those in which it is commonly used in the humanities, which is the primary concern of the present analysis. Since the tools and resources used do not allow for a disambiguation between the two meanings, an attempt has been made – heuristically – to get an approximation of the occurrences of *culture* in its scientific sense, by computing the number of occurrences of *culture* with the lemmas *cell* or *bacteria* in their co-text. This was done using the filter option and setting a broad co-text (15 words to the left and to the right of the node). The results seem to indicate that nearly 2,495 occurrences of *culture* can be related to its scientific meaning.[1]

The abridged sample from the Sketch Engine output reported in Figure 6.21 indicates the collocates of *culture* in order of salience for five patterns, which will be investigated in greater detail in the following pages.

culture *(noun)* ukWaC freq = 164112 (104.8 per million)

object_of	29697	1.4	subject_of	18968	1.5	modifier	97398	2.0	modifies	17783	0.4	and/or	60254	2.9
foster	335	7.73	influence	199	5.83	popular	3361	8.53	shock	741	8.57	religion	1436	7.93
promote	743	6.57	collide	29	5.39	contemporary	1276	7.81	vulture	145	7.82	heritage	833	7.71
experience	546	6.54	flourish	31	5.16	Western	887	7.75	clash	181	7.44	tradition	1267	7.65
embrace	180	6.54	fascinate	24	4.92	organisational	761	7.59	secretary	194	6.44	language	3178	7.61
strengthen	186	6.24	thrive	24	4.75	visual	917	7.35	religion	261	5.83	history	3648	7.58
celebrate	230	6.23	tend	62	4.64	American	1218	7.31	jamming	30	5.62	art	2446	7.48
embed	120	6.21	permeate	17	4.58	youth	944	7.3	Policing	26	5.5	politics	818	7.27
create	1205	6.04	emerge	66	4.53	diverse	668	7.07	fess	25	5.47	society	1653	7.04
change	991	6.04	evolve	42	4.53	different	3612	6.98	shift	101	5.38	literature	743	7.0
preserve	155	5.9	shape	45	4.39	western	503	6.92	ethnicity	41	5.35	leisure	465	6.96
reflect	361	5.87	underpin	26	4.27	pop	477	6.85	heritage	104	5.28	identity	742	6.88
rave	59	5.84	worship	14	4.17	Chinese	513	6.78	dish	92	5.26	lifestyle	419	6.83
prevail	74	5.84	persist	15	4.16	indigenous	378	6.76	medium	385	5.25	civilisation	220	6.57
respect	122	5.83	inspire	42	4.13	Japanese	468	6.74	change	873	5.14	custom	346	6.56
shape	136	5.78	enrich	18	4.12	ancient	555	6.64	filtrate	19	5.11	ethnicity	199	6.43
understand	504	5.72	dominate	38	4.06	dominant	367	6.62	minister	129	5.09	nationality	181	6.22
nurture	65	5.71	interact	17	3.98	Jewish	455	6.59	politics	131	5.03	background	513	6.07
transform	123	5.71	survive	41	3.94	corporate	590	6.58	etiquette	21	4.91	faith	421	6.05
pervade	53	5.69	merge	15	3.87	modern	909	6.57	gender	70	4.87	civilization	151	6.05
differ	97	5.51	infiltrate	10	3.86	compensation	417	6.54	tradition	146	4.86	gender	239	6.02
explore	264	5.44	condition	11	3.78	British	1001	6.46	custom	58	4.62	ethos	147	5.94
permeate	44	5.41	prevail	13	3.76	political	1022	6.44	supernatants	13	4.58	race	542	5.92
sustain	95	5.4	exist	90	3.73	tissue	419	6.36	history	417	4.56	geography	156	5.75
dominate	110	5.4	converge	10	3.71	European	725	6.33	geography	37	4.53	culture	583	5.74
enrich	57	5.38	embrace	21	3.7	Indian	324	6.26	language	341	4.51	belief	298	5.64

Figure 6.21. *A sample from the word sketch for* culture *from ukWaC*

4.3.1 *Culture* as object

According to data obtained from the Sketch Engine, in this corpus *culture* shows a tendency to occur as the object of verbs such as *foster, promote, create, change* (1st column), a list of collocates not so dissimilar from the list of collocates produced in terms of raw frequency from the BNC. Patterns such as those suggested by the verbs *assimilate, influence, absorb* found in the BNC seem instead to be less prominent here, with the exception of *prevail,* in the pattern *prevailing culture.* A quite interesting collocate for *culture* is again *dominate,* with *culture* seen as being dominated by something else (e.g. religious ideas/values) as shown in Figure 6.22.

As for the group of collocates including *foster* and its near-synonyms *promote, create, nurture, encourage,* the analysis of concordance lines for such verbs could provide evidence of discourses and discourse practices about culture in contemporary society: which culture is being, should be, or is said to be promoted? fostered? nurtured? encouraged? And who are the actors involved in the process?

Left context	Node	Right context
Beatles. It is an American form that *dominated* our	culture	in England . The Beatles appearances produced mass
they will none the less soon *dominate* our consumer	culture	. It is only 24 years since Britain got its first
'man of sorrows'. The image that has *dominated* our	culture	is that of a man being tortured to death on a cross
rights as possible and also to *dominate* the political	culture	to make it more difficult for upcoming rivals to
from Marxism. The English Revolution took place in a	culture	*dominated* by religious ideas and religious language
coexistence of two modes of production. Commodity	culture	was *dominated* by powerful cultural industries [2]
ıtisfaction. Hedonism, without pain, *dominates* Western	culture	, religious values are at a low ebb, and a humanistic
simple construction of stone and timber. Although Kafir	culture	was strongly *dominated* by men, women also could gain
order for these trends to become accessible for a	culture	*dominated* by materialism and rampant distractions
Symbolist sensibility that *dominated* Russian literary	culture.	in his account of the cultural reception of early
of its practitioners were raised in homes and/or a	culture	*dominated* by these religions. ... When the search
and high academic standards is now *dominating* school	cultures	. But how can we expect children to achieve high academic
simple construction of stone and timber. Although Kafir	culture	was strongly *dominated* by men, women also could gain
nbined with a rise in rudeness, a TV and DVD *dominated*	culture	and a lack of respect for authority. This wears him
outside, still the very kind of male *dominated* macho	culture	of the Police Service, which may well - Miss Weekes
put Joseph in charge of all of Egypt. Notes Western	culture	is somewhat *dominated* by celebrities. In the United
hich the Masculine Principle has come to *dominate* the	culture	absolutely, extirpating femininity even from the
came less from school than from a lively intellectual	culture	*dominated* by the radical Jewish intelligentsia of
innumerable small businesses, towards a supermarket	culture	*dominated* by a handful of large retailers. In 2000
luding the use of their heritage to *dominate* indigenous	cultures	and destroy native populations. Some of us are descendants

Figure 6.22. *A sample from the concordance lines for the collocation* dominate + culture

A look at concordances for the verb *foster* suggests, for instance, that the patterns in which culture is an object of this verb are often found in discourses about institutions (schools, departments, etc.) or workplaces, with the frequent collocation *enterprise culture*, a pervasive pattern also discussed in Stubbs (1996). A look at collocates computed by the Sketch Engine for patterns of co-occurrence of *foster* with *culture* suggests a strong collocation with *learning* and *enterprise*, as shown in Figure 6.23.

Collocation candidates

Page 1 Go Next >

	Freq	T-score	MI	logDice
p/n a	258	15.710	5.509	-1.647
p/n of	203	13.633	4.534	-2.622
p/n foster	189	13.747	15.828	8.641
p/n to	144	11.355	4.217	-2.939
p/n and	137	10.988	4.030	-3.126
p/n the	92	8.009	2.599	-4.556
p/n .	87	7.957	2.767	-4.388
p/n ,	83	7.684	2.675	-4.481
p/n fostering	76	8.718	16.008	8.765
p/n in	75	8.085	3.913	-3.243
p/n is	40	5.810	3.620	-3.536
p/n an	39	6.089	5.321	-1.835
p/n which	38	6.023	5.441	-1.715
p/n fostered	32	5.657	15.541	8.239
p/n that	30	5.025	3.598	-3.558
p/n fosters	24	4.899	16.180	8.736
p/n learning	23	4.780	8.245	1.088
p/n for	21	3.956	2.870	-4.286
p/n enterprise	20	4.471	11.426	4.257
p/n where	17	4.061	6.064	-1.092
p/n research	16	3.967	6.907	-0.250
p/n We	16	3.911	5.485	-1.671
p/n by	16	3.634	3.449	-3.706
p/n within	13	3.560	6.318	-0.838

Figure 6.23. *A sample of collocates for the pattern* foster + culture

And a click on *learning* or *enterprise* would reveal at a glance typical patterns like those shown in Figure 6.24 and Figure 6.25 below:

with only basic secondary education by 2010, *foster* a culture of lifelong *learning* , with support from social partners
reflection on practice Student support strategies: *Foster* a culture where *learning* is valued Assist in the development
to a 19+ Strategy and its implementation. *Foster* a culture of *learning* provider collaboration. Raise the profile
achieve them. NOF Training's aim is to help *foster* a culture of *learning* and of change and to this end it is committed
Befitting an organization that strives to *foster* a culture of continuous improvement and *learning* , AmeriCredit
desire for the organisation to strive to *foster* a culture of continuous *learning* and improvement. In fact,
some time and effort thinking about how to *foster* a culture of effectiveness and *learning* as an integral part
fail to create a learning society, or to *foster* a culture of *learning* . To this end, we recommend that Governmen
lifestyles and reduce health inequalities to *foster* a culture of *learning* and skills development, encourage existing
Norfolk's Future - Strategic Priority 2 aims to *foster* a culture of *learning* and skills development. Norfolk Learning
explored whether trade unions are able to *foster* a culture of *learning* within the workplace, and whether such
and homeless adults. Kaleidoscope aims to *foster* a culture of lifelong *learning* to help people develop their
and higher education and study, but also to *foster* a culture of life-long *learning* among the public in general
vironment that improves employee satisfaction. We *foster* a culture of continuous *learning* , and provide our staff with
volunteers is also given on a regular basis and we *foster* a culture of openess and positive *learning* , recognising that
learning and developing initiatives which *foster* a culture of lifelong *learning* in Hampshire. liaising with
practice concern valuing individuals, *fostering* a culture of life-long *learning* , enabling the Church to fulfil
enhance community capacity building by *fostering* a culture of lifelong *learning* and re-skilling. Learning provided
Lecture. Sir Thomas Gresham's passion was in *fostering* a culture of "new *learning* ". I have therefore chosen a theme
colleagues and other health care professionals *fostering* a culture of life-long *learning* in the health service; appreciating
address our national skills gap and *foster* a real culture of lifelong *learning* we have got to keep young people
optimise provision. Above all the is NTO will *foster* the culture of a *learning* workforce throughout the sector. Just
challenging, but risk free and enjoyable, *fostering* the culture of lifelong *learning* . Our hallmark is the practical

Figure 6.24. *A sample of collocates for patterns of co-occurrence of* culture *with* foster *and* learning

the New Deal, Denmark plans to *foster* an *enterprise* culture , Finland wants to reform its vocational training
positive progress in helping to *foster* an *enterprise* culture ; up from 40 per cent a year ago (FT, p.4). Martin
reducing carbon emissions, *fostering* an *enterprise* culture . Fostering an enterprise culture might be seen as
economy, and what we can do to *foster* that *enterprise* culture . In this new century, the nations that will succeed
policies and programmes designed to *foster* an *enterprise* culture . One example of this is the Manufacturing Advisory
and the growth of SMEs by *fostering* an *enterprise* culture across all discipline areas and at all levels of
debate, share information and *foster* an *enterprise* culture among innovators and business communities. The subjects
enterprise). Their aim is to *foster* an *enterprise* culture and encourage enterprising communities, particularly
secured lending with a view to *fostering* an *enterprise* culture and is likely to force both lenders and borrowers
privatisation of state schools, *fostering* an *enterprise* culture and the hiring and firing of teachers by private
training to raise productivity and *foster* an *enterprise* culture in Camborne, Pool and Redruth. It has also supported
industry department□s efforts to *foster* an *enterprise* culture in deprived areas scored only 28%. England□s regional
fostering an enterprise culture. *Fostering* an *enterprise* culture might be seen as a part of supply side economics
rules to control expenses if you want to *foster* a culture of *enterprise* . Instead his company has a thorough
velopment. Portsmouth Technopole is *fostering* a general culture of *enterprise* in the area, which includes a strong
approaches within young people early so as to *foster* a culture of *enterprise* offering young people (throughout their
with the advancement of knowledge helps to *foster* a culture of innovation and *enterprise* . Our strong links with
traffic congestion. We need to *foster* a new *enterprise* culture that will contribute to the creation of 50,000 new
Business School, created to *foster* an *enterprise* culture through staff and students of the University of Wolverhamp
within the County. Aim 2: To *foster* an *enterprise* culture which creates competitive businesses and contributes

Figure 6.25. *A sample of collocates for patterns of co-occurrence of* culture *with* foster *and* enterprise

It could also be observed that, in the frequency list of collocates in Figure 6.25 above, *enterprise* is immediately followed by the pronoun *we* and this reveals other interesting patterns, like *we foster a culture of/that/which* or *we want/try to foster a culture of/that/which*, in which *culture* is almost invariably followed by a post-modification, as seen in Figure 6.26 below:

Left context	Node	Right context
as enthusiastic and keen staff.	*We* try to *foster* a culture	of collaboration between staff and students and research
contribution made by our staff.	*We* try to *foster* a culture	of mutual trust and openness where staff can express
they are used to -- this is the best way to	*foster* a culture	of sharing. *We* also try to help the teachers to free
their professional development.	*We* try to *foster* a culture	that recognizes people's strengths and supports areas
involvement will be guaranteed.	*We* want to *foster* a culture	where artists are involved at the beginning, says
communication between copy and pictures.	*We* want to *foster* a culture	where the two work together as unit and get the
enquire for further details.	*We* continue to *foster* a culture	within the University in which staff development
that improves employee satisfaction.	*We foster* a culture	of continuous learning, and provide our staff with
commuicate ways to save water to residents	*We foster* a culture	of successful performance We strive for the best
Keilinschriften der Achaemeniden (1911), pp. 118-19	*We foster* a culture	of successful performance We strive for the best
help them overcome business challenges.	*We foster* a culture	that prizes consistency, a high level of service
'But our success depends on the team.	*We foster* a culture	where there are no glass ceilings and everyone's
and team spirit of its people.	*We* have *fostered* a culture	which promotes a "can do" attitude which benefits
management skills and activities.	*We* 're *fostering* a culture	that prioritises workloads and where people even
in the organisation	*We foster* an entrepreneurial culture	We enable our people to excel We deliver our promises
products in the market today.	*We foster* a performance culture	that recognises and rewards outstanding contribution

Figure 6.26. *A sample from the concordance lines for the pattern* we + foster + culture

The tendency of *culture* to occur with a post-modification will be discussed in more detail at the end of this chapter. What is interesting to note here is that these lines suggest that fostering a certain culture, especially in a workplace, school/university or company, is something which is not only done implicitly, as already noted in Gatto (2011), but also stated explicitly, Furthermore, the possibility of following the doc.id to the left of the concordance line in order to retrieve the original text could, in theory, help the linguist find out more about the real-life communicative situation in which the pattern was used. Yet this is not always possible, given the high volatility of the web and hence the extremely high speed at which pages appear and disappear. In some cases, however, the page is still available and makes it possible to observe how many of these occurrences come from specific sections within corporate websites devoted to the company's so-called 'culture and values', a sort of revised version of the traditional mission statement typical of a company's self-promotion.

In more general terms, this pattern confirms that the traditional – and in a sense 'absolute' – notion of culture as achievement in terms of intellectual/aesthetic refinement has given way, especially in the language of business and enterprise, to a notion of culture which is no more than a set of views and practices that are relevant only to a specific and relatively circumscribed community. This is confirmed by a small but significant lexico-grammar pattern foregrounded by the complete sketch of *culture* in which culture is followed by the preposition *within*, with a strong collocation with *organization*, *institution*, *NHS*, *department* (see Figure 6.27 overleaf).

pp_within-i	542	4.2
NHS	22	2.35
organisation	64	1.53
context	16	1.47
department	14	0.77
society	18	0.75
institution	11	0.55

Figure 6.27. *Collocates for patterns of co-occurrence of* culture *with the preposition* within

Another set of collocates of *culture* which deserves further investigation, are such verbs as *experience* and *explore* deserves further investigation. If we consider, for instance, the pattern *experience* + *culture* we notice the emergence of the word *cultures* in the plural (word sketches being available for lemmas only), as shown in Figure 6.28.[2]

students the opportunity to *experience* some amazing	culture	and unique geology, as well as a chance to learn
welcomes you to visit our great land, *experience* our	culture	and learn of our history. Our boundaries include
interesting food, and a chance to *experience* truly foreign	cultures	and vistas that haven't (yet) been overrun by Western
Play golf? Visit historical sites? *Experience* new	cultures	? Sit with a book in the sunshine? Go to museums and
America and the Middle East, *experiencing* different	cultures	and points of view. Jim is used to working in large
denying the benefits they bring *experiencing* different	cultures	and religions, understanding the incredible diversity
Play golf? Visit historical sites? *Experience* new	cultures	? Sit with a book in the sunshine? Go to museums and
sell to an American audience. *Experiencing* another	culture	first hand gives the knowledge you need to be successful
access routes through which they *experience* the foreign	culture	, the work place, the host family, their peers and
molded me into a world citizen. I *experienced* other	cultures	, religions, languages and customs. I was exposed
invaluable. You will be able to: *experience* a different	culture	make new friends and travel earn academic credits
onsequences of racial behaviour. Having *experienced* various	cultures	the children assemble for the finale. The ethos of
diving, and some to *experience* the unique aboriginal	culture	of the Yami people indigenous to Lanyu, but we also
chance to see the local sights and *experience* the	culture	of a region. From our cruises you can see scenery
opportunity to visit different countries and *experience* new	cultures	. For details of volunteering opportunities overseas
well as providing the opportunity to *experience* a new	culture	and country. Many volunteering placements have the
today's 'warm up' allows us to *experience* the local	culture	& landscape . This area is currently suffering with
benefit from learning new languages, *experiencing* a new	culture	and country and simply enjoying working abroad. For

Figure 6.28. *A sample from the concordance lines for the pattern* experience + culture

These concordance lines seem to reflect Williams' third meaning of culture, which can be associated with the anthropological/ethnographic approach inaugurated by Franz Boas, one of the first modern scholars to speak of cultures in the plural and to prompt an equation with a way life (American culture, Maori culture, etc.). This pattern has a quite consistent collocation with adjectives like *new, different, origin, other*, as seen in Figure 6.28 above. It must be acknowledged, however, that most of these concordance lines originate in academic sites and specialized sites dealing with the typically British experience of the gap year, a datum which relates to the choices made by the developers of ukWaC, who included academic sites (i.e. ac.uk sites) extensively in the crawl.

All in all, these occurrences testify to a radical shift in the meaning of culture, whereby culture is something to be experienced, rather than to be found in books (as Arnold would have argued) – again something quite distant from its more traditional meaning.

4.3.2 *Culture* as subject

The pattern in which *culture* is the grammatical subject of a clause is opened – in terms of salience – by two verbs, *influence* and *collide*. The verb *influence* is almost invariably used in the passive, again with a frequent collocation with *different*. In this case the grammatical function of the subject is equated with the agent in the passive form (see Figure 6.29).

Growing up, Palmer was *influenced* by two *different* cultures	and it is the memories of these and influences from
communication, it is used and *influenced* by *different* cultures	. Therefore, by raising cultural awareness in our
from Africa and the resulting blend of *different* cultures	has profoundly *influenced* the whole history of the
Apollonia. Cyrene was *influenced* by many *different* cultures	including those of the Carthaginians, Greeks, Egyptians
, Greece and England, her experience of *different* cultures	has most certainly *influenced* her music. Eliza Carthy
groups, we take a look at whether their *different* cultures	*influence* them with regard to abortion. Considering
the country has been *influenced* by many *different* cultures	, including the Romans, Vikings, Saxons, Normans and
to which other spiritual teachings from *different* cultures	have *influenced* the present day understanding of
childhood in India, and so was *influenced* by a *different* culture	when writing his timeless tale. What's more, the
people of Formentera were *influenced* by many *different* cultures	. These included the Visigoths, Byzantines and the
area and was heavily *influenced* by the *different* cultures	around him. A keen sportsman and student, Levi eventually
How increases in population, travel and *different* cultures	*influenced* the customs of naming children. Origins
society. Increases in population, travel and *different* cultures	*influenced* this custom and Surnames , were slowly
likely to be *influenced* by *different* organisational cultures	and there is insufficient discussion of this in the
chilli, as the sausage is *influenced* by *different* cultures	and lifestyles. This reinvention may be one of the
Asia, Europe and America and *influenced* by *different* cultures	, art movements, fashion and architecture...the world

Figure 6.29. *A sample from the concordance lines for the pattern* influence + culture

The second collocate is *collide*, a verb that evokes the unpleasant scenario where cultures do not always peacefully coexist, as shown in Figure 6.30 overleaf.

The number of occurrences for the collocation of *culture* with *collide* is balanced by the co-occurrence of *culture* with such verbs as *merge, interact*, and also *converge*, which evokes the peaceful coexistence of different

and write the cultural narratives of our times as cultures	*collide*	. The playwright in Europe as border crosser
the boundary. The dialogic clash that occurs when cultures	*collide*	- through speech genres, language levels,
the misunderstandings and wrongs committed when two cultures	*collide*	. In the late 1950s, a group of Aboriginal
the USA/UK setting in HELLRAISER (1987), where two cultures	*collide*	and produce something unique and unreal.
west: a land of extravagance and glamour, where two cultures	*collide*	to create one sensational night. Building
tries to make sense of a pivotal place where world cultures	*collide*	. Middle East Glamour and Glitz on the Gulf
). Madeleine confronts the difficulty of these two cultures	*colliding*	, and discovers the tumultuous outcome
weekend house party things really take off when the two cultures	*collide*	and the chemistry takes over. Meanwhile,
has always been a place where elements mingle and cultures	*collide*	. -- Max Rodenbeck, Cairo: The City Victorious
days from £1499 per person. A fussion of colours and cultures	*collide*	on this magical 33 night cruise to South
of addiction and the tragedy that can result when cultures	*collide*	. In the nineteenth century, Chinese society
on the only area at the festival where politics and culture	*collide*	will be announced at the end of May or check
surpasses all but the most extreme of "Romantics". As cultures	*collide*	, as labour competes, as worth is economic
strange but beguiling place where three contrasting cultures	*collide*	. It's in Germany, but only just. You can
circumcision! This is the story of what happens when two cultures	*collide*	within one family.. The summary: Being a
between two cultures. He saw the forces of a lunar-based culture	*colliding*	with those of the solar, agricultural culture
mysterious Kaahini...the past merges with the present, cultures	*collide*	and destiny unfolds Kaahini's secret. 'A
of opportunities for good-natured laughs as the two cultures	*collide*	, take the measure of, and in the end, understan
The film shows the results of what happens when two cultures	*collide*	. One of the key religious and moral themes
allowed us to fly cheaply and changed the rate at which cultures	*collided*	. Medical and dental ceramics allowed us

Figure 6.30. *A sample from the concordance lines for the pattern* collide + culture

cultures. Also worth mentioning is the presence of patterns which point to the 'resistance' of culture in certain conditions, as exemplified by such collocates as *persist* and *survive*.

Last but not least, it is important to highlight a quite obvious collocation of *culture* with *change*, a word which ranks in a middle position in the list of collocates in terms of raw frequency. All patterns of co-occurrence with *change*, as can easily be imagined, suggest a strong perception of the dynamic nature of culture, always in a state of flux (see Figure 6.31).

target in 90% of cases. How much has the	culture	*changed* ? Some FOI officials are refreshingly
confirmed. Have lessons been learned and has the	culture	*changed* sufficiently within the planning
based approach to regulation so that the	culture	*change* we all agree upon can be advanced
crucial change nowadays is that national	cultures	are rapidly *changing* themselves. They change
people in the traditional ways. The UK's bar	culture	is *changing* . On a typical night out you
n't get in. Identity really matters when a	culture	is *changing* quickly, and so theatre matters
public, we'd be world beaters. I think the	culture	has *changed* recently. The whole discipline
without a disciplinary base? How have research	cultures	*changed* the way we think of relations between
fifty years time, when language usage and	culture	have *changed* , your fantasy could have
projects this may have marked the fact that the	culture	had *changed* , the priorities had changed
physical remains of the processes by which	cultures	*change* . I remember the first time I read
components of the music. As the listening	culture	has *changed* , have spontaneity and improvisation
doing something, and I do not think that	culture	has *changed* , there are a few still at
English-Language Euro economy. The Celtic Tiger Irish	culture	is rapidly *changing* and expanding to include
scriptures spans 1,400 years! People and	cultures	*change* in that amount of time. Thus the
culture to more people or democratisation of	culture	*changing* perceptions of what constitutes
countries. How has this involvement with a youth	culture	*changed* you and your view of church? Church
tradition of the West has been shattered and	culture	has greatly *changed* . The Holocaust showed
grievance and disciplinary procedures. Systemic	culture	*change* A variety of techniques such as
build up a picture of how international	culture	has *changed* , and how people have reacted

Figure 6.31. *A sample from the concordance lines for the pattern* change + culture

4.3.3 Modifiers of culture

Particularly interesting is the list of pre-modifiers that accompany culture, significantly opened by *different* and *popular* in terms of raw frequency, and by *popular, contemporary, western* in terms of saliency. Each of these terms deserves more careful inspection than is feasible in the limited scope of this book. A telling collocation, which can be briefly examined, is *Western/western culture*, with the number of occurrences (in both lower and upper case) amounting to 1,390 hits. Indeed, a look at collocates for this pattern suggests that the most frequent collocates for *W/western culture* are its 'opposite', *E/eastern*, and then *modern*, *contemporary* and *Christian*. Moreover, concordance lines for patterns of co-occurrence of Western and Eastern suggest a consistent semantic preference for verbs referring to the overcoming of boundaries, such as *unite*, *mix*, *meet*, nouns like *fusion* and *melting pot*, adjectives like *hybrid*, and so on, as shown in Figure 6.32 below.

human awareness in both *Eastern* and *Western* cultures . They are drawn from consultations, readings
the gateway between *Eastern* and *Western* cultures , Turkey continues to make remarkable progress
the fabrics of both *Eastern* and *Western* culture . Once we reach genetic enlightenment and
surreal hybrids of *Eastern* and *Western* cultures , his confidently bizarre books are populated
gap between *Eastern* European and *Western* culture . Their lyrics spin darkly humorous tales
manuscripts representing both *Eastern* and *Western* cultures throughout his life. The Japanese collection
interacted with both *Eastern* and *Western* cultures throughout its 600-year history and, like
orientations between people of *Eastern* and *Western* cultures . Dr Laungani will also present a view of
Bates cited "a clash of *Eastern* and *Western* cultures " as he made an earlier exit than planned
chequered past-but with a twist *Western* culture meets *Eastern* in a bold and rich interpretation
and the meeting of *Eastern* and *Western* culture . Firmly anchored in the local reality of
show is a fusion of *Eastern* and *Western* cultures and music and is a sure fire hit guaranteed
the world where the *Eastern* and *Western* cultures meet. It is the most popular place in the
phenomenon within both *Eastern* and *Western* cultures . Over the centuries, abstaining from food
commenting on the clash of *Eastern* and *Western* culture and consumerism. Cai Yuan and J J Xi Two
Kedleston Hall that unites *Eastern* and *Western* cultures ; Lacemaking - Lichfield College City &
between his loyalty to *Eastern* and *Western* culture . City of Djinns: A Year in Delhi by William
designed to embrace both *Eastern* and *Western* cultures . Fabric applications, prints and colours
creating a fusion between *Eastern* and *Western* cultures . 'The Garden of Sensual Delights' was how
exhibition in a fusion of *Eastern* and *Western* cultures and their individual outlooks in creating
remains a melting pot of *eastern* and *western* cultures . From its quaint, traditional . The perfect
identify with post-Mao *eastern* or *western* cultures . and there are problems over the dichotomy
time-honored recipes from both *eastern* and *western* cultures . Served in a cozy atmosphere, diners may
centuries the surrounding *eastern* and *western* cultures China, Europe, India and Persia exchanged
remains a unique mix of *eastern* and *western* culture and you can fly there direct on one of
an intermingling of *eastern* and *western* cultures . Roman officials, businessmen and colonists
Kong remains a mix of *eastern* and *western* cultures from traditional Chinese heritage to high
at a crossroads of *eastern* and *western* culture , of ancient and modern spiritual disciplines
, 31 mins), drawing *eastern* and *western* cultures together via satellite. Perfromer/Audience
different aspects of *eastern* and *western* culture ... a charming and expertly told story...
ancient *eastern* principles to suit *western* culture . I can help you to understand yourself

Figure 6.32. *A sample from the concordance lines for the pattern* western/Western + eastern/Eastern + culture

These patterns testify to the dynamic relations between cultures which is characteristic of contemporary society, while also testifying to the persistence of such dichotomies as East vs West in framing our worldview.[3]

4.3.4 *Culture* as modifier

Another typical pattern highlighted by the word sketch is the one in which *culture* is itself used as a modifier. In this category attention should be drawn to *shock*, a collocation already attested in the BNC and now ranking first in order of saliency. The notion of *culture shock* hardly needs any explanation in a world that is experiencing increasing mobility. Significantly, however, one of the most prominent collocates for *culture shock* in ukWaC is *reverse*, which originates in the phrase *reverse culture shock* (see Figure 6.33 below), a form not yet attested in the BNC, probably because the experience itself had not yet been fully conceptualized.

spend time in Prague, experience *reverse* culture *shock* when they go back to the US, and
England, but also back to university was a culture *shock* in *reverse* . I found myself missing
have finally started to get over *reverse* culture *shock* . I was able to find some material
the UK, plus a discussion of ' *reverse* culture *shock* ', which many students experience
placement, the greater will be the *reverse* culture *shock* on return! Being home You have to
comment) These are the plusses and minuses of culture *shock* in *reverse* , very like the things
returning home (and coping with *reverse* culture *shock*) can be just as difficult as getting
promise it will only happen during my *reverse* culture *shock* ! I promise....youll just have to
you can experience a kind of " *reverse* culture *shock* ", together with a sense of loss
are sometimes referred to as ' *reverse* culture *shock* '. Some people feel disappointed
are sometimes referred to as *reverse* culture *shock* '. Some people feel disappointed
living in a new environment there is *reverse* culture *shock* as the returning missionary has to
what ways did they suffer from " *reverse* culture *shock* "? When they returned to the States
will not suffer too greatly from *reverse* culture *shock* . God of illumination, You call us
feeling any lasting effects of *reverse* culture *shock* (except still calling Benjamin's
Shock I didn't experience much *reverse* culture *shock* but the mobile phone technology here
minority views How to prepare for *reverse* culture *shock* Take addresses of people you want
re-adjustment has been called ' *reverse* culture *shock* '. How could it affect you? Personal
views. How can you prepare for *reverse* culture *shock* ? RELATED LINKS Alumni It helps just
It helps just to be aware that *reverse* culture *shock* is a common reaction and that you

Figure 6.33. *Concordance lines for* reverse culture shock *(sample)*

In this way ukWaC not only provides evidence of a relatively new linguistic formation, but in doing so it points to the emergence of a new social and psychological condition, resulting from a change in society itself. The very existence of a *reverse culture shock* is related to novel ways of experiencing mobility and migration, which may no longer entail a permanent relocation of the subjects involved, but rather produce continuous dislocations and relocations.

Also interesting is the collocation *culture clash*, where the notion of 'clash' seems to have been extended to encompass not only radical juxtapositions between civilizations, but also everyday differences in worldviews and opinions, as suggested in some of the concordance lines reported below (Figure 6.34) in which a culture clash is no more than the juxtaposition of different views in ICT.

smoothly. "I don't think there will be a big	culture *clash*	, because so many ex-Oracle people
of passion disrupts all the scheming and	culture *clashes*	- and opens up new possibilities
those of the settled community, and the two	cultures *clash*	." The Government guidelines are
most common barrier was considered to be	culture *clash*	, experienced in the case of 52%
plus without compromising values and the	culture *clashes*	which can provoke when dealing
Turing, and nor did his social space, with	culture *clashes*	between pure science, engineering
ıtertaining album full of exotic noises and cool	culture *clashes*	. A new Ilarvirus found in rose
wrote in the Washington Post of witnessing a	culture *clash*	at a diplomatic dinner. The speech
everything about him provoked conflict: the	culture *clash*	of his free-ranging scientific mind
ınchester. There was a particularly Mancunian	culture *clash*	. Alan Turing could not 'direct'
Minnelli in a cross-generational gay icon	culture *clash*	. Originally unleashed in 1989 and
to a screen as a computer graphics user.	Culture *clash*	: the soft machine in a hard place
As usual, Alan Turing walked into another	culture *clash*	, this time the most dramatic of
just about sums them up. It's a strange	culture *clash*	which nevertheless fails to prevent
serious attempts at experimental musical	culture *clash*	, and it's this that saves Revival
feel better soon- i know you will. ab Two	cultures *clash*	in cyberspace This is already the
camel-hair coat worn by Capote establish the	culture *clash*	between urbane Manhattan and the
stars in Oscar Wilde's classic tale of the	culture *clash*	between an American family and a
therefore set for lots of lame stereotypical	culture *clashes*	between the loud-mouthed, sloppy
repetition, 'noisy' stories. Christianity meets	culture	online Does Christianity *clash* with culture

Figure 6.34. *Concordance lines for* culture clash *(sample)*

In terms of raw frequency, the list of nouns modified by *culture* is instead opened by *change*, with collocations mainly pointing to the public domain of institutions and enterprises (e.g. *organisational, management, development*). The most typical patterns seem to be *to bring about a cultural change*, and *a cultural change is needed/required*, often occurring in conditional sentences.

As also seen in the BNC, the patterns in which culture is a modifier also include nouns like *dish, medium*, and *supernatant*, relating to the scientific meaning of culture. Here, they seem to include terms like *religion, history, language, traditions*. Yet, by inspecting each of these patterns the user becomes aware of one of the typical limitations of this system, i.e. a failure in recognizing the comma between one word and the following word, which leads to a misinterpretation of the sequence noun + comma + noun as being instead a noun phrase, as shown in Figure 6.35 overleaf.

but proud parent. In time the traditions, culture	, *language* of her family will be transmitted
disability, religion, conscience, belief, culture	, *language* and birth. The Constitution also
support the Tibetan people, help preserve the culture	, *language* , history, art and most importantly
without segregating students by ability, race, culture	, *language* , or other variables and (b)
staff within them, embrace this diversity of culture	, *language* , and ability and make it part
centred on their interests, understandings, culture	, *language* , and so on. This is so because
is but one component) and contexts. Like culture	, *language* is a metaphor, a 'useful fiction
the role of education in preserving the culture	, *language* and religious beliefs of all
and the whole world must abandon their own culture	, *language* and national identity and assimilate
part of more general debates on history, culture	, *language* and identity in the post colonial
school take the initiative to know about the cultures	, *languages* and lifestyles of the Gypsy
questions which relate to issues of identity, culture	, *language* , religion, society, citizenship
nderground system. For information on Brazil, its culture	, *language* , people and etiquette please
, which aims to promote knowledge of the culture	, *language* and history of Russia and the
You may need some information on Turkish culture	, *language* and etiquette Note that this
You may need some information on Turkish culture	, *language* and etiquette The French Department
European partnership in terms of differences in cultures	, *languages* and structures. But our aim,
may need some information on Argentina's culture	, *language* and etiquette The place names
may need some information on Argentina's culture	, *language* and etiquette RSS Feed | Further
information on doing business in Brazil, its culture	, *language* , people and etiquette please

Figure 6.35. *Concordance lines for* culture + language *(sample)*

4.3.5 The pattern *culture* and/or NOUN

Finally, the pattern '*culture* and/or noun' deserves a word of comment. Here *culture* is found in such typical pairs as *language and culture*, *history and culture*, *culture and society*, and *culture and religion*. Results are again significantly consistent with results from the BNC, and this is certainly an area in which earlier unqualified uses of the word *culture* are still prominent, while elsewhere in the word sketch under analysis, the notion of *culture* seems to have been fragmented into myriads of subcultures. In this pattern, *culture* seems to be used once again in its comprehensive meaning of 'achievement', and pairs with other words to focus on different aspects and perspectives.

4.4 *A culture of*: The changing face of culture in contemporary society

The patterns analysed so far testify to the liveliness of the word *culture* in contemporary society. While keeping its traditional meaning, culture has also entered different contexts and has been fragmented in a myriad of more or less accepted sub-categorizations, which suggest that its core 'Arnoldian' sense coexists and contends with new meanings and with looser ways of defining culture. This is nowhere more evident than in the extremely rich and varied array of post-modifiers devised over the years for the word, and to which both the BNC and ukWaC abundantly testify (see Figure 6.36). Particularly significant in this respect is the pattern *a culture of*, which seems to turn the word *culture* into an extraordinarily capacious and inclusive category that can be used for anything.

pp_of-p	737	1.2	pp_of-i	14837	1.7
contentment	7	7.66	secrecy	127	7.49
racism	13	7.47	openness	153	7.34
dependency	7	6.68	blame	58	6.2
poverty	6	5.2	impunity	34	6.06
discourse	5	5.01	entrepreneurship	35	5.7
organisation	20	4.62	dependency	49	5.62
resistance	5	4.47	peace	217	5.45
cell	11	3.94	consumerism	23	5.34
society	23	3.83	spin	36	5.12
Europe	7	3.22	complacency	20	5.05
region	7	3.15	innovation	106	4.97
education	11	2.99	disbelief	19	4.94
station	7	2.94	disrespect	14	4.78
Britain	6	2.66	individualism	16	4.74
police	7	2.61	violence	110	4.74
community	8	2.51	tolerance	35	4.69
country	12	2.4	accountability	38	4.65
language	5	2.2	suspicion	30	4.59
management	5	2.09	microorganism	13	4.56
class	5	2.03	learning	154	4.52
period	6	1.99	deceit	13	4.49
school	10	1.97	cynicism	14	4.48
people	19	1.69	excellence	49	4.45
world	8	1.66	enterprise	74	4.45
group	7	0.97	bacterium	36	4.42

Figure 6.36. *The pattern* a culture of *in the BNC and in ukWaC*

While these collocates might seem to confirm Stubbs' intuition that the pattern has a relatively negative semantic prosody (1996: 106), owing to collocations with words bearing negative connotations (like *racism*, *poverty*, *dependence* in the BNC, or *secrecy*, *blame*, *impunity*, *consumerism* in ukWaC), there is ample evidence that the pattern can equally accommodate positive notions, like *peace*, *openness*, *community*, *excellence*. Furthermore, even patterns which might carry inherently negative connotations, like the collocation between *culture* and *impunity*, are mitigated by their co-occurrence with words suggesting an opposition (*challenge*, *end*, *change*, *combat*, *eradicate*) as seen in the concordance lines below.

epetitive cycles of violences which created the culture of *impunity* , exclusion, systematic killings
Gacaca was established to put an end to the culture of *impunity* , to find out the truth about
Confronting Impunity, Jan. 2004 , reports that "a culture of *impunity* " exists within the DRC where
torture in its prisons, while pursuing a culture of *impunity* for the perpetrators of such
done little to disarm militias or end the " culture of *impunity* " there. He said Sudan's authorities
series of ongoing legal challenges to the culture of *impunity* which has surrounded state
for her eldest son but also to end the " culture of *impunity* " which allows heavily armed
for over 65 years, as well as the growing culture of *impunity* and disregard for basic rights
of indiscriminate killings by army and a culture of *impunity* (06/09/05) Aljazeera.net: Sharon
is to be peace in west Africa, that the culture of *impunity* that has prevailed in the region
of law and accountability and a resulting culture of *impunity* . Ideally, Mr. Habré would
in October in northern Bogra district. "A culture of *impunity* is growing in Bangladesh due
protection encourages the Israeli government culture of *impunity* and dismissal of overwhelming
and are capable of swift escalation. The culture of *impunity* is exemplified by land grabs
the government in Khartoum to operate in a culture of *impunity* . Asset and travel sanctions
general. Hope for a genuine change to the culture of *impunity* on which Mexican politics thrives
government has not done enough to combat the culture of *impunity* which has reigned since 1986
government has not done enough to combat the culture of *impunity* which has reigned since 1986
issue in Rwanda was bad governance, the culture of *impunity* and social injustices by successive
of their conflicts, hence eradicating a culture of *impunity* . The participation of the

Figure 6.37. *The pattern* culture of impunity *in ukWaC*

Furthermore, it should be observed that, especially in ukWaC, the pattern *a culture of* includes many examples of phrases in inverted commas, which seem to create a culture virtually *ex-nihilo*, reducing culture to little more than an attitude, as in the examples reported in Figure 6.38.

were shown by and to everyone. Creating a culture of 'allowing' seems to me to be the only option
of car insurance companies who criticise a culture of 'bigger is best' when it comes to buying
addressing social issues and engendering a culture of 'collective responsibility' and the promotion
on self-assessment and the development of a culture of 'continuous improvement'. The QSTG identified
well-meaning Westerners are in danger of creating a culture of 'disaster tourism' which actually makes
Evaluation of impact - How could you develop a culture of 'evaluation for learning', to provide a
Hatfield Primary Care Trust aims to create a culture of ' excellence in customer care' to try and
executed after May 1923. Dolan alludes to a culture of 'fighting for its own sake' in the IRA,
digestive function in pets. A probiotic is a culture of 'friendly' bacteria which grow in the gut
you're hearing the same old stories (30). a culture of 'getting by' Amongst the constraints alluded
1995, 28) suggests this is "leading towards a culture of 'getting by' " amongst academic staff.
(1) by practising lecturers establishing a culture of 'Good Practice', and (2) by the creation
theory in the practice and (b) establish a culture of 'Good Practice'. The first of these points

Figure 6.38. *A sample from the concordance lines for the pattern* a culture of *from ukWaC*

Here again the word *culture* seems to have become a sort of neutral term that can keep the company of many different words: a culture of corruption, a culture of accountability, a culture of violence, a culture of peace, and even a culture of 'buy it now pay for it later'. As suggested by the various collocates for the pattern *a culture of* shown in Figure 6.38 above, this lexico-grammar pattern really has the power of turning culture into a sort of *vox media* that can be used for anything.

This pattern could certainly be further explored using the full potential of the tools at hand. For instance, by using regular expressions we could retrieve only patterns in which *a culture of* is followed by a noun, or a verb, or by an adjective followed by a noun (see Figures 6.39, 6.40 and 6.41 respectively).

and national parliaments, and introducing	a culture of debate	and discussion. Unfortunately for her,
development in these animals. To develop	a culture of peace	there needs to be a culture of debate,
These are important strands in establishing	a culture of responsibility	on our roads. In this context, it is also
in other ways we have sought to create "	a culture of compliance	" that makes operating in accordance with
have strong leadership and strong systems,	a culture of achievement	with high expectations and intensive support
are moving towards working with a model of	a culture of singularity	(singular to a logic of its own organisation
improving police performance, establishing	a culture of accountability	and changing where necessary and appropriate
Regent House. 2. The General Board maintains	a culture of secrecy	in matters where there ought to be transparency
leadership is shaped by the instrumentalities of	a culture of trust	. In his insightful discussion on the issue
to worry about the others, but it creates	a culture of disinterest	and uninvolvement, which, in turn, restricts
prove their manhood, egged on by peers or	a culture of violence	, or driven by a desire to avenge atrocities
to universities and small magazines, and	a culture of promotion	and hype, the world of the Sunday books
. The Innovation Strategy aims to create	a culture of innovation	by encouraging businesses to innovate by
can be a response to the needs to create	a culture of peace	and human rights. There were other workshops
practices were more generally integrated into	a culture of curiosity	and collection. Moreover, the mobility
writings of others will be endangered by	a culture of originality	at all costs. Others think that it will
desire and approval.' 9 Relating the rise of	a culture of celebrity	to the decline of religion (a core symptom
city council are accused of presiding over	a culture of fear	where Black workers who "rock the boat"
identified âmanagement shortcomings and	a culture of over-spending	with no incentive to reduce costsâ (FT

Figure 6.39. *A sample from the concordance lines for the pattern* a culture of + *NOUN*

individual and group values are recognized (	a culture of welcoming	, living together, that is appealing for
pupils about attribution. If you create	a culture of taking	knowledge and looking at it, reflecting
social enterprises? back to top Creating	a culture of volunteering	and mentoring What more can Government
euro; in order to continue to encourage	a culture of giving	, and to avoid a possible downturn in giving
eadership in regeneration through encouraging	a culture of learning	and the acquisition of core skills. · Identifying
eremonies, but is also charged with stimulating	a culture of learning	and to advance the knowledge of the history
an initiative lies in the development of	a culture of accepting	the use of private citizens by the police
to tutors too, who would wish to engender	a culture of documenting	reactions and ideas associated with the
mi-naked women on billboards selling cars, and	a culture of imported	(female) and indigenous (tourist-oriented
action, we need to do much more to create	a culture of giving	time. Our next task is to encourage new
for people who are blind and to enhance	a culture of learning	in the information age. Further details
action, we need to do much more to create	a culture of giving	time. Our next task is to encourage new
thereby tapping new markets and creating	a culture of saving	amongst low income families. And so many
the current position. There seems to be	a culture of blaming	the infantry when the fault lies with the
unfunded targets, unfunded pay reforms, and	a culture of bullying	and intimidation2 have left the NHS in
. The theme for the Forum is âbuilding	a culture of volunteering	and citizenship through sportâ and will
reastmilk substitutes, the industry had created	a culture of bottle-feeding	, depriving babies of the ideal baby food

Figure 6.40. *A sample from the concordance lines for the pattern* a culture of + VERB

community. It is hard for those of us steeped in	a culture of materialistic individualism	to understand fully what Africa is all
provide good value for money, and to promote	a culture of good performance	: Have proper procedures and controls necess
outcome-based service planning techniques	a culture of continuous improvement	and striving for excellence 2.3 The County
more intensive professional learning within	a culture of continuous deliberation	, and that it has to be continually tested
clear how very gettable we are, even in	a culture of high alert	. To anyone with imagination (or who knows
was more acceptable and everyday. It was	a culture of verbal belligerence	, too: somewhere behind Swift's virulent
terrorist bombs, and no one could stop them. So	a culture of free exchange	and mutual help has come into being in
more visible week by week as we encourage	a culture of open access	. References GNU EPrints archive software
manner in which a combination of technology,	a culture of instant gratification	and the commercial fragmentation of the
other health care professionals fostering	a culture of life-long learning	in the health service; appreciating the
means 'mirror' - is dedicated to cultivating	a culture of independent media	in Afghanistan" A fledgling free press:
means 'mirror' - is dedicated to cultivating	a culture of independent media	and information in Afghanistan. Reza had
Government in Britain is distinguished by	a culture of administrative centralism	, whichalong with departmentalismpresents
manner in which a combination of technology,	a culture of instant gratification	and the commercial fragmentation of the
available simultaneously, providing for	a culture of dynamic publishing	of research results. Back in 1994, the
every facet of the corporation, and achieve	a culture of continual improvement	to assure total customer satisfaction.
society We are at the forefront of creating	a culture of human rights	in the delivery of public services at a
Karnataka and other Indian states, there is	a culture of organic agriculture	, and she is currently talking to local
students active in this area. It promotes	a culture of social science	research and provides the opportunity for

Figure 6.41. *A sample from the concordance lines for the pattern* a culture of + *ADJ + NOUN*

It goes without saying that it is necessary to be extremely cautious before drawing conclusions, if any, from investigations like these. And it is still open to discussion whether the tools and data sets like those described and discussed in this chapter can be profitably used in the context of research aimed at gaining a deeper understanding of discourse and society, which are generally carried out on the basis of smaller and more controlled corpora, as we see today. What is certain is that, thanks to these resources and tools, a huge amount of data has been made available to the research community and a rewarding exploration can only come as the result of teamwork in the context of a multidisciplinary approach.

Conclusion

As this chapter has shown, charting the latest achievements of the web as corpus, the development of new methods for corpus linguistics is not simply a matter of new corpora and new tools, but rather of changing ways of conceiving corpora and corpus tools under the impact of the web. While the notion of the *web-as-corpus* might be giving way to a complementary view of the *corpus-as-web*, other significant changes are occurring in terms of availability and distribution of tools and resources, including a shift of both from products to services. Furthermore, the huge amount of data made available for corpus linguistics investigation through large web corpora requires tools capable of supporting the linguist's analytical approach, by providing raw quantitative data on which to exercise a theoretically informed and culturally conscious interpretative effort. All this seems to connect the changes taking place in contemporary corpus linguistics to similar changes taking place in society at large, and perhaps represents the best way to sum up the real significance of the achievements presented in the present work.

Study questions and activities

Go to www.sketchengine.co.uk and register for a free one-month trial. If necessary, familiarize with the tool through the guide 'Getting Started with the Sketch Engine' (http://trac.sketchengine.co.uk/wiki/SkE/GettingStarted). When you are ready, choose one of the large corpora made available through the system (e.g. ukWaC, or a corpus for your own language, if you are not from an English-speaking country).

- Produce concordances for one or two words whose collocational profile is of particular interest to you. How does the system's output help you find out more about these words?
- Now go to the Word Sketch function. To what extent is the information obtained qualitatively different from that obtained through ordinary concordance lines?
- Create a list of synonyms for one of the words you have used for the exercises above and then find out synonym candidates for that word through the Thesaurus function implemented in the Sketch Engine. Are there any significant differences? Can you explain them?
- Using the Sketch Difference function, compare English words with similar meanings but different usages (e.g. big/large, little/small, travel/journey, traveller/tourist, migrant/refugee, man/woman etc.) and comment on the tool's output.

Suggestions for further reading

Baroni, M., S. Bernardini, A. Ferraresi, E. Zanchetta et al. (2009), 'The WaCky Wide Web: A Collection of Very Large Linguistically Processed Web-Crawled Corpora', *Language Resources and Evaluation*, 43(3), 209–26.

Bennett, T., Grossberg, L. and Morris, M. (2005), *New Keywords: A Revised Vocabulary of Culture and Society.* New York: John Wiley & Sons.

Kilgarriff, A. et al. (2004), 'The Sketch Engine', in *Proceedings Euralex,* Lorient: France, 105–16.

Pearce, M. (2008), 'Investigating the Collocational Behaviour of MAN and WOMAN in the BNC using Sketch Engine', *Corpora*, 3,1, 1–29
Wild, K., A. Church, D. McCarthy and J. Burgess (2013), 'Quantifying Lexical Usage: Vocabulary pertaining to Ecosystems and the Environment', *Corpora*, 8, 53–79.

Notes

1 I wish to thank Maria Monno for suggesting this solution.

2 I wish to thank Maria Monno for calling my attention to this specific aspect.

3 This point is also raised in Monno 2012: 119.

7

From Download to Upload: The Web as Corpus in the Web 2.0 Era

Introduction

The aim of this final chapter is to comment briefly on the relevance to web-as-corpus issues of some changes that have occurred in the World Wide Web in the nearly 15 years since it emerged as a widely accessible global phenomenon. More specifically, the main focus will be on those changes that have occurred as a result of the development of technological affordances generally known under the label Web 2.0, which turned the web into the ubiquitous, participatory reality of today. Section 1 briefly surveys some aspects of Web 2.0, focusing on the blurring of distinctions between producers and consumers of web content, introducing the new category of *prosumers*. Section 2 provides an overview of recent uses of Wikipedia as a corpus, pointing to possible future developments. Section 3 comments on the new horizons opened up by collective intelligence and cloud computing, with the hope that paradigms involving cooperation over the internet will become the norm in corpus linguistics all over the world.

1. From download to upload: Web users as *prosumers*

Investigating the impact that the technological affordances comprising the so-called Web 2.0 may have had on specific web-as-corpus issues requires a preliminary step to focus on what actually makes up a Web 2.0 environment. Although there has been significant debate about the concept of Web 2.0

and the term itself has been criticized for its incorrect implication of a new stage in internet development, rather than simply signifying a different use of existing technologies, the constellation of features that we currently associate with Web 2.0 has undoubtedly qualitatively changed the ways in which people use web technologies (Warschauer and Grimes 2007: 2). As a famous video by anthropologist Robert Wesch illustrates, Web 2.0 technologies have made the creation and distribution of user-generated content easy and free for everybody, thanks to a change in the code (the example that Wesch gives is HTML being replaced by XML) that enables the separation of form and content. In so doing, this technology has raised fundamental issues which are relevant to communication and society at large, ultimately contributing to new forms of interaction between man and machine as well as between human beings themselves (Wesch 2007).

In this new context, one of the most prominent aspects of how the web has changed is the dramatic increase in user-generated content published online. Only a few years ago, the basic assumption behind the web was that the majority of users only needed to download content published by a tiny minority of computer-savvy operators who had all the technical skills and 'authority' required to upload content to the web, whether for scientific, political or commercial purposes. Even the bandwidth on cable and phone lines, Kelly (2005) suggests, was asymmetrical so as to respond to these clearly imbalanced needs. Download rates thus exceeded upload rates, the dogma being that ordinary people were mere consumers of web content, not producers. Today, as we all know, most users are as likely to upload content as to download. The new paradigm is participation, not mere consumption, and this blurring of clear-cut distinctions between producers and consumers of web content is also related to changes which have invested the realm of economy and have been investigated with reference to society at large. One such change is the emergence of the new category of prosumers (Toffler 1981), a blend of the words 'producer' and 'consumer'.

Some effects that this move away from the hierarchical structure of the Web 1.0 may have had on the nature and use of the web as corpus have already been discussed. Especially when using the web as a corpus through ordinary search engines, the possibility of coming across evidence of attested usage which comes not from 'edited' sources but from direct upload of content by the most disparate users has dramatically increased. Only a few years ago, not many occurrences would have been found on the web for new verbal coinages by teenagers, whose access to the publication of web content would have been deemed impossible, whereas today social networks actually give immediate worldwide resonance to youth jargon and memes, making it possible for researchers to study 'epidemics' in their real-time diffusion (Freitag 2012). Furthermore, the possibility of accessing and producing concordances from subsections of the web, including blogs and tweets, makes it relatively easy to explore the language used in informal personal communication or the language accompanying the upload of user-generated content. It should be noted, moreover, that the accessibility of the web as an instant repository of user-generated content has contributed to the spread of languages other than English, making the web a truly multilingual environment. In this respect, Wikipedia especially, with its entries generally in at least two or three languages and often many more, has greatly contributed to the decentralization of English as the *lingua franca* of the web, making it much easier to find quantitatively and qualitatively consistent web content for many languages and many topics. Finally, the technological affordances that have made it so easy to share information and collaborate at all levels are providing the platform for new ways to cooperate which will undoubtedly play an increasing role in corpus linguistics as well. All these aspects will need to be objects of investigation over the next few years. For the purpose of the present book, however, only two aspects will be explored in greater detail in the following pages.

2. Web 2.0 as corpus: The case of Wikipedia as a multilingual corpus

As seen in the previous section, the key issue in the so-called second generation of the web is the simple fact that users have taken an increasingly active role. Almost all users are now able to 'create new content, share it, link to it, search for it, tag it, and modify it' (Levene 2010) – Wikipedia, Facebook, Twitter and YouTube being the most significant, and now classic, examples of this Copernican revolution.

From a corpus linguistics perspective, particularly significant is the role played by wikis as prototypical Web 2.0 tools, of which Wikipedia is the most widespread application. By allowing real-time publication of individual content without any previous editorial revision, wikis have unleashed a number of centrifugal forces which have led to a dynamic merging of the traditionally distinct functions of audience and authorship. Furthermore, the ability for users to edit and re-edit web pages in real time actually displays the inherent instability of texts, while de-emphasizing the role of individual authorship. Wikis thus provide material evidence of the dynamic and inherently social nature of language, and allow discourse to emerge that is continually negotiated and articulated through a community of users (Ray and Graeff 2008: 39–40).

In this respect, a very interesting phenomenon is the attention that Wikipedia has attracted in the context of Natural Language Processing, Computational Linguistics, and recently also Corpus Linguistics, both as a collection of monolingual encyclopaedic corpora and as a virtual multilingual 'comparallel', or 'comparable-cum-parallel' (Bernardini et al. 2011; Zanettin 2012) corpus. Indeed, when seen from a corpus perspective, Wikipedia defies all definitions, challenging clear-cut traditional distinctions between 'parallel' and 'comparable' corpora by offering the user a collaboratively constructed resource, in which texts can entertain a rather loose translation relation with other texts in the same corpus, at least at some stage in their life.

Wikipedia currently hosts more than 300 languages covering the most disparate areas of human knowledge, and many works have been published in the last few years that focus on its use and exploitation for multilingual tasks in natural language processing. The most typical concern the extraction of bilingual dictionaries (Yu and Tsujii 2009; Tyers and Pieanaar 2008), alignment and machine translation (Adafre and de Rijke 2006), as well as multilingual retrieval information (Pottast et al. 2008). In corpus linguistics, Wikipedia articles have long found a place as a good source of corpus-like information and have been used to extract seeds for the creation of domain-specific corpora through semi-automated methods (see Chapter 5). Since the number of entries for the most common languages in Wikipedia is relatively high, it is generally considered as a reliable multilingual resource (Gamallo Otero and Gonzalez Lopez 2010: 21) and several approaches have been implemented to exploit its potential from a corpus linguistics perspective on a larger scale. Indeed, recently Wikipedia entries have been used as the starting point for the creation of large web corpora for many languages, as in the Corpus Factory Project (Kilgarriff et al. 2010).

Wikipedia being the largest repository of similar texts in many languages, much attention is also being paid to the possibility of exploiting the comparability of Wikipedia articles to create multilingual comparable corpora. Methods to mine Wikipedia for comparable texts, according to the two basic parameters of variation in languages and topics, are described in Gamallo Otero and Gonzalez Lopez (2010), while attempts are being made to create parallel corpora from Wikipedia by identifying translation pairs (Mohammadi and Ghasem Aghaee 2010) – a research field that still poses many challenges, particularly owing to the great instability of Wikipedia texts and to the extremely loose relations between translated texts.

3. The corpus in the cloud? The challenges that lie ahead

We have already traced a change in the way in which corpus resources and tools are accessed and distributed, from a conventional product – developed and sold as a package – to a service, where the software and the corpus are hosted on the vendor's web servers and delivered to customers, who use it on demand over the internet. This change is undoubtedly an effect of the centrality of the web in contemporary society, and has partly affected – as we have seen – the way in which corpora are used today: no longer as 'finished products' to be purchased and locally 'owned' by each single user, but rather as services offered either for free or under licence (Kilgarriff 2010). Along with traditional corpus linguistics work, performed with both the corpus and the tool installed locally, a radically different approach has emerged, which allows for corpus queries to be submitted from an ordinary web browser to a corpus stored on a remote server. This is the change underlying the development of what McEnery and Hardie (2012: 43) term 'fourth generation concordancers' like BNCweb (Hoffmann et al. 2008), corpus.byu.edu (Davies 2005) or the Sketch Engine (Kilgarriff 2004). This has two obvious advantages: the user does not need to install any special software, and the user does not need to store local copies of the corpora, thus partly solving the problems of copyright.

While innovative in the way they provide access to corpus resources, these services still run on conventional web servers. By contrast, a new trend, which is typically connected to Web 2.0 as a new working environment, is related to the concept of cloud computing, and will undoubtedly play an important role in the way in which corpus resources are produced, distributed and accessed in the future. In the new paradigm, exemplified by the metaphor of the cloud, resources may be geographically distributed, may come from a multitude of computing systems and may be delivered to a variety of devices. Some examples of this new trend were at the basis of the 2012 LREC Conference on Collaborative Resources (Wilcock 2012; Green 2012).

But the change that will affect the practices of corpus linguistics probably more than anything else is the possibility of cooperating, sharing and creating new resources, through what is generally known as 'collective intelligence'. Defined as 'the emergence of new ideas as a result of a group effort' (Levene 2010), collective intelligence is likely to change the face of corpus linguistics over the next few years, together with changing methods based on the principles of crowd-sourcing, i.e. enabling more people to enter cooperative projects. The open source software movement is a typical example. The key ingredients of collaborative programming – 'swapping code, updating instantly, recruiting globally' (Kelly 2005) – could never have worked without the emergence of new tools for sharing and cooperating. The changes that have occurred in the web have fostered an approach based on involvement and interactivity at levels once thought unfashionable or impossible, turning 'small actions into powerful forces'. And this is something from which the web-as-corpus community, and indeed the corpus linguistics community as a whole, can greatly profit.

Suggestions for further reading

Bernardini, S., S. Castagnoli, A. Ferraresi, F. Gaspari and E. Zanchetta (2011), 'Turning Wikipedia into Comparapedia: Towards a new type of comparable corpus for language professionals'. *Corpus Linguistics Conference 2011*. University of Birmingham, 20-22 July 2011.

Kelly, K. (2005), 'We Are the Web, Wired, 13.08, August 2005.

Wesch, M. (2007), *Web 2.0: The machine is us/ing us.* [Video] Avaialble at http://www.youtube.com/watch?v=6gmP4nk0EOE [accessed 1 June 2013].

Wilcock, G. (2012), 'Annotated Corpora in the Cloud: Free Storage and Free Delivery'. *Proceedings of Collaborative Resource Development and Delivery*, Workshop in The 8th International Conference on Language Resources and Evaluation (LREC) 2012, Istanbul, Turkey.

Conclusion

The steps taken throughout this book have shown how the notion of the web as a corpus is grounded on a *de facto* intersection between the corpus linguistics approach and the emergence of the web as a huge self-generating collection of authentic text in machine-readable format. Even at first glance, the act of searching for information through a digital database via an ordinary search engine, and reading the results 'vertically', which is what typically happens in the simplest web search, may appear strikingly similar to what happens when searching a corpus through a concordancer. Indeed, a common search engine results page may recall a concordance list, in which the search item is highlighted within a small amount of co-text. Though this is by no means the same format as the Key Word In Context typical of linguistically oriented tools, it does seem that web search modalities have made reading 'vertically', 'fragmented', and looking for 'repeated events' – the features that set the act of reading through a corpus apart from the common act of reading a text (Tognini Bonelli 2001: 3) – an everyday experience for readers beyond the corpus linguistics community. This superficial similarity cannot conceal, however, the fundamental difference between searching a deliberately collected corpus using specific tools, and searching the web by means of a commercial search engine.

In the ten years since the earliest attempts at bridging the gap between corpus linguistics and the web were made, the way we conceive of a corpus has broadened to accommodate, side by side, the somewhat 'reassuring' standards subsumed under the corpus-as-body metaphor, and the new horizons of the corpus-as-web. On the one hand, the notion of a linguistic corpus as a 'body of texts' still rests on issues such as finite size, balance, part-whole relationship, and permanence; on the other hand, the idea of a 'web of texts' has brought about notions of non-finiteness, flexibility, de-centring/re-centring, and provisionality. In terms of methodology, this latter conception questions issues which could be taken for granted when working with traditional corpora, such as data stability, the reproducibility of the research, and the reliability of the results, but has also created the conditions for the development of specific tools that have helped make the 'webscape' a more hospitable space for corpus research. Either by exploiting to the full the potential of ordinary search engines, or by reworking their output format to make it suitable for linguistic analysis (e.g. WebCorp); by allowing the creation of quick, flexible, small, specialized and customized multilingual corpora from the web (e.g. WebBootCaT) on demand, or by creating new resources and tools that can reproduce the standards of traditional corpus research with huge amounts of web data (e.g. WebCorp*LSE* and Sketch Engine), all the tools and methods devised in corpus linguistics under the impact of the web seem to have finally redirected the way in which corpus work is conceived in the new millennium, along those lines envisaged by Martin Wynne as characterizing all linguistic resources in the twenty-first century: multilinguality, dynamic content, distributed architecture, virtual corpora, connection with web search (Wynne 2002).

As the issues, methods, resources and tools discussed in this book have shown, the notion of the web as corpus can thus be seen as the outcome of the wider process of redefinition in terms of flexibility, multiplicity and 'mass-customization' which corpus linguistics is undergoing, along with other fields of human activity, in a sort of 'convergence of technologies and standards in several related fields which have in common the goal of delivering linguistic content through electronic means' (Wynne 2002: 1207). It is due to this convergence, indeed, that it has become feasible to argue that changes in corpus work, under the impact of the web, are also related to the new styles and approaches to the sharing/distribution of knowledge, goods and resources more generally that has become an everyday experience in contemporary society. In this respect, the shift of many language resources from locally owned finished products to online services is one of the most evident paradigm shifts. Finally, the role played by the technical affordances of the so-called Web 2.0 in prompting new working styles that favour collaboration and exchange, along with the emergence of cloud computing, seem to foreshadow promising developments in terms of collaborative development of resources and cooperative research efforts.

By way of conclusion, it is perhaps worth stressing once again that while the web as corpus is undoubtedly a promising research field, it does not question the fundamental tenets of more 'traditional' corpus linguistics methods. As Baroni and Ueyama (2006) suggest, it is only 'a matter of research policy, time constraints and funding' that determines whether a certain project requires building a thoroughly controlled conventional corpus, or if it is better to resort to some way or method which takes advantage of the web's controversial status as linguistic corpus. And, in more general terms, it will be the priorities and objectives of each research project that will ultimately orient the researcher towards the more appropriate resources and tools. What is certain is that, as in any other field of human knowledge, linguistic research can only profit from the tensions created between established theoretical positions and tools and methods devised from the needs of practicality and pragmatism. It seems more than desirable, then, that 'traditional' corpus linguistics and studies on the web as corpus should coexist for some time to come, thus providing the linguistic community with a wider spectrum of resources to choose from.

References[1]

Adafre S. F. and de Rijke, M. (2006), 'Finding similar sentences across multiple languages in Wikipedia'. *Proceedings of the 11th Conference of the European Chapter of the Association for Computational Linguistics*, 62–9.

Aijmer, K. and Altenberg, B. (eds) (1991), *English Corpus Linguistics. Studies in Honour of Jan Svartvik*. London: Longman.

—(eds) (2004), *Advances in Corpus Linguistics*. Amsterdam: Rodopi.

Anderson, W. and Corbett, J. (2009), *Investigating English with online corpora*. Basingstoke: Palgrave Macmillan.

Arnold, M. (1869), *Culture and anarchy: an essay in political and social criticism*. London: Smith Elder.

Aston G., Bernardini, S. and Stewart, D. (eds) (2004), *Corpora and Language Learners*. Amsterdam: Benjamin.

Aston, G. and Burnard, L. (1998), *The BNC Handbook: Exploring the British National Corpus with SARA*. Edinburgh: Edinburgh University Press.

Atkins S., Clear, J. and Osler, N. (1992), 'Corpus Design Criteria', *Literary and Linguistic Computing*, 7, (1), 1–16

Baeza-Yates R. and Ribeiro-Neto, B. (2011), *Modern Information Retrieval*. Addison-Wesley.

Baker, P. (2006), *Using Corpora in Discourse Analysis*. London: Continuum.

—(2009), *Contemporary Corpus Linguistics*. London: Continuum.

Banko, M. and Brill, E. (2001), 'Scaling to Very Very Large Corpora for Natural Language Disambiguation', in *Proceedings of the 39th Annual Meeting of the Association for Computational Linguistics*, 26–33. Available at http://acl.ldc.upenn.edu/P/P01/P01-1005.pdf

Baroni, M. and Bernardini, S. (2004), 'BootCaT: Bootstrapping corpora and terms from the web', in *Proceedings of LREC 2004*. Lisbon: ELDA, 1313–1316. Available at http://sslmit.unibo.it/~baroni/publications/lrec2004/bootcat_lrec_2004.pdf

—(2006), *Wacky! Working Papers on the Web as Corpus*. Bologna: Gedit. Available at http://wackybook.sslmit.unibo.it/

Baroni, M., Bernardini, S., Ferraresi, A. and Zanchetta, E. (2009), 'The WaCky wide web: a collection of very large linguistically processed web-crawled corpora', *Language Resources & Evaluation*, 43, 209–26.

Baroni, M. and Kilgarriff, A. (eds) (2006), *Proceedings of the 2nd International Workshop on Web as Corpus (EACL06)*. Trento: Italy.

—(2006), 'Large linguistically-processed Web corpora for multiple languages', in Baroni, M. and Kilgarriff, A. (eds), 87–90. Available at http://www.aclweb.org/anthology-new/E/E06/E06-2001.pdf

Baroni, M., Kilgarriff, A., Pomikalek, J. and Rychly, P. (2006), 'WebBootCat: a Web Tool for Instant Corpora', in *Proceeding of the EuraLex Conference 2006*.

Alessandria: Edizioni dell'Orso, 123–32. Available at http://www.kilgarriff.co.uk/Publications/2006-BaroniKilgPomikalekRychly-ELX-WBC.doc

Baroni, M. and Ueyama, M. (2006), 'Building general- and special-purpose corpora by Web crawling', in *Proceedings of the NIJL International Symposyum, Language Corpora: Their Compilation and Application*, 31–40. Available at http://clic.cimec.unitn.it/marco/publications/bu_wac_kokken_formatted.pdf

Battelle, J. (2005), *The Search: How Google and Its Rivals Rewrote the Rules of Business and Transformed Our Culture.* London: Nicholas Brealey Publishing.

Bennett, T., Grossberg, L. and Morris, M. *New Keywords: A Revised Vocabulary of Culture and Society.* New York: John Wiley & Sons.

Bergh, G. (2005), 'Min(d)ing English language data on the Web. What can Google tell us?', in *ICAME Journal*, 29, 25–46. Available at http://gandalf.aksis.uib.no/icame/ij29/ij29-page25-46.pdf

Bergh, G. and Zanchetta, E. (2009), 'Web Linguistics', in Ludeling, A. and Kyto, M., *Corpus Linguistics.* Berlin: Walter de Gruyter.

Bernardini, S. (2002), 'Exploring new directions for discovery learning', in Kettemann, B. and Marko, G. (eds), 165–82.

—(2004), 'Corpora in the classroom: an overview and some reflections on future developments', in J. Sinclair (ed.), 15–36.

—(2006), 'Corpora for translator education and translation practice. Achievements and challenges', in *Proceedings of LREC 2006.* Available at http://mellange.eila.univ-paris-diderot.fr/bernardini_lrec06.pdf

Bernardini, S., Castagnoli, S., Ferraresi, A., Gaspari, F. and Zanchetta, E. (2010), 'Introducing Comparapedia: A New Resource for Corpus–Based Translation Studies'. *UCCTS Conference.* Edge Hill University, 27–9 July 2010.

Bernardini, S., Ferraresi A. and Gaspari, F. (2010), 'Institutional academic English in the European context: a web-as-corpus approach to comparing native and non-native language', in Á. L. López and R. C. Jiménez *English in the European Context.* Frankfurt am Main: Peter Lang.

Bernardini, S. and Ferraresi, A. (2013). 'Old needs, new solutions. Comparable corpora for language professionals', S. Sharoff, R. Rapp, P. Zweigenbaum and P. Fung (eds), *BUCC: Building and using comparable corpora.* Dordrecht: Springer.

Biber, D. (1992), 'Representativeness in Corpus Design'. Reprinted in J. Sampson and D. McCarthy (eds), 174–97.

Biber, D., Conrad, S. and Reppen, R. (1998), *Corpus Linguistics. Investigating Language Structures and Use.* Cambridge: Cambridge University Press.

Biber, D. and Kurjian, J. (2007), 'Towards a taxonomy of web registers and text types: A multi-dimensional analysis', in M. Hundt et al. (eds), 109–32.

Boase, E. (2005), *Stereotyping the Web: Genre Classification of Web Documents.* Unpublished M.Sc. Dissertation. Colorado: Colorado State University.

Bolter, J. D. and Grusin, R. (2000), *Remediation. Understanding New Media.* Cambridge, MA: MIT Press.

Bowker, L. and Pearson, J. (2002), *Working with Specialized Language: A Practical Guide to Using Corpora.* London: Routledge.

Bray, T. (1996), 'Measuring the Web', in *Proceedings of the fifth international World Wide Web conference on Computer networks and ISDN systems,*

993–1005. Available at http://www.tbray.org/ongoing/When/199x/1996/05/07/OVERVIEW.HTM

Brezina, V. (2012), 'Google Scholar as a linguistic tool: new possibilities in EAP', in C. Gkitsaki and R. Baldauf (eds), *The Future of Applied Linguistics: Local and Global Perspectives.* Newcastle upon Tyne: Cambridge Scholars Publishers, 26–48.

Brin, S. and Page, L. (1998), 'The Anatomy of a Large-Scale Hypertextual Web Search Engine', *Computer Networks and ISDN Systems*, 30 (1), 107–17. Available at http://infolab.stanford.edu/pub/papers/google.pdf

Broder, A. (2002), 'A taxonomy of web search', *ACM SIGIR Forum Archive*, 36(2), 3–10. Available at http://www.acm.org/sigir/forum/F2002/broder.pdf

—(2006), 'From query based Information Retrieval to context driven Information Supply'. Workshop on The Future of Web Search, Barcelona, 19–20 May 2006. Videolecture available at http://videolectures.net/fws06_broder_qbirc/

Buendia, L. (2013), 'The Web for Corpus and the Web as Corpus in Translator Training', *New Voices in Translation Studies*, (10), 54–71.

Burnard, L. and McEnery, T. (eds) (2000), *Rethinking Language Pedagogy from a Corpus Perspective*. Frankfurt am Main: Peter Lang.

Calvo, H. and Gelbukh, A. (2003), 'Improving Prepositional Phrase Attachment Disambiguation Using the Web as Corpus'. *Progress in Pattern Recognition, Speech and Image Analysis: 8th Iberoamerican Congress on Pattern Recognition*, CIARP. Available at http://www.gelbukh.com/CV/Publications/2003/CIARP-2003-PP-attachment.pdf

Carter, R., McCarthy, M., Mark, G. and O'Keeffee, A. (2011), *English Grammar Today*. Cambridge: Cambridge University Press.

Castagnoli, S. (2006), 'Using the Web as a Source of LSP Corpora in the Terminology Classroom', in M. Baroni and S. Bernardini (eds), 159–72.

Catone, J. (2011), 'The Staggering Size of the Internet'. Available at http://mashable.com/2011/01/25/internet-size-infographic/

Cavaglià, G. and Kilgarriff, A. (2001), 'Corpora from the Web'. Fourth Annual CLUCK Colloquium, Sheffield, UK, January 2001. Available at ftp://ftp.itri.bton.ac.uk/reports/ITRI-01-11.pdf

Chakrabarti, S. (1999), 'Hypersearching the Web', in *Scientific American*, 280 (6), 54–60. Available at http://econ.tepper.cmu.edu/ecommerce/hypersearch.pdf

—(2003), *Mining the Web. Discovering Knowledge from Hypertext Data*. San Francisco: Morgan Kaufmann.

Chinnery, M. G. (2008), 'You've Got some GALL: Google-Assisted Language Learning'. *Language Learning & Technology*, Vol.12, 1, 3–11.

Chomsky, N. (1962), *Paper given at the 3rd Texas Conference on Problems of Linguistic Analysis in English* (1958). Austin: University of Texas.

Church, K. W. and Hanks, P. (1990), 'Word association norms, mutual information, and lexicography. *Journal of Computational Linguistics*, 16, 1, 22–9.

Ciaramita, M. and Baroni, M. (2006), 'Measuring Web-corpus randomness: A progress report', in M. Baroni and S. Bernardini (eds), 127–58.

Connor, U. and Upton, T. (eds) (2004), *Corpus Linguistics in North America 2002: Selections from the Fourth North American Symposium of the American Association for Applied Corpus Linguistics*. Amsterdam: Rodopi.

Cook, P. and Hirst, G. (2012), 'Do Web Corpora from Top-Level Domains Represent National Varieties of English?', in *Proceedings, 11th International Conference on Statistical Analysis of Textual Data / 11es Journées internationales d'Analyse statistique des Données Textuelles* (JADT 2012), 281–91. Available at http://www.cs.toronto.edu/~pcook/CookHirst2012.pdf

Crowston, K. and Kwasnik, B. (2004), 'A Framework for Creating a Facetted Classification for Genres: Addressing Issues of Multidimensionality', in *Proceedings of the 37th Hawaii International Conference on System Sciences*. Available at http://csdl2.computer.org/comp/proceedings/hicss/2004/2056/04/205640100a.pdf

Crowstone, K. and Williams, M. (1997), 'Reproduced and Emergent Genres on the World Wide Web', in *Proceedings of the 30th Hawaii International Conference on System Sciences: Digital Documents*. Available at http://csdl2.computer.org/comp/proceedings/hicss/1997/7734/06/7734060030.pdf

Crystal, D. (2006), *Language and the Internet*. Cambridge: Cambridge University Press (2nd edn).

—(2011), *Internet Linguistics. A Student's Guide*. London: Routledge.

De Schryver, G. (2002), 'Web for/as corpus: a perspective for the African languages', in *Nordic Journal of African Studies*, 11(2), 266–82. Available at http://www.njas.helsinki.fi/pdf-files/vol11num2/schryver.pdf

Di Martino, G., Lombardo, L. and Nuccorini, S. (eds) (2011), *Challenges for the 21st Century. Dilemmas, Ambiguities, Directions. Papers from the 24th AIA Conference*, Vol. II. Roma: Edizioni Q.

EAGLES (Expert Advisory Group on Language Engineering Standards), (1996), 'Preliminary recommendations on text typology'. Available at http://www.ilc.cnr.it/EAGLES/texttyp/texttyp.html

Fairon C., Naets, H., Kilgarriff, A. and De Schryver, G. (2007), *Building and Exploring Web Corpora (WAC3 – 2007)*. Louvain-la-Neuve: Presses Universitaires de Louvain.

Ferraresi, A. (2007), *Building a very large corpus of English obtained by Web crawling: ukWaC*. MA Thesis, University of Bologna. Available at http://trac.sketchengine.co.uk/wiki/Corpora/UKWaC

—(2009), 'Google and beyond: web as corpus methodologies for translators', *Revista Tradumàtica*.7. Available at http://webs2002.uab.es/tradumatica/revista/num7/articles/04/04.pdf

Ferraresi, A., Zanchetta, E., Baroni, M. and Bernardini, S. (2008), 'Introducing and evaluating ukWaC, a very large web-derived corpus of English', in S. Evert, A. Kilgarriff and S. Sharoff (eds), *Proceedings of the 4th Web as Corpus Workshop (WAC-4) – Can we beat Google?*, Marrakech, 1 June 2008. Available at http://wacky.sslmit.unibo.it/lib/exe/fetch.php?media=papers:wac4_2008.pdf

Firth, J. R. (1957), *Papers in Linguistics 1934–1951*. London: Oxford University Press.

Fletcher, W. (2001), 'Concordancing the Web with KWiCFinder'. *American Association for Applied Corpus Linguistics, Third North American Symposium on Corpus Linguistics and Language Teaching*, Boston, MA, 23–25 March 2001. Available at http://www.kwicfinder.com/FletcherCLLT2001.pdf

—(2004a), 'Facilitating the Compilation and Dissemination of Ad-Hoc Web Corpora', in G. Aston et al. (eds), 271–300.

—(2004b), 'Making the Web More Useful as a Source for Linguistic Corpora', in U. Connor and T. Upton (eds), 191–205.

—(2007), 'Concordancing the Web. Promise and problems, tools and techniques', in M. Hundt et al. (eds), 25–46.

—(2012), 'Corpus analysis of the World Wide Web', in C. A. Chapelle (ed.), *Encyclopedia of Applied Linguistics*. Oxford: Wiley-Blackwell.

Francis, N. W. (1992), 'Language corpora B.C.', in J. Svartvik (ed.), 17–33.

Freitag, D., Chow, E., Kalmar, P., Muezzinoglu, T. and Niekrasz, J. (2012), 'A Corpus of Online Discussions for Research into Linguistic Memes'. *Proceedings of the 7th Web As Corpus Workshop*, 14–22. Available at http://www.ai.sri.com/~niekrasz/papers/Freitag2012.pdf

Gabrielatos, C. (2007), *'Selecting query terms to build a specialised corpus from a restricted-access database'. ICAME Joural*, 31: 5–44.

Gamallo Otero, P. and Gonzalez Lopez, I. (2008), 'Wikipedia as a Multilingual Source of Comparable Corpora'. Workshop on Building and Using Comparable Corpora, LREC 2010: 19–26. Available at http://gramatica.usc.es/~gamallo/artigos-web/LREC2010Web.pdf

Gartner Research (2011), 'Solving 'Big Data' Challenge Involves More Than Just Managing Volumes of Data'. Available at http://www.gartner.com/it/page.jsp?id=1731916

Gatto, M. (2009), *From Body to Web. An Introduction to the Web as Corpus. Roma – Bari*: Editori Laterza University Press on-line

—(2010), 'From language to culture and beyond', in *Proceedings of the 3rd Workshop on Building and Using Comparable Corpora*, Malta, 22 May 2010. Available at http://www.fb06.uni-mainz.de/lk/bucc2010/documents/Proceedings-BUCC-2010.pdf

—(2011), 'Sketches of CULTURE from the web. A preliminary study', in G. Di Martino, L. Lombardo and S. Nuccorini (eds), 285–93.

—(2011a), 'The body and the web. The web as corpus ten years on', *ICAME JOURNAL*, 35: 35–58.

Inktomi Research Institute (2000), *Web Surpasses One Billion Documents*. Available at http://web.archive.org/web/20011003203111/www.inktomi.com/new/press/2000/billion.html

Geluso, J. (2011), 'How Can Search Engines Improve Your Writing', *CALL-EJ*, 12, 1, 10. Available at http://callej.org/journal/12-1/Acar_2011.pdf

—(2011a), 'Phraseology and frequency of occurrence on the web: native speakers' perceptions of Google-informed second language writing'. *Computer Assisted Language Learning*, 26, 2: 144–57.

Ghani, R., Jones, R. and Mladenic, D. (2001), 'Building Minority Language Corpora by Learning to Generate Web Search Queries'. *Knowledge and Information Systems*, 1, 7. Available at http://www.cs.cmu.edu/afs/cs/project/theo-4/text-learning/www/corpusbuilder/papers/CMU-CALD-01-100.pdf

Granger, S. and Petch-Tyson, S. (eds) (2003), *Extending the scope of corpus-based research: new applications, new challenges*. Amsterdam: Rodopi.

Green, N. D. (2012), 'Building parallel corpora through social network gaming'. Proceedings of Collaborative Resource Development and Delivery, Workshop in the 8th International Conference on Language Resources and Evaluation (LREC) 2012, Istanbul, Turkey. Available at http://www.lrec-conf.org/proceedings/lrec2012/workshops/22.LREC 2012 Collaborative Resources Proceedings.pdf

Grefenstette, G. (1999), 'The WWW as a resource for example-based MT tasks'. *Translating and the Computer*, 21, ASLIB, London. Available at http://www.academia.edu/910203/The_WWW_as_a_resource_for_example-based_MT_tasks

Grefenstette, G. and Nioche, J. (2000), 'Estimation of English and non-English language use on the WWW', in *Proceedings of the RIAO* (Recherche d'Informations Assistée par Ordinateur), Paris, 12–14 April 2000, 237–46. Available at http://arxiv.org/ftp/cs/papers/0006/0006032.pdf

Halliday, M. A. K. (1991), 'Towards probabilistic interpretations', in M. A. K. Halliday and J, J. Webster Computational and Quantitative Studies (2006). London: Continuum, 39–62.

—(1991a), 'Corpus studies and probabilistic grammar', in K. Aijmer and B. Altenberg (eds), 30–43.

—(1993), 'Quantitative studies and probabilities in grammar', in M. Hoey (ed.), 1–25.

Harris, R. H. (2003), *The Linguistics War*. Oxford: Oxford University Press.

Hemming, C. and Lassi, M. (2002), 'Copyright and the Web as Corpus'. Available at http://hemming.se/gslt/copyrightHemmingLassi.pdf

Henziger, M. and Lawrence, S. (2004), 'Extracting Knowledge from the World Wide Web'. *Proceedings of the National Academy of Sciences*, 101, 5186–91. Available at http://www.pnas.org/content/101/suppl.1/5186.full

Hoey, M. (ed.) (1993), *Data. Description. Discourse*. London: HarperCollins.

Hoey, M., Mahlberg, M., Stubbs, M. and Teubert, W. (eds) (2007), *Text, discourse, corpora: theory and analysis*. London: Continuum.

Hundt M., Nesselhauf, N. and Biewer, C. (eds) (2007), *Corpus Linguistics and the Web*. Amsterdam: Rodopi.

Hunston, S. (2002), *Introducing corpora in applied linguistics*. Cambridge: Cambridge University Press.

Indurkhya, N. and Damerau, F. (eds) (2010), *The Handbook of Natural Language Processing* (2nd edn). London: CRC Press T&F Group.

Inktomi Research Institute (2000), *Web Surpasses One Billion Documents.* Available at http://web.archive.org/web/20011003203111/www.inktomi.com/new/press/2000/billion.html

Jakubíček, M., Kilgarriff, A., Kovář, V., Rychiý, P., and Suchomel, V. (2013). 'The Ten Ten Corpus Family'. In 7th International Corpus Linguistics Conference CL 2013. Lancaster: 125–7.

Johns, T. (2002), *Data-Driven Learning: The Perpetual Challenge*, in Kettemann, B. and Marko, G. (eds), *Teaching and Learning by Doing Corpus Analysis*. Proceedings of the Fourth International Conference of Teaching and Language Corpora, Graz, 19–24 July 2000. Amsterdam: Rodopi, 107–17.

Kehoe, A. and Gee, M. (2007), 'New corpora from the web: making web text more "text-like"', in P. Pahta, I. Taavitsainen, T. Nevalainen and J. Tyrkkö (eds), *Studies in Variation, Contacts and Change in English. Volume 2: Towards Multimedia in Corpus Studies,* University of Helsinki (e-journal). Available at http://www.helsinki.fi/varieng/series/volumes/02/kehoe_gee/

—(2009), 'Weaving Web data into a diachronic corpus patchwork', in A. Renouf and A. Kehoe (eds), *Corpus Linguistics: Refinements and Reassessments*. Amsterdam: Rodopi, 255–79.

Kehoe, A. and Renouf, A. (2002), 'WebCorp: Applying the Web to Linguistics and Linguistics to the Web'. *WWW2002 Conference*, Honolulu, Hawaii. Available at http://www2002.org/CDROM/poster/67/

—(2006), 'Diachronic linguistic analysis on the web with WebCorp', in A. Renouf and A. Kehoe (eds), 297–308.

Keller, A. and Lapata, M. (2003), 'Using the web to obtain frequencies for unseen bigrams'. *Computational Linguistics*, 29(3), 459–84. Available at http://www.aclweb.org/anthology-new/J/J03/J03-3005.pdf

Kelly, K. (2005), 'We Are the Web', *Wired*, 13 August 2005. Available at http://www.wired.com/wired/archive/13.08/tech.html

Kennedy, G. (1998), *An Introduction to Corpus Linguistics*. London: Longman.

Kessler, B., Nunberg, G. and Schütze, H. (1997), 'Automatic detection of text genre'. Available at http://www.aclweb.org/anthology-new/P/P97/P97-1005.pdf

Kettemann, B. and Marko, G. (eds) (2002), *Teaching and learning by doing corpus linguistics. Papers from the Fourth International Conference on Teaching and Language Corpora*, Graz, 19–24 July 2000. Amsterdam and Atlanta, GA: Rodopi.

Kilgarriff, A. (2001), 'Web as corpus', in *Proceedings of the Corpus Linguistics Conference (CL 2001)*, University Centre for Computer Research on Language Technical Paper, Vol. 13, Special Issue, Lancaster University, 342–4. Available at http://ucrel.lancs.ac.uk/publications/CL2003/CL2001%20conference/papers/kilgarri.pdf

—(2007), 'Googleology is Bad Science', *Computational Linguistics*, 33, 1, 147–51. Available at http://www.mitpressjournals.org/doi/abs/10.1162/coli.2007.33.1.147

—(2010), 'Corpora by Web Services'. *LREC workshop on Web Services and Processing Pipelines*, Malta. Available at http://trac.sketchengine.co.uk/attachment/wiki/AK/Papers/2010-K-WSPPmalta-CorporaByWebSevices.pdf

Kilgarriff, A., Avinesh PVS and Pomikálek, J. (2011), Bootcatting Comparable Corpora. *Proceedings of the 9th International Conference on Terminology and Artificial Intelligence*, 123–6.

Kilgariff, A. and Baroni, M. (2006), *Proceedings of the 2nd International Workshop on Web as Corpus*, Trento, 3 April 2006.

Kilgarriff, A. and Grefenstette, G. (2003), 'Introduction to the Special Issue on the Web as Corpus', in *Computational Linguistics*, 29, 3, 333–47. Available at http://acl.ldc.upenn.edu/J/J03/J03-3001.pdf

Kilgarriff, A. and Kosem, I. (2012), 'Corpus tools for lexicographers', in S. Granger and M. Paquot (eds), *Electronic lexicography*. Oxford: Oxford University Press.

Kilgarriff, A., Reddy S., Pomikálek, J. and Avinesh PVS (2010), 'A Corpus Factory for Many Languages', in *Proceedings of the Seventh International Conference on Language Resources and Evaluation* (LREC '10): 904–10.

Kilgarriff, A., Rychly, P., Smerz, P. and Tugwell, D. (2004), 'The Sketch Engine', in *Proceedings Euralex*, Lorient, France, 105–16. Available at http://trac.sketchengine.co.uk/attachment/wiki/SkE/DocsIndex/sketch-engine-elx04.pdf?format=raw

Kilgarriff, A. and Sharoff, S. (eds) (2012), *Proceedings of the Seventh Web as Corpus Workshop.* http://sigwag.org.uk/attachment/wiki/WAC7/wac-7-proc.pdf.

Kristeva, J. (1986), The Kristeva-Reader, T. Moi (ed.). Oxford: Blackwell.

Kübler, N. (2004), 'Using WebCorp in the classroom for building specialized dictionaries', in K. Aijmer and B. Altenberg (eds), 387–400.

Kwasnik, B., Crowston, K., Nilan, M. and Roussinov, D. (2000), 'Identifying document genre to improve Web search effectiveness', in *Bulletin of the American Society for Information Science & Technology*, 27(2), 23–6. Available at http://www.asis.org/Bulletin/Dec-01/kwasnikartic.html

Lapata, M. and Keller, A. (2004), 'The Web as a Baseline: Evaluating the Performance of Unsupervised Web-based Models for a Range of NLP Tasks', in *Proceedings of the Human Language Technology Conference of the North American Chapter of the Association for Computational Linguistics*, Boston, Massachusetts, 121–8. Available at http://acl.ldc.upenn.edu/hlt-naacl2004/main/pdf/5_Paper.pdf

Laviosa, S. (1997), 'How Comparable Can "Comparable Corpora" Be?', *Target,* 9(2): 289–319.

—(2002), *Corpus-Based Translation Studies: Theory, Findings, Applications.* Amsterdam: Rodopi.

Lawrence, S. and Giles, C. L. (1999), 'Accessibility of Information on the Web' in *Nature,* 400, 107–9.

Lee, D. (2001), 'Genres, Registers, Text Types, Domains, and Styles: Clarifying the Concepts and Navigating a Path Through the BNC Jungle', *Language Learning and Technology*, 5, 3, 37–72. Available at http://llt.msu.edu/vol5num3/pdf/lee.pdf

Leech, G. (1992), 'Corpora and theories of linguistic performance', in J. Svartvik (ed.), 105–22.

—(2003), 'Adding Linguistic Annotation', in *Developing Linguistic Corpora: a Guide to Good Practice*, M. Wynne (ed.). Oxford: Oxbow Books: 17–29. Available at http://ahds.ac.uk/linguistic-corpora

—(2007), 'New resources or just better old ones? The Holy Grail of representativeness', in M. Hundt et al. (eds), 133–50.

Leistyna, P. and Meyer, C. (eds) (2003), *Corpus Analysis: Language Structure and Language Use*. Amsterdam: Rodopi.

Levene, M. (2010), *An introduction to search engines and web navigation.* New York: John Wiley & Sons.

Lew, R. (2009), 'The Web as corpus versus traditional corpora: Their relative utility for linguists and language learners', in *Contemporary Corpus Linguistics*, P. Baker (ed.). London: Continuum.

Lindquist, H. (2009), *Corpus Linguistics and the Description of English.* Edinburgh: Edinburgh University Press.

Louw, B. (1993), 'Irony in the Text or Insincerity in the Writer? The Diagnostic Potential of Semantic Prosodies', in M. Baker, G. Francis, and E. Tognini-Bonelli (eds), *Text and Technology*. Philadelphia/Amsterdam: John Benjamins.

Lüdeling, A., Evert, S. and Baroni, M. (2007), 'Using Web data for linguistic purposes', in M. Hundt et al. (eds), 7–24.

Mahlberg, M. (2005), *English General Nouns. A corpus theoretical approach.* Amsterdam/Philadelphia: John Benjamins.

Mair, C. (2007), 'Change and variation in present-day English: integrating the analysis of closed corpora and web-based monitoring', in M. Hundt, et al., 233–48.

—(2012), 'From opportunistic to systematic use if the web as corpus', in T. Nevalainen and E. C. Traugott (eds), 245–55.

Manca, E. (2004), 'The Language of Tourism in English and Italian: Investigating the Concept of Nature between Culture and Usage'. *ESP. Across Cultures* 1, 53–65.

Maniez, F. (2007), 'Using the Web and computer corpora as language resources for the translation of complex noun phrases in medical research articles', in *Panace@: Revista de Medicina, Lenguaje y Traducción*, 9, 26, 162–7.

Manning, C. D. and Schütze, H. (1999), *Foundations of Statistical Natural Language Processing*. Cambridge, MA: MIT Press.

McCarthy, A. M. and O'Keefee, M. (2010), *The Routledge Handbook of Corpus Linguistics*. London: Routledge.

McEnery, A. and Hardie, A. (2012), *Corpus Linguistics: Theory, Method, and Practice*. Cambridge: Cambridge University Press.

—(2012a), 'Support website for *Corpus Linguistics: Method, theory and practice*'. Available online at *http://corpora.lancs.ac.uk/clmtp*

McEnery, A. and Xiao, M. (2006), *Corpus-based language studies: an advanced resource book*. London: Routledge.

McEnery, T. and Wilson, A. (2001), *Corpus Linguistics*, Edinburgh: Edinburgh University Press.

McGuigan, B. (2011), 'How big is the Internet?'. Available at http://www.wisegeek.com/how-big-is-the-internet.htm

Meyer, C. et al. (2003), 'The World Wide Web as linguistic corpus', in P. Leistyna and C. Meyer (eds), 241–54.

Mehler, A., Sharoff, S. and Santini, M. (2010), *Genres on the Web: Computational Models and Empirical Studies*. Dordrecht, Heidelberg, London and New York: Springer.

Michel, J.-B., Liberman Aiden, E., Aiden, A. P., Veres, A., Gray, M. K., Pickett, J. P., Hoiberg, D., Clancy, D., Norvig, P., Orwan, J., Nowak, M., Pinker, S. (2010), 'Quantitative Analysis of Culture Using Millions of Digitized Books'. *Science*, 331 (6014): 176–82.

Monno, M. (2012), *Sketches of 'culture' in ukWaC. A preliminary study*. Unpublished Dissertation in English Language and Translation (supervisor: M. Gatto), Bari: Facoltà di Lingue e Letterature Straniere.

Mohammadi, M. and Ghasem, A. (2010), 'Building parallel bilingual corpora from Wikipedia', in *Proceedings of the 2010 Second International Conference on Computer Engineering and Applications*, 264–8. Washington, DC: IEEÈ Computer Society.

Morley, A. (2006), 'WebCorp: A Tool for Online Linguistic Information Retrieval and Analysis', in A. Renouf and A. Kehoe (eds), 283–95.

Mouhobi, S. (2005), 'Bridging the North South Divide', in *The New Courier* (UNESCO), November 2005. Available at http://unesdoc.unesco.org/images/0014/001420/142021e.pdf#142065

Munat, J. (2007), *Lexical Creativity, Texts and Contexts*, Amsterdam: John Benjamins.

Murphy, B. and Stemle, E. W. (2011), 'PaddyWaC: A Minimally-Supervised Web-Corpus of Hiberno-English', *Proceedings of EMNLP 2011, Conference on Empirical Methods in Natural Language Processing*, 22–9.

Nakov, P. and Hearst, M. (2005a), 'A Study of Using Search Engine Page Hits as a Proxy for n-gram Frequencies', *Proceedings of RANLP '05*. http://biotext.berkeley.edu/papers/nakov_ranlp2005.pdf

—(2005b), 'Search Engine Statistics Beyond the n-gram: Application to Noun Compound Bracketing', *Proceedings of* CoNLL-2005, Ann Arbor, MI. http://biotext.berkeley.edu/papers/conll05.pdf

Nevalainen, T. and Traugott, E. C. (eds) (2012), *The Oxford Handbook of the History of English*, Oxford: Oxford University Press.

Norvig, P. (2008), 'Theorizing from Data: Avoiding the Capital Mistake', Videolecture. Available at http://www.youtube.com/watch?v=nU8DcBF-qo4

Ntoulas, A., Junghoo, C. and Olston, C. (2004), 'What's New on the Web? The Evolution of the Web from a Search Engine Perspective', in *WWW 2004*. ACM Press, 1–12. Available at http://www2004.org/proceedings/docs/1p1.pdf

Oja, D. and Parsons, J. J. (2012), *Computer Concepts: Illustrated*. Standford, CT: Cengage Learning.

Ohlan, M. (2004), *Introducing Corpora in Translation Studies*. London: Routledge.

Parser, E. (2011), *The Filter Bubble. How the New Personalized Web Is Changing What We Read and How We Think*. New York: Penguin Group US.

Pastore, M. (2000), *Web Pages by Language*. Available at http://www.clickz.com/clickz/news/1697080/web-pages-language

Pearce, M. (2008), 'Investigating the Collocational Behaviour of MAN and WOMAN in the BNC using Sketch Engine', *Corpora*, 3, 1, 1–29.

Pearson, J. (2000), 'Surfing the Internet: Teaching Students to Choose their Texts Wisely', in L. Burnard and T. McEnery (eds), 235–9.

Pottast, M., Stein, B. and Anderka, M. (2008), 'A Wikipedia-based multilingual retrieval model', in *Advances in Information Retrieval*. Proceedings of 30th European Conference on IR Research, ECIR 2008, Glasgow, UK 522–30.

Ray, A. and Graeff, E. (2008), 'Reviewing the Author-Function in the Age of Wikipedia', in C. Eisner and M. Vicinus, *Originality, imitation, and plagiarism: teaching writing in the digital age*. University of Michigan Press: 39–47.

Rayson, P. et al. (eds) (2001), *Proceedings of the Corpus Linguistics 2001 Conference*, Lancaster: UCREL.

Rayson, P., Charles, O. and Auty, I. (2012), 'Can Google count? Estimating search engine result consistency', in A. Kilgarriff and S. Sharoff (eds), *Proceedings of the Seventh Web as Corpus Workshop* (WAC7), 24–31. Available at http://sigwac.org.uk/wiki/WAC7

Renouf, A. (ed.) (1998), *Explorations in Corpus Linguistics*. Amsterdam: Rodopi.

—(2003), 'WebCorp: providing a renewable data source for corpus linguists', in Granger, S. and Petch-Tyson, S. (eds), 39–58.

—(2007), 'Tracing lexical productivity in the British Media', in Munat, J. (ed), 61–89.

—(2013), 'A Finer Definition of Neology in English: the life-cycle of a word', in H. Hasselgård, S. O. Ebeling and J. Ebeling (eds), *Corpus Perspectives on Patterns of Lexis*. Amsterdam/Philadelphia: John Benjamins.

Renouf, A. and Keohe, A. (2013) 'Filling the gaps: Using the WebCorp Linguist's Search Engine to supplement existing text resources'. International Journal of Corpus Linguistics, 18: 2, 167–98.

Renouf, A. and Kehoe, A. (eds) (2006), *The Changing Face of Corpus Linguistics*, Amsterdam: Rodopi.

Renouf, A., Kehoe, A. and Banerjee, J. (2005), 'The WebCorp Search Engine: a holistic approach to Web text Search', *Electronic Proceedings of CL2005*, University of Birmingham. Available at http://www.corpus.bham.ac.uk/PCLC/cl2005-SE-pap-final-050705.doc

Renouf, A., Kehoe, A. and Banerjee, J. (2007), 'WebCorp: an integrated system for web text search', in M. Hundt et al. (eds), 47–67.

Renouf, A., Kehoe, A. and Mezquiriz, D. (2004), 'The Accidental Corpus: issues involved in extracting linguistic information from the Web', in K. Aijmer and B. Altenberg (eds), 403–19.

Risvik, K. M. and Michelsen, R. (2002), 'Search engines and web dynamics', in Computer Networks, 39, 289–302. Available at http://www.iconocast.com/zresearch/se-dynamicweb1.pdf

Resnik, P. and Smith, N. (2003), *The Web as Parallel Corpus. Computational Linguistics* (Special Issue on the Web as a corpus), 29 (3), 349–80.

Rosenbach, A. (2007), 'Exploring constructions on the Web: a case study', in M. Hundt et al. (eds), 167–90.

Rychly, P. (2008), 'A lexicographer-friendly association score', in Sojka, P. and Horák, A. (eds), *Proceedings of Second Workshop on Recent Advances in Slavonic Natural Languages Processing*, RASLAN 2008, 6–9. Brno: Masaryk University.

Sampson, J. and McCarthy, D. (eds) (2005), *Corpus Linguistics. Readings in a Widening Discipline*. London: Continuum.

Sánchez-Gijón, P. (2009), 'Developing documentation skills to build do-it-yourself corpora in the specialised translation course', in A. Beeby, P. Rodríguez Inés and P. Sánchez-Gijón (eds), *Corpus Use and Translating: Corpus use for learning to translate and learning corpus use to translate*. Amsterdam: John Benjamins, 109–27.

Santini, M. (2004), 'Identification of Genres on the Web: a Multi-Faceted Approach'. In M. P. Oakes (ed.), *Proceedings of the ECIR 2004 (26th European Conference on IR Research)*, University of Sunderland (UK), 5–7 April 2004.

—(2005), 'Web pages, text types and linguistic features: some issues', *ICAME Journal*, Vol. 30, 67- 86. *Available at http://icame.uib.no/ij30/ij30-page67-86.pdf*

—(2007), 'Characterizing Genres of Web Pages: Genre Hybridism and Individualization', in *Proceedings of the 40th Annual Hawaii International Conference on System Sciences (HICSS '07)*. Available at http://csdl2.computer.org/comp/proceedings/hicss/2007/2755/00/27550071.pdf

Santini, M., Mehler, A. and Sharoff, S. (2010), 'Riding the Rough Waves of Genre on the Web', in A. Mehler et al., *Genres on the Web: Computational Models and Empirical Studies*, 3–25.

Scannell, K. (2007), 'The Crúbadán Project: Corpus building for under-resourced languages', in Fairon, C. et al., 5–16. Available at http://borel.slu.edu/pub/wac3.pdf

Schafer, R. and Bildhauer, F. (2013). Web Corpus Construction. San Francisco: Morgan & Claypool.

Scheffler, P. (2007), 'When Intuition Fails us: the World Wide Web as a Corpus', *Glottodidactica*, Vol. 33, 137–45. Available at https://repozytorium.amu.edu.pl/jspui/handle/10593/2285

Scott, M. (2010), *WordSmith Tools Step by Step. Version 5.0.* Available at http://www.lexically.org/wordsmith/step_by_step_guide_English.pdf

—(2010a), *WordSmith Tools Manual. Version 5.0.* Available at http://www.lexically.net/downloads/version5/WordSmith.pdf

Scott, M. and Trimble, C. (2006), *Textual Patterns. Keywords and corpus analysis in language education.* Amsterdam/Philadelphia: John Benjamins.

Sengupta, S. (2012), 'U.N. Affirms Internet Freedom as a Basic Right', *The New York Times*, Technology, 6 July 2012. Available at http://bits.blogs.nytimes.com/2012/07/06/so-the-united-nations-affirms-internet-freedom-as-a-basic-right-now-what/

Sha, G. (2010), 'Using Google as a super corpus to drive written language learning: a comparison with the British National Corpus', *Computer Assisted Language Learning*, 23(5), 377–93.

Sharoff, S. (2006), 'Creating general-purpose corpora using automated search engine queries', in M. Baroni and S. Bernardini (eds), 63–98.
—(2007), 'Classifying Web corpora into domain and genre using automatic feature identification', in C. Fairon et al. (eds), 83–94.
Shei, C. C. (2008), 'Discovering the hidden treasure on the Internet: using Google to uncover the veil of phraseology', *Computer Assisted Language Learning*, 21(1), 67–85.
Sinclair, J. (1991), *Corpus, Concordance, Collocation.* Oxford: Oxford University Press.
—(1992), 'The automatic analysis of corpora', in J. Svartvik (ed.), *Directions in Corpus Linguistics*. Berlin: Mouton de Gruyter, 379–97.
—(ed.) (2004), *How to Use Corpora in Language Teaching*. Amsterdam: John Benjamins.
—(2005), 'Corpus and Text. Basic Principles', in Wynne, M. (ed.), *Developing Linguistic Corpora: a Guide to Good Practice*, Oxford: Oxbow Books, 1–16. http://ahds.ac.uk/linguistic-corpora/
Stewart, D. (2010), *Semantic Prosody*. London: Routledge.
Stubbs, M. (1996), *Text and Corpus Analysis. Computer assisted studies of language and culture.* Oxford and Cambridge, MA: Blackwell.
—(2002), *Words and Phrases*. Oxford: Blackwell Publishing.
—(2007), 'On texts, corpora and models of language', in M. Hoey, M. Mahlberg, M. Stubbs and W. Teubert (eds), 127–62.
Sullivan, D. (2005), 'Search Engine Sizes', *Search Engine Watch*, 28 January 2005. Available at http://searchenginewatch.com/showPage.html?page=2156481
—(2009), 'Google's Personalized Results: The "New Normal" That Deserves Extraordinary Attention'. Available at http://searchengineland.com/googles-personalized-results-the-new-normal-31290
—(2011), 'Hoe Google Instant's Autocomplete Suggestions Work'. Available at http://searchengineland.com/how-google-instant-autocomplete-suggestions-work-62592
Svartvik, J. (ed.) (1992), *Directions in Corpus Linguistics. Proceedings of Nobel Symposium 82 Stockholm, 4–8 August 1991*. Berlin: Mouton de Gruyter.
Teich, E. (2003), *Cross-linguistic variation in system and text: a methodology for the investigation.* Berlin: Mouton de Gruyter.
Teubert, W. (2005), 'My version of corpus linguistics', *International Journal of Corpus Linguistics*, 10, (1), 1–13.
—(2007), 'Parole-linguistics and the diachronic dimension of the discourse', in M. Hoey et al. (eds), 57–88.
Toffler, A. (1981), *The Third Wave.* New York: Bantam Books.
Tognini Bonelli, E. (2001), *Corpus Linguistics at Work.* Amsterdam: John Benjamins.
Tyers, M. F. and Pieanaar, J. A. (2008), 'Extracting Bilingual Word Pairs from Wikipedia', in *LREC-SALTMIL Workshop*, Marrakech, Morocco.
Ueyama, M. (2006), 'Evaluation of Japanese web-based reference corpora: Effects of seed selection and time interval', in M. Baroni and S. Bernardini (eds), 99–126.
Van Rijsbergen, C. J. K. (1979), *Information Retrieval.* Available at http://www.dcs.gla.ac.uk/Keith/Preface.html
Varantola, K. (2003), 'Translators and disposable corpora', in *Corpora in translator education.* Manchester: St Jerome, 55–70.
Ventola, E. (ed.) (1991), *Functional and Systemic Linguistics: Approaches and Uses*, Berlin: Walter de Gruyter.

Véronis, J. (2005), *Google's missing pages: mystery solved?* Available at http://aixtal.blogspot.com/2005/02/web-googles-missing-pages-mystery.html

Volk, M. (2002), 'Using the Web as Corpus for Linguistic Research', in R. Pajusalu and T. Hennoste (eds), *Tahendusepüüdja. Catcher of the Meaning. A Festschrift for Professor Haldur Oim*, Publications of the Department of General Linguistics 3. University of Tartu. Available at http://www.ifi.uzh.ch/cl/volk/papers/Oim_Festschrift_2002.pdf

Xiao, R. (2010), 'Corpus Creation', in Indurkhya, N. and Damerau, F. (eds), *The Handbook of Natural Language Processing* (2nd edn). London: CRC Press T&F Group, 147–65.

Warschauer, M. and Grimes, D. (2007), 'Audience, Authorship, and Artifact: the Emergent Semiotics of Web 2.0'. *Annual Review of Applied Linguistics*. 27, 1–23.

Wesch, M. (2007), *Web 2.0: The machine is us/ing us*. [Video] Available at http://www.youtube.com/watch?v=6gmP4nk0EOE

Wilcock, G. (2012), 'Annotated Corpora in the Cloud: Free Storage and Free Delivery'. *Proceedings of Collaborative Resource Development and Delivery*, Workshop in the 8th International Conference on Language Resources and Evaluation (LREC) 2012, Istanbul, Turkey. Available at http://www.ling.helsinki.fi/~gwilcock/Pubs/2012/CRDD-2012.pdf

Wild, K., Church, A., McCarthy, D. and Burgess, J. (2013), 'Quantifying Lexical Usage: Vocabulary pertaining to Ecosystems and the Environment', *Corpora*, 8, 53–79.

Williams, R. (1966), *Culture and Society: 1780–1650*. Oxford: Oxford University Press.

—(1985), *Keywords. A Vocabulary of Culture and Society*. Oxford: Oxford University Press.

Wu, S., Franken, M. and Witten, I. (2009), 'Refining the use of the Web (and Web search) as a language teaching and learning resource', *International Journal of Computer Assisted Language Learning*, 22(3), 247–65.

Wynne, M. (2002), *The Language Resource Archive of the 21th century*. Oxford Text Archive. Available at http://gandalf.aksis.uib.no/lrec2002/pdf/271.pdf

Wynne, M. (ed.) (2005), *Developing Linguistic Corpora: a Guide to Good Practice*. Oxford: Oxbow Books. Available at http://ahds.ac.uk/linguistic-corpora/

Yates, S. J. and Sumner, T. R. (1997), 'Digital Genres and the New Burden of Fixity', in *Proceedings of the Hawaiian International Conference on System Sciences (HICCS 30)*, VI, 3–12. Available at http://csdl2.computer.org/comp/proceedings/hicss/1997/7734/06/7734060003.pdf

Yu, K. and Tsujii, J. (2009), 'Extracting bilingual dictionary from comparable corpora', in *Proceedings of NAACL-HLT*: 121–4.

Zanettin, F. (2002), 'DIY Corpora: the WWW and the Translator', in B. Maia, J. Haller and M. Ulrych (eds), *Training the Language Services Provider for the New Millennium*. Porto: Facultade de Letras, Universidade do Porto, 239–48. Available at http://www.federicozanettin.net/DIYcorpora.htm

—(2009), 'Corpus-based Translation Activities for Language Learners'. *The Interpreter and Translator Trainer* (ITT), 3, (2), 209–24.

—(2012), *Translation-Driven Corpora. Corpus Resources for Descriptive and Applied Translation Studies*. Manchester: St Jerome.

Zanettin, F., Bernardini, S. and Stewart, D. (eds) (2003), *Corpora in Translator Education.* Manchester: St. Jerome.
Zipf, G. K. (1935), *The psychobiology of language.* New York: Houghton Mifflin.
Zuraw, K. (2006), 'Using the Web as a Phonological Corpus: a case study from Tagalog', in M. Baroni and A. Kilgarriff (eds), 59–66.

Corpora

Bank of English (Sinclair 1987)
British National Corpus (Aston and Burnard 2008)
Coca (Davies 2009)
GloWbe (Davies 2013)
Internet Leeds Corpora (Sharoff 2006)
TenTen corpora (Jakubíček et al. 2013))
ukWaC (Ferraresi 2007)
Software and other corpus resources:
AntConc (Anthony 2005)
BootCaT (Baroni and Bernardini 2004)
BNCweb (Hoffmann et al. 2008)
Corpus.byu.edu (Davies 2005)
Sketch Engine (Kilgarriff 2004)
WebAsCorpus (Fletcher 2007)
WebConc (Hüning 2001, 2002)
WebCorp*Live* (Kehoe and Renouf 2002)
Wordsmith Tools (Scott 2004)

Online tutorials

WebCorp Linguist's Search Engine Masterclasses, http://wse1.webcorp.org.uk/mc/
Sketch Engine, http://www.youtube.com/user/TheSketchEngine?feature=watch

Note

1 All Internet URLs included in the references have been last accessed in June 2013.

Index